HOW RICH SHOULD THE 1% BE?

How rich should the 1% be? And, most importantly, when does the distance in economic resources between the richest citizens and 'us', the average citizenry, become a concern for justice?

This volume explores how excessive economic inequality gives the best-off considerably more political influence than average citizens, thereby violating political equality. It argues that the gap between the best-off and the worst-off should not be reduced because it is good, but rather as an inescapable instrument to protect citizens from the risk of material domination. For this reason, it defends the 'principle of proportionality': economic inequality should not exceed a certain range or proportion to enable both the best-off and the worst-off to be co-authors of the legal, political, and socioeconomic rules that govern the 'social' relations in which they are involved.

Further, the book discusses material domination and explains how money influences politics and what are the remedies for this phenomenon; how social justice should face and harmonise power, poverty, efficiency, individual merit, and economic liberties; and, most importantly, how to determine income and wealth limit ratios in a liberal democracy.

A thoughtful investigation on the interdependencies of money and justice and their influence our socio-political systems, this volume will be of great interest to students and researchers of political theory, political philosophy, economics and development, economics theory and philosophy, and social policy.

Nunzio Alì is a postdoctoral researcher at the Department of Political and Social Sciences at the University of Catania, Italy, and a former postdoctoral researcher at the Department of Political Science at the University of São Paulo, Brazil (2018–2020). He holds a PhD in Philosophy from the Federal University of Santa Catarina, Brazil (2018), and is the coordinator of the *Colloquium Philosophy & Global Affairs* (Department of Political and Social Sciences – University of Catania). His main research interests concern theories of justice, economic inequality, power, and human rights.

HOW RICH SHOULD THE 1% BE?

Proportional Justice and Economic Inequality

Nunzio Alì

Routledge
Taylor & Francis Group
LONDON AND NEW YORK

Cover image: Getty Images

First published 2023
by Routledge
4 Park Square, Milton Park, Abingdon, Oxon OX14 4RN

and by Routledge
605 Third Avenue, New York, NY 10158

Routledge is an imprint of the Taylor & Francis Group, an informa business

British Library Cataloguing-in-Publication Data
A catalogue record for this book is available from the British Library

ISBN: 978-0-367-75698-7 (hbk)
ISBN: 978-1-032-03864-3 (pbk)
ISBN: 978-1-003-18942-8 (ebk)

DOI: 10.4324/9781003189428

Typeset in Bembo
by SPi Technologies India Pvt Ltd (Straive)

CONTENTS

ACKNOWLEDGEMENTS

Since the beginning of my studies, I have been interested in theories of justice and economic inequality, and the project on Proportional Justice has been present for the entirety of my academic path. Thus, this book would have proved impossible without all those people who tirelessly helped, guided and fostered me through these years of study and research.

The list is extensive, but I cannot help but first express my thanks to the teachers who have actively oriented and contributed to my scientific formation and the genesis of this book. I would like to begin with my mentor, Professor Luigi Caranti, who deserves my gratitude for the merit of initiating me into political philosophy and for supporting me, in many ways and without ever giving the impression of doubting my path, since I was a graduate student. I am also, and mainly, in debt to him for the precious intellectual partnership and collaboration in developing some benchmark arguments on Proportional Justice, ones we have presented in a couple of previous publications. Thanks also to Professor Luigi Caranti for permitting me to include some of our conclusions in this book. Great thanks goes to Professor Alessandro Pinzani for his supervision, patience, and for all the advice during my four-year PhD at the Department of Philosophy of the Federal University of Santa Catarina, Brazil. His immense intellectual support, and generous friendship, was priceless in helping me to carry out my PhD thesis on the idea of proportionality, which provided the inspiration for this book. Thanks also to Professor Denilson Luís Werle for having accompanied me throughout the entire gestation of the PhD thesis. I am very grateful to my supervisor, Professor Álvaro de Vita, during my former postdoctoral position at the Department of Political Science at the University of São Paulo, Brazil. His teachings gave me the opportunity to improve my understanding of the writings of John Rawls, and, more extensively, of distributive theories of justice in general.

I certainly cannot forget all the colleagues with whom I have shared this long academic and personal-life adventure. Thankfully you are many, but at the least I want to mention Lucas Petroni, Raissa Ventura, and Ivan Rodrigues for their comments, long conversations, and, above all, for their indissoluble friendship; the colleagues who participate in the research groups *Desigualdade e Justiça* at the *Centro Brasileiro de Análise e Planejamento* (CEBRAP – São Paulo), *Justiça e Democracia* at the Federal University of Santa Catarina, and the European Union's exchange project: *Kant in South America* (KANTINSA). All of your contributions have proved indispensable to the making of this book. Another big thanks goes to Rissa Miller for her professional, accurate, and patient editing and proofreading.

Furthermore, I must dutifully admit that without the funds and scholarships from public agencies I have received in these many years of research I would not have had the financial provision to write this book. This project has received funding from the European Union's Horizon 2020 research and innovation programme under the Marie Skłodowska-Curie Grant Agreement No. 777786, from the Grant #2018/04606-4 of the São Paulo Research Foundation (FAPESP), and from the CAPES Foundation.

Finally, I will never be able to repay all of the help I have received from my parents and my sister. To them, I am forever grateful. Most of all, thanks to Diana Piroli, my intellectual and emotional partner, who carefully read and discussed every line of the draft of the manuscript with me. Without the unforgettable moments we spent together, our travels in Latin America and Europe, the endless nights of working, every time you didn't hesitate to listen to my frustration and fears, or abiding my idiosyncrasies, and all the glasses of wine and cachaça that made our philosophical discussions a lot more fun, this book could never have been conceived. You are to me what the blossoming flowers are to the Atacama Desert.

INTRODUCTION

What Is Wrong, If Anything, with Economic Inequality?

It has been just 10 years since the *Occupy Wall Street* movement began with the occupation of Zuccotti Park (located in New York City's Wall Street financial district) on 17 September, 2011.[1] Much has been written and said about this movement's merits and shortcomings, and opinions still differ. Regardless, what is hardly disputable is that it marked a turning point in the debate around the level that economic inequality, in the USA and in liberal democracies in general, had reached at the dawn of the 21st century. Resurrected even earlier by the 2008 financial crisis, the issue of economic inequality gained a new centrality, not only among scholars but also in terms of public debate. Many thought that the contemporary level of economic inequality was incompatible with, and in fact causally related to, high levels of unemployment, job insecurity, and an increase in extreme poverty. Most importantly, the main question concerning distributive justice stopped being whether the poor had a decent level of resources and became whether or not the gap between the super-rich and the rest of society was acceptable.

Another issue advanced by *Occupy* was that of the dangerous relationship between money and politics. Excessive economic inequality gives leverage to the best-off that can be easily converted into political power. Political power, in turn, reinforces their socioeconomic position and increases the distance from those at the bottom of distribution. This vicious circle generates a drift towards oligarchy, captured by the shift from the principle 'one person, one vote' to that of 'one dollar, one vote'. The very many (the poor and the middle class) end up being ruled by the very few (the super-rich). The slogan for which *Occupy* is known – 'We are the 99%' – denounced this state of affairs. The elite's economic power not only distorts electoral campaigns, but also influences the public political agenda. The gap between the richest and the rest of society was at last perceived as a, and perhaps

DOI: 10.4324/9781003189428-1

the, fundamental political problem of our times. Certainly, it is the most important one for liberal democracy.

Finally, *Occupy* was also revolutionary from the perspective of the remedies suggested. The idea was there was no alternative to reducing socioeconomic inequality: indulging in the belief, popular since the 1980s, that democracy could survive with any distance between rich and poor, was perceived as foolish.

After over a decade, what can we say about the concerns of the people gathered in Zuccotti Park? The evaluation has to be twofold in nature. On the one hand, we know now, perhaps better than then, that in the last 40 years a *disproportionate* share of the total national income and wealth has been captured by the top end of the distribution, at the global and domestic level, across authoritarian as well as democratic regimes, albeit to different manners and degrees. Much empirical research shows a consolidated trend towards a sharp increase in the economic concentration of wealth towards the top resulting in the state of affairs known as the "New Inequality" or the "New Gilded Age".[2] According to the *World Inequality Report 2018* (Alvaredo et al. 2018), in those countries with the highest levels of income inequality, the share going to the top 1% ranges between 20% and 28% of the total national income: South Africa (19.2%), Russia and the USA (20.2%), India (21.7%), Turkey (23.4%), and Brazil (27.8%). The magnitude of the current economic inequality appears in all its evidence when we realise that the richest 1% get a percentage of the total national income that is double or more than the percentage received by the entire bottom 50% of the population. In these countries, a person who belongs to the top 1% earns, on average, 30 or even 40 times more than a person who belongs to the bottom 50%. The phenomenon is even more pronounced regarding wealth inequality. To mention just a few cases, in the United States, the richest 1% owns 38.6% of total national wealth, in Russia the percentage is 42.6%, while in Europe the percentage of total national wealth obtained by the top 1% varies between 20% and 24%. By contrast, in most developed countries, the bottom 50% owns around 5% of total national wealth. As observed by Piketty (2014: 258), if this trend is not stopped, many liberal capitalistic societies will soon reach a level of wealth inequality in which the top 10% owns 90%, and the top 1% owns 50% of national wealth, a state of affairs already experimented with in Europe during the period of the Belle Époque. The current economic inequality reaches a very extreme level when we take into account the individual wealth of the richest people in the world (see Bloomberg Billionaires Index 2022). The latest report by Oxfam (Ahmed et al. 2022: 10) estimates that 'the 10 richest men in the world own more than the bottom 3.1 billion people'. Furthermore, the current pandemic and its very unequal social repercussions have only reinforced this already astonishing wealth inequality; in summary, 'the wealth of the 10 richest men has doubled, while the incomes of 99% of humanity are worse-off, because of COVID-19' (Ahmed et al. 2022: 10). On the other hand, *Occupy* was also right to illuminate the fact that money translates easily into political power. This phenomenon is confirmed by empirical research (in particular in the USA), which provides strong evidence that the most affluent citizens enjoy a significantly bigger share of political influence than the one left to the middle class and, a fortiori, to the poor.[3]

For sure, these findings give us reasons to pursue a reduction of economic inequality that go beyond a defence of political equality. For example, we now know that current levels of economic inequality are detrimental to the economy itself and to the social well-being of democratic societies.[4] These reasons, plausible as they are, are not the claims against economic inequality pushed by the *Occupy* movement. That movement *highlighted* a more fundamental question, one of basic justice. The idea expressed was that a reduction in economic inequality was not just one of many desiderata to fight for in a democratic context, but rather, albeit hardly expressed in these terms, that a decrease in economic inequality was a precondition to having any democratic debate whatsoever. It concerned limits and background requisites that the public and political confrontation and deliberation should respect and satisfy. This leaves room for a specific normative work which is no longer limited to the scope of empirical scientists, but primarily engages political philosophy.

From an intellectual point of view, this is the greatest legacy of *Occupy*: the offering of a perspective that is interested in keeping a certain *proportion* between the resources of the rich and poor within a democracy. A perspective that was, and still is, overlooked by the distributive theories that were, and still are, unable to explain why Jeff Bezos' level of wealth is unjust (not merely astonishing, unethical, disturbing, and the like) and, most importantly, *when* his distance from 'us', the average citizenry, becomes a concern for justice.[5] If you think that this is an exaggerated and ungenerous evaluation, allow me a brief overview of the state of the art in current theories of justice.

If we draw a line punctuated by the most relevant normative positions on the acceptability of material inequality, at one end of this spectrum rest anti-egalitarian theories that deny that material equality poses any specific concern relating to justice. They do ask whether Bezos' wealth is just or not, but the interest is exclusively focused on whether or not the best-off satisfy certain criteria to occupy that position. Some ask whether their wealth is the result of individual merits (pure desert-based theories), others whether this entails the maximisation of the total sum of utility in the society (unrestricted utilitarianism), and yet others whether the wealth was acquired through free, un-coerced property exchange (right-libertarianism). Clearly, these views may recommend some egalitarian redistribution, for various extrinsic reasons, but their default position is that neither the astronomical amount of Bezos' wealth, nor, most importantly, the inequality that accompanies it generates any concern for the matter of justice.

On the opposite end, we have theories that perceive substantive equality as intrinsically good, hence the focus is not on how wide the economic gap, nor on how wealthy an individual is, but rather on the sheer fact that there is a difference. According to this perspective, which can be labelled intrinsic-telic egalitarianism, a reduction of the difference would be in and of itself an improvement. Here the objection to Bezos' wealth is that some fellow citizens have less than he does and justice requires reducing this inequality as much as possible. Although intrinsic-telic egalitarianism concerns itself with how each person's level compares with the level of other people, it is highly problematic because it sustains a diminution of inequality simply for the sake of equality as a moral/ethical value, even if this does not improve the personal condition of anyone (a non-person-affecting conception). An intrinsic-telic concern for inequality is indeed notoriously exposed to the levelling-down objection: one is committed to demand that some inequality be removed even if the change worsens the condition of some and improves the condition of no one (Parfit 2000: 110). This counter-intuitive result could still be tolerated only under the assumption that all citizens share the ethical gist of intrinsic egalitarianism, an assumption that seems to be incompatible with nothing less than reasonable pluralism and disagreement among different and competing comprehensive views in a democratic society, which, as Rawls would say, is nothing but a natural and inevitable result of the exercise of basic liberties.

The common solution to bypass the levelling-down objection and advance some egalitarian demands is to argue that inequality is not in itself, or *per se*, bad or unjust. It is what it generates that makes it so. This is usually termed non-intrinsic egalitarianism. We have a reason to reduce or eliminate inequality only when, and only because, doing so benefits those who are less advantaged in a certain relevant form. Unsurprisingly, the vast majority of egalitarian theories belong to the non-intrinsic camp.

One way to deal with economic inequality from a non-intrinsic perspective is to maintain that

> when some people are worse off than others, through no fault or choice of their own, they have a special claim to be raised up to the level of the others, but they have no claim that others be brought down to their level.
>
> (Parfit 1997: 211)

The problem is not inequality *per se*, but inequality when this translates into an unjustifiable shrinking of someone's share. This is the path followed by the major theories that provide a specific distributive principle or criterion. For example, inequality is to be countered if a society does not secure the maximisation of the position of the worst-off (difference principle), priority to the benefits of the worst-off (prioritarianism), a sufficient socioeconomic threshold (sufficientarianism), or the compensation of brute luck (luck-egalitarianism). Being super-rich is morally wrong as long as at least one of these distributive principles is not met, regardless of the gap between Bezos and other fellow citizens. Being concerned with people's absolute levels, and often only with the bottom of distribution, these criteria are rather comfortable with a view of justice that includes no principled limits to inequality.

Focusing on people's absolute levels of material resources entails another important feature. If a society has vast material inequality, people are often economically and politically powerless or subject to exploitation and marginalisation, even if the criteria indicated above are met. Clearly, distributivists do not deny the moral and political significance of the problem, but they tend to believe that it is possible, in fact appropriate, to keep the question of distribution separate from the question of political and socioeconomic power and inclusion. Other philosophers, in particular relational egalitarians, are dissatisfied with this separation and advocate for a paradigm shift. They no longer associate social justice with a distributive 'picture', but with a relational one according to which social relations should be the primary question. The relational conception of justice focuses on how people are treated in terms of intersubjective relations rather than in terms of what people have. Inequality is now objectionable when it is the result of unjustified hierarchical social relations. From a relational egalitarian perspective, we have several reasons to condemn inequality between Bezos' wealth and what others have. According to Scanlon (2018), for example, inequality might: (1) create humiliating differences in status, (2) give the rich unacceptable forms of power over those who have less, (3) undermine equality of economic opportunity, (4) undermine the fairness of political institutions, (5) result from violation of a requirement of equal concern for people's interests, (6) arise from economic institutions that are unfair.

Since the focus is on intersubjective relations, relational accounts are better equipped than distributive accounts to deal with the normative significance of the *distance* in economic resources between the best-off and worst-off. The economic gap between the best-off and worst-off becomes a chief concern. And yet, surprisingly, even within the relational school nothing is said about the acceptable limits of the magnitude of the gap, nor do we find a distributive principle or criterion to command redistribution simply because we have no indication whatsoever as to when inequality becomes too much. This theoretical deficit could be explained by two features of relational egalitarianism.

On the one hand, as a consequence of their shift from merely distributive concerns, relational egalitarians tend to water down distributive criteria. You will not find in relational egalitarianism something as determined and well defined as the difference principle. This seems to incentivise avoiding the problem of defining the limits of what is acceptable. On the other hand, the tendency in relational egalitarianism to provide a plurality of moral and political reasons for economic inequality generates a difficulty. If too much inequality is bad for multiple reasons, it may reach the level of too much at different thresholds, depending on the varying reasons for its acceptable limits. A gap that creates humiliating status inequality might be very different from one which undermines equality of economic opportunity or the fairness of political institutions, or other desiderata. This suggests that relational egalitarians should provide a sort of ranking of the values that inequality puts in danger. If, as is often the case, priority is assigned to the value of political equality, then citizens should enjoy equal (or roughly equal) influence over political decisions, and they should specify what kind of economic inequality generates that kind of threat. Unfortunately, they do not.

Of course, one may think that the threat to political equality, and in general to domination-free relations among citizens, may be circumvented by insulating money from politics. If this worked, then we could afford to remain ignorant of the acceptable limits on economic inequality, no matter how large it would be, and yet the mechanisms above would diffuse potentially degenerative effects of economic inequality. We shall see later in detail why these mechanisms are not credible. For now, let us just ask a simple question. Can one seriously believe that Jeff Bezos, from the position where he is now compared to common citizens, could have roughly the same political influence simply because we cap contributions on political campaigns or check his donations?

If the two main pictures of justice, the distributive and the relational, suffer from the failure to specify the limits of acceptable economic inequality, the recent proposal by Ingrid Robeyns (2017, 2022) marks a novelty that goes in the right direction: it provides a principle to limit wealth and a formula to specify exactly *how much is too much* in absolute terms, a quantitative commitment and a courageous gesture towards a figure quite uncommon in normative thinking. Like sufficientarianism, limitarianism entails a threshold, but this time the threshold focuses on the people situated at the top of the distributive ladder. Robeyns provides two main justifications for her position: the democratic argument and the argument from unmet urgent needs. The former is related to the sheer fact that there are unmet urgent needs for fellow citizens or fellow human beings. The latter is based on the idea that large inequalities in income and wealth undermine the ideal of political equality, given that wealthy people can translate their economic power into political influence.

Limitarianism's democratic argument makes an interesting move towards an adequate concern for the demand of the *Occupy* movement. Unfortunately, Robeyns' account (2017: 16–18) is mainly against 'having too much' of a set of capabilities in absolute terms rather than having too much of them with respect to others. According to limitarianism, under non-ideal circumstances, 'it is not morally permissible to have more resources than are needed to fully flourishing in life' (Robeyns 2017: 1). Then, once we have chosen the list of basic capabilities for a fully flourishing life in a specific context, we need to calculate how much money is necessary to buy these goods and services. The resulting amount, in absolute terms, corresponds to the riches line. Jeff Bezos should not have an individual wealth that surpasses this line.

What is one of the problems, if not *the* problem, with limitarianism? Extreme wealth and inequality, no matter how strictly linked, are two different phenomena that require different moral and political assessments. Indeed, if being rich or super-rich is morally wrong only as long as there are people who are not able to meet their urgent needs, how distant the rich and poor remain no longer matters once this problem is overcome. But the same is not true for the democratic argument. Given the competitive nature of the political and economic spheres, the ability to translate economic power into political power does not depend necessarily or even primarily on the absolute level of wealth enjoyed by the best-off, but on the magnitude of the economic gap from the worst-off. The main problem is not being above or below the threshold. Thus, Robeyns' limitarianism surprisingly misses the target. Granted, if the distance between those who are above the threshold and those who are below is small, the former group will not have the resources necessary to influence politics significantly more than the latter. But if the distance is large enough, political equality remains in danger. Limitarianism prescribes a severe limitation of individual wealth that is ineffective in reaching the goal of the democratic argument.

To summarise, all major orientations in contemporary normative theory either ignore the question of the permissible size of economic inequality between the best-off and the worst-off, or offer some reasons to deal with it that are vulnerable to the levelling-down objection, or provide instrumental reasons to worry about excessive inequality without even trying to define a distributive principle of justice capable of identifying when material inequality becomes political domination. But is this really a problem? Perhaps I have been misled by the *Occupy* movement, and thus exaggerating the problem. For example, the value of political equality matters to liberal democratic citizens, but so does an economic distribution which respects legitimate individual properties, the exercise of economic liberties, the free enjoyment of the fruits of such exercise, and the individual right to pursue one's own life plan. Alternatively, if to guarantee political equality one must give up the Rawlsian ambition to make economic inequalities instrumental to maximising the positions of the worst-off (whatever the gap with the best-off may be), perhaps we should not pay this price. After all, one could say: political equality means that we have the same right to vote, not that we have the same political influence. It is OK that our money heavily influences politics. At best we could do something, even if not fully effective, to insulate money from politics.

I believe that these compromises are intellectually unsatisfactory and politically dangerous. The question of the size of material inequality cannot be left at the door of justice. If it is true that excessive economic inequality gives leverage to the best-off that can be easily converted into political power, I claim that a compelling conception of social justice is necessary to provide a material distributive principle that *explicitly* prescribes that economic inequality must not exceed a certain range or *proportion*. In other words, social justice needs what I call the 'principle of proportionality'. A distributive principle that allows us to say that Bezos' wealth is neither unjust in itself nor unjust because it overcomes an absolute top threshold, nor because it might be reduced to raise people's absolute material levels up to a certain threshold or as much as possible, but rather that Bezos' wealth is unjust when the distance between his economic resources and those of the worst-off citizens in the USA reaches a range capable of exposing the latter to the risk of what I call 'material domination'. Here the appeal is to a conception of domination that aims to restore and reformulate the classical one according to which, it will be recalled, individuals are dominated if they obey the foreign will of others as opposed to 'obeying only oneself' (Rousseau: 1997). Domination occurs precisely, in my view, when a person or a group does not have adequate power to be co-authors of the primary rules of society. Obviously, domination is not caused solely by material factors. The most evident form of domination occurs in a society in which a group is formally excluded from certain positions in government or denied equal political rights. This form of domination occurs even in a society with perfect material equality. For this reason, the approach of 'proportional justice' should be applied to all those key power resources that allow citizens to be co-authors of primary rules. Now, let me briefly explain and clarify the main ideas by which I intend to defend the approach of proportional justice and, more precisely, the distributive principle of proportionality.

Why We Need Proportional Justice

To be honest from the start, the idea that inequality in material resources should be contained within some ratio is not new. Indeed, its origin can be traced back to Plato and Aristotle. In *The Laws* (1960), Plato argued that no one should be more than four times richer than the poorest member of the society while Aristotle in the *Politics* (1998) favoured 'proportional equality', thereby condemning extreme material inequalities because they produce a situation in which the poor and the rich are not able to establish a just constitution and government. In modern times, the most authoritative proponent of proportional justice is likely Rousseau. In a famous passage of *The Social Contract* Rousseau (1997: 78) holds that 'no citizen be so very rich that he can buy another, and none so poor that he is compelled to sell himself'. Surprising, in the contemporary debate of distributive justice, the idea that proportional justice concerns inequality between the best-off and the worst-off is quite lost.

To be clear, when these classical authors appeal to this idea of proportional justice, they refer to the domain of political and social justice, rather than to that of ethics, retributive justice or 'local' issues of redistributive justice which are, instead, the domain whereby contemporary scholars often advocate the idea of proportionality.[6] Of course, we have undefeatable reasons to disagree with Plato and Aristotle for the way they unjustifiably exclude certain categories of individuals (mainly slaves and women) from a political society, and with Rousseau for the way he conceives individual self-determination (not to mention his discriminatory judgements on women). But, while we can draw very different conclusions, I think they are correct in one basic assumption; i.e. when we take into account a (political) society as a whole, the terms of material distribution cannot be dissociated from the question of 'political authority'. To 'go back' to contemporary times, this is the same basic assumption that moved John Rawls in identifying as the primary subject of social justice what, since *A Theory of Justice* (1971), he called the basic structure of society (or background justice); or what I prefer to call the 'primary rules' of society. Here, with the notion of primary rules, I want to make more explicit the contents of the basic structure of society; that is, a complex network of basic or ground rules – understood in broad terms as political, legal, socioeconomic, epistemic, and cultural – that govern the social relations in which individuals are involved, and, as Rawls (1971: 7) says, 'its effects [on individuals' life prospects] are so profound and present from the start'. Thus, in my view, once 'distributive' justice inevitably focuses on the primary rules of society, the main normative question turns out to be: who has the power to establish, shape and stabilise primary rules over the time? Not accidentally, this question is the topic of Chapter 1.

From a normative point of view, the first task is to clarify that the moral question of who has the power to establish and shape the primary rules cannot be reduced to a normative problem that arises only in the presence of a special kind of 'actor', such as a government or other political authority. In other words, it is a 'moral' problem that cannot be ignored even in a libertarian ideal world, like that of an island in which property has moved from one individual to another with no breach of the three principles specified by Nozick (1974: 150–153), up to the point that the entire island is owned by one of its inhabitants. In this scenario, what happens is that,

> providing it is difficult or expensive enough to leave the island, the owner can impose on the other inhabitants any condition she fancies. If they are to be allowed to earn their livelihood, they may have to work abysmally long hours, for example, or give up their religion, or wear scarlet underwear.
>
> (Van Parijs 1995: 14)

Clearly, it means that the inhabitants live under the owner's will. Note that the foreign will is not imposed on the inhabitants by means of violence and coercion as external interferences or physical obstacles and threats. The owner of the island has the material power to offer a job on his own terms. Although the inhabitants are materially disempowered, they still can say: No thanks! Of course, then, the consequence of this refusal might be to live in extreme poverty, or even starve. In this sense, we can argue that the inhabitants are materially dominated by the owner. This imaginary scenario is able to introduce intuitively the notion of material domination.

First of all, the specific 'circumstances'[7] of the libertarian island leads us to infer that the inhabitants are involved in social relations that cannot be considered 'voluntary' (leaving the island is objectively highly costly and risky) and in which there is only one game in 'town'; they are obliged to play by the rules of this game. In the imaginary scenario of the libertarian island, even in the absence of a political authority and genuine political rules, inhabitants are involved in social relations governed by socioeconomic rules. The owner of the island has the material power with respect to other inhabitants to establish and shape these rules at will. Note that nothing changes if the owner is morally virtuous; that is, if he tries to track inhabitants' preferences, ideas and interests. In this case, inhabitants may enjoy better living conditions, but they ultimately stand on the goodwill of the owner. They continue to be dominated because their moral 'deliberative' autonomy (co-authorship) is disrespected; that is, they do not have a voice in shaping the rules, or better primary rules, that govern social interaction and cooperation in which they are involved.

Second, although the case of the island appears as too distant from reality and the risk of material domination accordingly quite remote, the normative point is that this risk cannot be avoided even if all individuals are extended equal political status through the democratic procedures of the rule of law – formal political equality, political and voting rights, constitutional provisions or specific forums for public contestation. This means that this risk does not disappear even if we abandon the apolitical libertarian ideal of a society and we institute a (democratic) republican form of government. In other words, material domination concerns a form of domination that is not 'encoded in legal statuses such as "slave" or "serf" but that arise out of conditions of dependence and inequality among individuals who are legally recognized as free and equal persons' (Neuhouser 2013: 203). Most importantly, neither can the risk of material domination be avoided if some version of the insulation strategy is enforced. The insulation strategy aims, indeed, to insulate the political democratic process from the power of money by a set of methods to cap private contributions to candidates and parties, severely curtail television and radio advertising, and guarantee public slots in the media devoted to representing the views of all different candidates. But even the most ambitious and comprehensive proposal of insulation strategy in the current debate – that provided by Julia Cagé, *The Price of Democracy: How Money Shapes Politics and What to Do about It* (2020) – is entirely impotent against those mechanisms through which money indirectly influences the political system and, above all, public opinion.

To sum up, we need to deeply rethink the way the theories of justice commonly justify the terms of material distribution. Given the competitive and relational nature of economic and political powers, the significance of power ensuing from wealth depends not simply on how much one has in absolute terms, but on the comparative difference between what some have and what others do not. As a result, the worst-off in a society could and should reject 'social' arrangements that leave them so distant from the best-off that they risk domination, *regardless of their absolute shares of economic resources*. For example, the fact that in absolute terms Westerners today have more resources than mediaeval kings is no guarantee that they are not dominated. In fact, the risk of material domination is with us, as the empirical studies cited above show. No democratic theory of justice can afford the luxury of allowing social mechanisms that lead to a group of citizens dominating another. Otherwise, we would endorse a distributive view that conceives citizens as passive recipients of goods, rather than as active subjects of justice.

Power and Inequality: The Risk of Domination

At this point in the discussion, one essential thing appears evident: theories of justice need to take into account the question of power. Surprisingly, however, power is not viewed as the central concept in discussions of social and distributive justice. Fortunately, in more recent times and with increasing vigour, power has become a component of the debate on social justice. Thus, giving continuity and yet drawing some alternative conclusions on this debate, in Chapter 2, I provide a specific conceptualisation of power and domination that aspires to be adequate and useful from the perspective of political and distributive justice.

Up to this point, I said that domination occurs when a person or a group does not have the adequate power to be co-authors of the primary rules of society. In Chapter 2, I define more rigorously what I mean by domination. Two elements of my definition need clarification and specification. First of all, what do I mean by 'adequate' power? Or exactly when can power be considered 'adequate' to avoid domination. Secondly, what is the nature of this power? More precisely, how is power exercised or effective, over whom, and through what means or resources. These two questions are roughly related to the effort in the contemporary literature to distinguish the concepts of power and domination, opting for a 'neutral' conceptualisation of power, meanwhile the concept of domination is employed in case someone falls under an arbitrary power. Thus, the debate on domination has run along two related lines of investigation. The first line concerns understanding how power is exercised; while the second line of investigation aims to identify the arbitrary exercise of power – and it is here that the normative challenge exists. In this way, I believe that the conception of power and domination I appeal to might be able to obtain two fundamental steps forward with respect to the current debate.

In the debate on the question of how power is exercised, scholars usually conceive of two different manners: (a) relational as *interagentive* and (b) structural as *impersonal*. According to the relational model, power is always and exclusively understood as interagentive, i.e. between identifiable agents: A has the capacity to interfere and alter the free actions, choices and ideas of B. To be clear, the relational account does not overlook the existence and impact of social structures, but it simply assumes that 'structures do not "exercise" power as persons do; rather, they rely on and provide opportunities for exercising it' (Forst 2017: 45). On the contrary, according to the structural account, power is not exclusively located in agents, but rather also and mainly exercised by social structures themselves without identifiable agents, insofar as these structures operate with several impersonal mechanisms. The result is that, the structural (or systematic) form of domination cannot be traced back to power asymmetries resulting from unequal distribution of resources; e.g., wealth, knowledge, recognition (Azmanova 2020: 46).

I believe that, put in these terms, this common distinction between interagentive and structural domination is somewhat misleading. On the one hand, interagentive theorists risk taking for granted the primary question of how social structures are established and shaped. They overlook that both A and B agents' actions, interests and ideas are not only influenced but also *partially* formed by social structures. Again, I prefer to identify 'social structures' with the notion of 'primary rules'. The point is not who has power within identifiable agents' relationships, like the famous and classic 'master–slave relationship', rather who has power with respect to others to set otherwise primary rules. On the other hand, once structural theorists advocated the idea that individuals might be dominated by an impersonal form of power, they are exposed to the trap of a deterministic view, and hence the risk of making the conception of non-domination politically impracticable or potentially paternalistic and authoritarian.

It is possible to avoid the unproductive contraposition between interagentive and structural power, if we realise that 'social power' is located in agents, but it is attributed to them only through their '*relative*' capacity, by mobilising 'key power resources', to establish, shape, and stabilise primary rules. In other words, primary rules determine a certain asymmetrical distribution of key power resources and, in turn, only through these resources can individuals establish, change, or stabilise those primary rules. From this perspective, first, what I call 'social power' cannot be associated with all kinds of individual power resources, but only with those resources that are indispensable to establish and shape primary rules. Second, social power can be deconstructed into subfields of power according to those key resources that we take into account, such as political power, epistemic power, symbolic power (or status power), authority power (or power of official positions), and material power. I sustain that a conception of social power should embody these essential features. It follows that:

> Social power exists as the capacity of a social actor A, by mobilising certain 'key power resources', to make social actor B or C think and act in a certain way by establishing, shaping, and stabilising primary rules that govern 'social' relations in which both A and B or C are involved.

Now, we can move on to the question of when power can be considered 'adequate' to avoid domination. In this respect, if my conception of social power is consistent, the main implication is that we can derive that a social actor's capacity to establish and shape primary rules is directly *proportional* to key power resources that he disposes of with respect to others. From this perspective, contrary to what most scholars seem to assume, the concept of non-domination cannot be, in principle, insensitive to the size of the inequality of power resources between citizens. However, the alternative does not necessarily imply that any inequality in key power resources should be impermissible. For example, it is implausible to assume that even a tiny economic inequality entails material domination. Pursuing perfect equality in material resources among citizens is an unrealistic, undesirable and above all unnecessary normative prescription. However, although this normative consideration about equality is true, it does not mean that we can be blind about the size of material inequality between Jeff Bezos and those US citizens that occupy the bottom of the distribution. Perhaps we may have some uncertainty about the exact magnitude of inequality that entails material domination, but we can be reasonably sure about the fact that under current US primary rules the already astonishing wealth inequality can still increase unboundedly and, therefore, exposes the US' worst-off citizens to the *risk of material domination*. Thus, this forces us, in order to avoid the *risk of domination*, to establish a certain theoretical and empirical 'limit' range (or proportion) for each of these key power resources. We need a normative account that explicitly embodies this prescription, and this is what the proportionality approach does.

Proportional Justice as a Political Conception

It is certain that proportional justice appeals to a moral standpoint in condemning unbounded inequality. However, as I said, it is important to spell out the domain of this moral view. Hence, in Chapter 3, I will draft, following the path paved by Rawls in *Political Liberalism*, the main features of what we may call a 'political conception of distributive justice', one that in my own view takes the form of proportional justice. The main purpose is to clarify that by endorsing a Rawlsian-inspired political conception of justice does not mean to abandon substantive distributive requirements. It is not true, unlike what some believe (Shoelandt and Gaus 2018), that the inevitable result of a political conception of justice, given the fact of pluralism, is that of watering down the distributive justice that concerns material resources or goods. At the least, it is possible to provide a principle of material distribution from a 'freestanding' point of view: the principle of proportionality.

According to Rawls (2005), a political conception of justice is confined to a specific domain of morality which is independent of epistemology, metaphysics and any particular comprehensive doctrine (moral, religious, ethical, etc.). For this reason, Rawls (2005: 38) defines it as 'the domain of the political'. A political conception of justice is presented as freestanding; it means that we cannot expect to find an agreement among reasonable citizens if this 'political' content, but always moral (Rawls 2005: xlvii, 395), includes principles that are grounded on a particular comprehensive doctrine. In the context of a democratic regime, the principles of a political conception of justice have the function to impose background requisites that the public and political confrontation and deliberation should satisfy. This means that the result of public deliberation and confrontation, whatever it would be, cannot deprive citizens of certain 'goods'. As we know, Rawls (1971) calls these goods 'social primary goods'.

What I suggest calling a 'political conception of distributive justice' is conceived for the same purpose. I will not enter into the debate on whether Rawls' primary goods are all those 'goods' we need to ensure the background requisites of a political conception of distributive justice, but instead focus on what matters about the nature of these 'goods', and that is that they should be understood as 'key power resources'. From this perspective, these 'resources' (material and immaterial) should be distributed according to what I call the approach of proportional justice. Evidently, I do not have the space and time to focus on each of these key power resources. This book concerns the distribution of material power that, in my account, corresponds to economic resources in terms of income and wealth. Hence, what I call the (distributive) principle of proportionality applies to material resources. At this point, the reading can easily ascertain that the prescription that economic inequality must not exceed a certain range or *proportion* is grounded on the freestanding moral/political idea that the worst-off in a society should not be exposed to the risk of material domination. Hence, the principle of proportionality can be presented as a freestanding principle.

I have already provided a concise, but quite convincing overview of how all major distributive principles available in the contemporary literature are unable to adequately deal with the question of the size of inequality. There is no need to dwell on this point, and yet I would like to emphasise that, unlike what some might still suspect, the principle of proportionality is not equivalent to the principle of equality (here understood as equality of outcome), and therefore it is far from superfluous or redundant. Although both of them take directly into account the distance between the most and the least advantaged, what the principle of proportionality prescribes cannot be inferred from the principle of equality. The latter can only tell us to pursue the greatest possible equality. Instead, according to the principle of proportionality, we are not informed by reasons of justice to pursue a more equal material distribution than that of a certain well-specified limit ratio that allows us to avoid the risk of material domination. I am quite convinced that this feature can also make all the difference in the public debate.

The Permissible Range: Towards a Definition

The final aim, and effort, of the book is present in as much detail as possible the (distributive) principle of proportionality. In Chapter 4, I will try to provide a compelling, yet not fully complete and exhaustive, guidance regarding the acceptable size of the economic gap. Of course, it can be done if one is ready to accept the degree of precision allowed by the nature of the problem. The first, and the most important, thing is to define the constraints that the range should respect, which also serve as indications of how the range ought to be sought.[8] What follows is a first attempt:

1. The limits of permissible inequality are to be expressed through two ratios: one between the wealth of the best-off segment of the population and the wealth of the worst-off segment; the other between the incomes of the same segments (post-tax and transfer benefits). One should distinguish between wealth and income, not only out of conformity with current scientific standards, but because wealth inequality is more pronounced, produces more economic inefficiency, and more effectively impacts economic and political power than inequality of labour income.
2. Ratios come with a technical problem, similar to the one well known about the threshold. Imagine we say that the richest segment's income cannot be 29 times higher than that of the worst-off segment. We would be saying that those who make 29.0001 more times than what the poor make will risk to dominate, while those who make 28.9999 will not. In any event, the general normative point – the necessity to establish some proportion in the resources of the best-off and worst-off – does not change. Notice that even if a satisfactory solution

to the 'threshold' problem or other technical problems is not available, one should be ready to sacrifice elegance for the sake of protecting the fairness of political equality through an unambiguous measure of the limit. After all, not only is the threshold problem widespread in any legislative body (think of tax brackets), but it is certainly not a problem peculiar to proportional justice given that many distributive accounts (think of limitarianism and sufficientarianism) suffer the same difficulty.

3. The permissible ratios should reflect what the best empirical science available at any time indicates as necessary to avoid the risk of material domination. In particular, any account of the limit will have to justify how the best-off and the worst-off segments of the population are identified. To compare the resources of the top 10% with those of the bottom 50% is one thing; to compare the resources of the top 1% and those of the bottom 20% is quite another. The justification must rest on empirical findings on the relation between money and political influence and other relevant facts such as the availability of welfare services. To have a certain income in a society that offers free access to healthcare, schools and college is quite different than having the same amount in a society without those services.
4. A specific justification will have to be provided if the account, as it is reasonable to assume, will focus on average income and wealth of the worst-off segment. For example, since the poorest individuals in the society earn and own less than the average of the bottom segment, they seem to remain at risk of domination even if the ratio is respected. This suggests the opportunity to make the bottom segment narrow enough to limit this risk. More importantly, the bottom segment should be defined in such a way that there are strong reasons to believe that the poorest in it are poorest not because of some modifiable societal arrangement but because of subjective factors unrelated to the shaping of primary rules. Once this is done, the criterion will take the following form: *no one should have an income (post-tax and transfer benefits) that exceeds the limit of being No. times higher than the average income of the bottom X% of the national population, and no one should possess a wealth (post-tax and transfer benefits) that is No. times higher than the average wealth of the bottom X% of the national population.*
5. The ratios should be prudent in the sense that we are authorised to adopt one only if there are strong reasons to believe that a more permissive limit would entail the risk of domination. In other words, the limit should be permissive enough to allow as much exercise of economic liberties and socioeconomic efficiency as possible. The only acceptable reason to limit one of these values is the risk of material domination.
6. The ratios should be realistic in the sense that they should not aim to make each citizen perfectly equal in terms of political influence. Differences in political influence, even considering only economic factors, will likely remain in any just socicty.
7. In principle, the ratios should be the same for all liberal democratic societies. However, the specificities of income and wealth distribution in each liberal

democracy may suggest the opportunity to cut different segments at the top and at the bottom, something which would obviously impact the final ratios. It follows that we may keep the general validity of the ratios as a regulative ideal (a sort of general formula of democratic distribution), while proceeding at this initial stage by focusing on one country at a time, privileging those countries in which data on wealth and income distribution are available and research on the relation between money and influence has produced some reliable results.

8. The ratios only apply to the domestic level. I am far from denying that we have obligations of justice to reduce material inequalities at the global level. I simply do not deal with the problem in this book.

These constraints also show how the principle of proportionality is able to deal with those normative issues concerning the wealth and income distribution that are fundamental to a liberal democracy. They are concerned with efficiency, absolute poverty, basic liberties, pluralism, and the set of distributive public policies and social reforms that are needed to avoid this risk. I believe that the principle of proportionality is better equipped to face all these main issues than other competitive distributive principles. Broadly, the way the principle of proportionality deals with all these related issues shows how it is possible to rebut some predictable objections to it.

To conclude, this book obviously cannot escape providing an attempt, and not a final answer, of how permissible ratios for income and wealth inequalities could be determined in a domestic context. A case study based on the contemporary United States seems to be an almost mandatory first choice, and one for which the preliminary empirical studies and data are available. The application of the above constraints seems to lead towards the following figure of income and wealth ratios which is, respectively, 1/29 for income inequality and 1/400 for wealth inequality. Precisely, given the recent income and wealth distribution in the USA, this means that to avoid the risk of domination no one should have an income (post-tax and benefits) that exceeds USD13,100*29, and no one should have a wealth that exceeds USD10,000*400.[9]

I admit that determining a fair and effective ratio with precision is extremely difficult. Indeed, no one should be surprised if in the end the permissible range for income inequality and wealth inequality in the United States will be different from the 1/29 and 1/400 I proposed. A compelling definition of permissible ratios most certainly requires future, and more accurate, multidisciplinary research than what I can offer in this book. In any case, although we can, and will, disagree on exactly how large the permissible income or wealth ratio which protects us from the *risk of material domination* must be, the approach of proportional justice aspires to defend and convince as reasonably as possible, in both the academic and public debates, that we have no excuse to abstain from defining and defending one. We can no longer accept that, in our liberal democracies, unbounded economic inequality is the accepted status quo.

Notes

1 See Flank (2011), van Gelder (2011), Chomsky (2012, 2013), and Writers for the 99% (2012). Similar social movements have also spread in Europe, for example Movimiento 15-M (Indignados). In the same period other political movements emerged around the globe, such as the Arab Spring movements and the Iranian Green movement.
2 See Keister (2000), Kelly (2009), Volscho and Kelly (2012), Rosanvallon (2013), Piketty (2014, 2020), Galbraith (2012, 2014), Dorling (2014), Drennan (2015), Reich (2016), Wolff (2017), Alvaredo et al. (2018), Piketty et al. (2018), Milanovic (2019), and Saez and Zucman (2019).
3 See West and Loomis (1998), Phillips (2002), Krugman (2002), Graetz and Shapiro (2005), Bartels (2008), Acemoglu and Robinson (2008), Winters and Page (2009), Winters (2011), Gilens (2005, 2012), Gilens and Page (2014, 2017), McCarty, Poole and Rosenthal (2016), Hacker and Pierson (2010), Jacobs and Shapiro (2000), and Cagé (2020).
4 See McAdams (2007), Wilkinson and Pickett (2010), Lansley (2012), Bowles (2012), Stiglitz (2012, 2015), and Atkinson (2015). Some have argued that the current level of economic inequality fuels political resentment and the rise of populist movements in liberal democracies, see Frank (2005), Cramer (2016), Hochschild (2016), Mounk (2018), and Cagé (2020).
5 Jeff Bezos was the world's richest person for the fourth year running until 2021 (see Dolan 2021). Recently, his first-place position has been overtaken by Elon Musk (see Bloomberg Billionaires Index 2022). Here, Bezos is taken as an example only for his amount of wealth and economic power, and not for some individual characteristics as a wealthy person or entrepreneur.
6 This other domain to apply 'proportional justice' is, in fact, the same that Aristotle identified in *Nicomachean Ethics* (2004).
7 Following Rawls (1971), I call them subjective and objective circumstances of justice.
8 These constraints have already been presented in a similar shape in Alì and Caranti (2021) and Caranti and Alì (2021).
9 Data Piketty et al. (2018), Saez and Zucman (2016), Leiserson, McGrew and Kopparam (2019).

Bibliography

Acemoglu, Daron and James A. Robinson. 2008. 'Persistence of Power, Elites, and Institutions', *American Economic Review*, 98(1): 267–293.

Ahmed, Nabil, Anna Marriott, Nafkote Dabi, Megan Lowthers, Max Lawson, and Leah Mugehera. 2022. *Inequality Kills: The Unparalleled Action Needed to Combat Unprecedented Inequality in the Wake of COVID-19*. Oxford: Oxfam GB.

Alì, Nunzio and Luigi Caranti. 2021. 'How Much Economic Inequality is Fair in Liberal Democracies? The Approach of Proportional Justice', *Philosophy & Social Criticism*, 47(7): 769–788.

Alvaredo, Facundo, Lucas Chancel, Thomas Piketty, Emmanuel Saez, and Gabriel Zucman (eds.). 2018. *World Inequality Report 2018*. Cambridge: Belknap Press.

Aristotle. 2004. *Nicomachean Ethics*. Trans. and ed. by Roger Crisp. Cambridge: Cambridge University Press.

Aristotle. 1998. *Politics*. Trans. by C. D. C. Reeve. Cambridge: Hackett Publishing Company.

Atkinson, Anthony B. 2015. *Inequality: What Can Be Done?* Cambridge: Harvard University Press.

Azmanova, Albena. 2020. *Capitalism on Edge: How Fighting Precarity Can Achieve Radical Change Without Crisis or Utopia*. New York: Columbia University Press.

Bartels, Larry M. 2008. *Unequal Democracy: The Political Economy of a New Gilded Age*. Princeton: Princeton University Press.

Bloomberg. 2022. 'Bloomberg Billionaires Index.' *Bloomberg*, 15 March, https://www.bloomberg.com/billionaires/ (accessed on 15 March 2022).

Bowles, Samuel. 2012. *The New Economics of Inequality and Redistribution*. Cambridge: Cambridge University Press.

Cagé, Julia. 2020. *The Price of Democracy: How Money Shapes Politics and What to Do About It*. Trans. Patrick Camiller. Cambridge: Harvard University Press.

Caranti, Luigi and Nunzio Alì. 2021. 'The Limits of Limitarianism: Why Political Equality is Not Protected by Robeyns' Democratic Argument', *Politica & Società*, 1: 89–116.

Chomsky, Noam. 2013. *Occupy: Reflections on Class War, Rebellion and Solidarity, 2nd Edition*. New York: Zuccotti Park Press.

Chomsky, Noam. 2012. *Occupy*. London: Penguin Books.

Cramer, Katherine J. 2016. *The Politics of Resentment: Rural Consciousness in Wisconsin and the Rise of Scott Walker*. Chicago: University of Chicago Press.

Dolan, Kerry A. 2021. 'Forbes' 35th Annual World's Billionaires List: Facts And Figures 2021.' *Forbes*, 6 April 2021, https://www.forbes.com/sites/kerryadolan/2021/04/06/forbes-35th-annual-worlds-billionaires-list-facts-and-figures-2021/?sh=6c4f852d5e58 (accessed on 10 July 2022)

Dorling, Danny. 2014. *Inequality and the 1%*. London: Verso.

Drennan, Matthew P. 2015. *Income Inequality: Why It Matters and Why Most Economists Didn't Notice*. New Haven: Yale University Press.

Flank, Lenny (ed.). 2011. *Voices From the 99 Percent: An Oral History of the Occupy Wall Street Movement*. Florida: Red and Black Publishers.

Forst, Rainer. 2017. *Normativity and Power: Analyzing Social Orders of Justification*. Oxford: Oxford University Press.

Frank, Thomas. 2005. *What's the Matter with Kansas? How Conservatives Won the Heart of America*. New York: Henry Holt and Company.

Galbraith, James K. 2014. *The End of Normal: The Great Crisis and the Future of Growth*. New York: Simon & Schuster.

Galbraith, James K. 2012. *Inequality and Instability: A Study of the World Economy Just before the Great Crisis*. Oxford: Oxford University Press.

Gilens, Martin. 2012. *Affluence and Influence: Economic Inequality and Political Power in America*. Princeton: Princeton University Press and Russell Sage Foundation.

Gilens, Martin. 2005. 'Inequality and Democratic Responsiveness', *Public Opinion Quarterly*, 69(5): 778–796.

Gilens, Martin and Benjamin Page. 2017. *Democracy in America? What Has Gone Wrong and What We Can Do About It*. Chicago: University of Chicago Press.

Gilens, Martin and Benjamin Page. 2014. 'Testing Theories of American Politics: Elites, Interest Groups, and Average Citizens', *Perspectives on Politics*, 12(3): 564–581.

Graetz, Michael J. and Ian Shapiro. 2005. *Death by a Thousand Cuts: The Fight Over Taxing Inherited Wealth*. Princeton: Princeton University Press.

Hacker, Jacob S. and Paul Pierson. 2010. *Winner-Take-All Politics: How Washington Made the Rich Richer-and Turned Its Back on the Middle Class*. New York: Simon & Schuster Paperbacks.

Hochschild, Arlie R. 2016. *Strangers in Their Own Land: Anger and Mourning on the American Right*. New York: The New Press.

Jacobs, Lawrence R. and Robert Y. Shapiro. 2000. *Politicians Don't Pander: Political Manipulation and the Loss of Democratic Responsiveness*. Chicago: University of Chicago Press.

Keister, Lisa A. 2000. *Wealth in America: Trends in Wealth Inequality*. New York: Cambridge University Press.

Kelly, Nathan J. 2009. *The Politics of Income Inequality in the United States*. New York: Cambridge University Press.

Krugman, Paul. 2002. 'For Richer: How the Permissive Capitalism of the Boom Destroyed American Equality', *The New York Times Magazine*, 20 October 2002, https://www.nytimes.com/2002/10/20/magazine/for-richer.html (accessed on 15 March 2022).

Lansley, Stewart. 2012. *The Cost of Inequality: Why Economic Equality is Essential for Recovery*. London: Gibson Square Books.

Leiserson, Greg, Will McGrew and Raksha Kopparam. 2019. 'Net Worth Taxes: What They Are and How They Work', *Washington Center for Equitable Growth*, 21 March 2019, https://equitablegrowth.org/research-paper/net-worth-taxes-what-they-are-and-how-they-work/ (accessed on 15 March 2022).

McAdams, Richard H. 2007. 'The Economic Costs of Inequality', *John M. Olin Program in Law and Economics*, Working Paper no. 370: 1–33.

McCarty, Nolan, Keith T. Poole and Howard Rosenthal. 2016. *Polarized America: The Dance of Ideology and Unequal Riches. Second Edition*. Cambridge: The MIT Press.

Milanovic, Branko. 2019. *Capitalism, Alone: The Future of the System That Rules the World*. Cambridge: Belknap Press.

Mounk, Yascha. 2018. *The People vs. Democracy: Why Our Freedom Is in Danger and How to Save It*. Cambridge: Harvard University Press.

Neuhouser, Frederick. 2013. 'Rousseau's Critique of Economic Inequality', *Philosophy & Public Affairs*, 41(3): 193–225.

Nozick, Robert. 1974. *Anarchy, State, and Utopia*. Oxford: Blackwell Publishers.

Parfit, Derek. 2000. 'Equality or Priority?', in Matthew Clayton and Andrew Williams (eds.), *The Ideal of Equality*, pp. 81–125. New York: St. Martin's Press.

Parfit, Derek. 1997. 'Equality and Priority', *Ratio*, 10(3): 202–221.

Phillips, Kevin. 2002. *Wealth and Democracy: A Political History of the American Rich*. New York: Broadway Books.

Piketty, Thomas. 2020. *Capital and Ideology*. Trans. by Arthur Goldhammer. Cambridge: Harvard University Press.

Piketty, Thomas. 2014. *Capital in The Twenty-First Century*. Trans. by Arthur Goldhammer. Cambridge: Harvard University Press.

Piketty, Thomas, Emmanuel Saez and Gabriel Zucman. 2018. 'Distributional National Accounts: Methods and Estimates for the United States', *The Quarterly Journal of Economics*, 133(2): 553–609.

Plato. 1960. *The Laws*. New York: E.P. Dutton and Co.

Rawls, John. 2005. *Political Liberalism. Expanded Edition*. New York: Columbia University Press.

Rawls, John. 1971. *A Theory of Justice. Original Edition*. Cambridge: Harvard University Press.

Reich, Robert B. 2016. *Saving Capitalism: for the Many, Not the Few*. New York: Icon Books.

Robeyns, Ingrid. 2022. 'Why Limitarianism?' *The Journal of Political Philosophy*, 30(2): 249–270.

Robeyns, Ingrid. 2017. 'Having Too Much', in Jack Knight and Melissa Schwartzberg (eds.), *NOMOS LVI: Wealth. Yearbook of the American Society for Political and Legal Philosophy*, pp. 1–44. New York: New York University Press.

Rosanvallon, Pierre. 2013. *The Society of Equals*. Trans. by Arthur Goldhammer. Cambridge: Harvard University Press.

Rousseau, Jean-Jacques. 1997. 'The Social Contract', in Victor Gourevitch (ed. and trans.), *The Social Contract, and Other Later Political Writings*, pp. 39–152. Cambridge: Cambridge University Press.

Saez, Emmanuel and Gabriel Zucman. 2019. *The Triumph of Injustice: How the Rich Dodge Taxes and How to Make Them Pay*. New York: W. W. Norton & Company.

Saez, Emmanuel and Gabriel Zucman. 2016. 'Wealth Inequality in the United States since 1913: Evidence from Capitalized Income Tax Data', *The Quarterly Journal of Economics*, 131(2): 519–578.

Scanlon, Thomas M. 2018. *Why Does Inequality Matter?* Oxford: Oxford University Press.

Shoelandt, Chad Van and Gerald Gaus. 2018. 'Political and Distributive Justice', in Serena Olsaretti (ed.), *The Oxford Handbook of Distributive Justice*, pp. 283–305. Oxford: Oxford University Press.

Stiglitz, Joseph E. 2015. *Rewriting the Rules of the American Economy: An Agenda for Growth and Shared Prosperity*. New York & London: W. W. Norton & Company.

Stiglitz, Joseph. 2012. *The Price of Inequality: How Today's Divided Society Endangers Our Future*. New York & London: W. W. Norton & Company.

van Gelder, Sarah (ed.). 2011. *This Changes Everything: Occupy Wall Street and the 99% Movement*. San Francisco: Berrett-Koehler Publishers.

Van Parijs, Philippe. 1995. *Real Freedom for All: What (If Anything) Can Justify Capitalism?* Oxford: Oxford University Press.

Volscho, Thomas W. and Nathan J. Kelly. 2012. 'The Rise of the Superrich: Power Resources, Taxes, Financial Markets, and the Dynamics of the Top 1 Percent, 1949–2008', *American Sociological Review*, 77(5): 679–699.

West, Darrell M. and Burdett A. Loomis. 1998. *The Sound of Money: How Political Interests Get What They Want*. New York: W. W. Norton & Company.

Wilkinson, Richard and Kate Pickett. 2010. *The Spirit Level: Why Equality is Better for Everyone*. London: Penguin Press.

Winters, Jeffrey A. 2011. *Oligarchy*. Cambridge: Cambridge University Press.

Winters, Jeffrey A. and Benjamin Page. 2009. 'Oligarchy in the United States?' *Perspectives on Politics*, 7(4): 731–751.

Wolff, Edward N. 2017. *A Century of Wealth in America*. Cambridge: Harvard University Press.

Writers for the 99%. 2012. *Occupying Wall Street: The Inside Story of an Action that Changed America*. New York: Haymarket Books.

1

WHO HAS THE POWER TO ESTABLISH AND SHAPE PRIMARY RULES?

Why the Size of Material Inequality Matters

Since the inception of the classical idea of distributive justice, distributive principles have been thought to assign the way in which the benefits and burdens of a society or among individuals are distributed, and consequently what types of inequality are bad or unjust, and therefore how they should be eliminated or mitigated. From this perspective, any principle that determines how a certain 'good' should be distributed or divided among two or more claimants can be considered a distributive principle of justice. The term 'good' can be understood as including almost everything: money, human organs, job or educational opportunity, public authority, power, basic rights and liberties, or as the avoidance of some specific burdens. Put in these broad terms, distributive principles can concern an innumerable, almost endless, variety of issues. The list of possible distributive principles could be very long; and, of course, our concern for inequality can be very different depending on which of these principles we opt for. However, there is no reason to believe that the same set of principles of justice should be adopted for every domain of morality and for every type of normative judgment. For example, nothing forces us to think that the distributive principles that apply the basic structure of society (Rawls 1971) should be the same as those which apply to individuals who live in a 'Divided World' (Parfit 2000). For this reason, I believe that it is impossible to establish which of the distributive principles are more valid or plausible than others without making the scope and object of our investigation clear and well defined.

Regarding the scope of distributive justice, we can immediately distinguish between the type of philosophical question we want to answer; in other words, the ultimate aim of our normative investigation. First of all, we can simply be interested in providing normative arguments and principles for moral judgments or evaluations. In this case, we focus on axiological theories. This means that we focus on the relative goodness of states of affairs, but it does not automatically follow that

DOI: 10.4324/9781003189428-2

we have reasons to act in order to bring about a better state of affairs, *all things considered* (see G. A. Cohen 2008; Temkin 2017). In this sense, we separate our evaluative judgments from judgments that 'make claims about what we have reason to do' (Scanlon 1998: 2). Of course, these kinds of moral judgments can also guide individuals' conduct and behaviour, but they do not have the ambition to solve conflicts that emerge from divergent interests and moral ideas and values when our conduct inevitably has serious effects and consequences on others. Thus, when we have the intention to solve or mitigate these kinds of conflict in a way that gives individuals or social institutions strong reasons to act, we have moved into the domain of morality that Scanlon (1998) calls a non-metaphysical domain of 'what we owe to each other'. From this perspective, distributive justice is a regulatory idea, or, as G. A. Cohen (2008: 302) says, justice concerns 'rules of social regulation'. From this perspective, distributive justice means social and political justice. It is in this case that the question of 'authority' must be addressed.

Suppose we dispose of a theory of distributive justice or a set of distributive principles of justice: what is the relationship between the theory or the principles and the subjects of justice, whether they are all human beings or a specific group of individuals? We should assume that if we are confident about the content of distributive justice, official individuals or some social institutions will be authorised to enact it. In other words, we can use our power to pursue, satisfy or ensure the principles of distributive justice. This is how distributive justice can be understood to mean social and political justice. However, we cannot deal with the question of 'authority' unless we expressly clarify the object of our investigation; in other words, we must clarify what kinds of conflict are at stake and in which circumstances they emerge. These circumstances are roughly those that Rawls (1971: 126–130; 2001: 24, 84; 2005: 66) calls the subjective and objective circumstances of justice. I define the subjective circumstances of justice as those in which conflicts and disagreements about norms and principles that govern our social relations cannot be reconciled by appealing to our social virtues. This means that radical pluralism is potentially at stake. Meanwhile, the objective circumstances of justice are those in which social relations cannot be considered 'voluntary' and in which, by contrast and to some degree, we are forced to share, because getting out of them is objectively highly costly and risky. This means that domination is potentially at stake.[1] Let me show how these circumstances determine the way in which we should conceive distributive justice.

I said that any principle that determines how a certain 'good', for instance a material resource, should be distributed or divided among two or more claimants can be considered a distributive principle of justice. But a premise is fundamental here. To argue about justice, it is necessary that claimants consider themselves as moral beings or justificatory beings (Forst 2012). There are numerous ways to understand this moral attitude.[2] I assume that they are moral beings insofar as they are reasonable persons (Scanlon 1982, 1998; Rawls 1982, 2005). I believe that the idea of reasonableness appeals to our deepest sense of 'practical/political' morality in our social relations, when it is understood as taking the effects or consequences of our actions on others very seriously. According to Rawls (2005: 49, 395), reasonable persons as those who are ready 1) to propose principles and standards as fair terms of cooperation and to abide by them willingly, given the assurance that others will likewise do so, and 2) to discuss the fair terms that others propose. On the contrary, a person is unreasonable to give no weight to the interests of others in deciding which principle or norms to accept.[3]

However, I need to make two important clarifications. In my view, being a reasonable person means to endorse a 'universal' moral attitude, something that should not necessarily be restricted only to liberal democratic societies, as a simple liberal virtue of tolerance.[4] Moreover, the idea of reasonableness cannot be too indeterminate; otherwise it provides no criteria or requirements to evaluate a reasonable rejection of a principle. Thus, I assume that the idea of reasonableness, understood as taking the effects or consequences of our actions on others very seriously, means that reasonable persons, first of all, know that their actions can, both directly and indirectly, cause harm or injury to others; that is, no use of violence, coercion, or domination to impose their will and opinion on others. Secondly, reasonable persons also know that they are able to eliminate or alleviate the suffering condition of others, even if this condition does not depend on our direct and indirect actions. This implies the common requirements of social virtues such as: sympathy, beneficence, love, care, recognition, solidarity, etc.[5]

Now, imagine a group of individuals who are tasked with dividing a certain limited or scarce material resource produced through their social interactions and cooperation. However, under accurate reflection, they realise that this material resource comes into the world only due to a set of social rules (political, legal, socioeconomic, cultural etc.) that govern their social interactions and cooperation. Thus, one thing appears clear: they gather that, in this case, these social rules are *the primary object of distributive justice*. In other words, these rules (political, legal, socioeconomic, cultural etc.) determine the question of 'how these goods come into the world in the first place and of who decides on their allocation and how this allocation is made' (Forst 2014: 34). For the purpose of my argument, it is sufficient to keep in mind that the members of this group (as reasonable persons) rule out, by default, imposing their will and opinion on others through means of violence, coercion or domination in order to take that resource for themselves. In other words, they want to offer reasons or justifications to others to defend their distributive views.

Now, the members of this group might have a 'shared understanding' of how to distribute this 'good'; something similar to what Walzer (1983) supposed must be the ground for distributive justice. For example, they may share a comprehensive religious or ethical view that gives them guidance on how to establish and shape these rules and consequently how to assign or 'distribute' this 'good'; for instance, if they have a holy book and there is a member among them who is able to interpret it, or if they share the same form of life wherein the most valued aim is to become as courageous and capable as warriors. This comprehensive religious or ethical view might give them normative guidance to solve the conflicts of distributive justice.

Thus, they can easily solve the problem of distribution in a number of ways. They might believe that this resource should be equally divided, or that each one should receive a certain amount of it and the rest should be assigned by lot, or that a greater part of it should go to those who are more blessed or more capable warriors.

Unfortunately, things can be more complicated, and they might seriously disagree about religious and ethical views. Some members might hold different religious views and different forms of life. This is a serious problem for them, because they are moral (reasonable) beings; they cannot impose their will and opinion on others. However, beyond their deep religious and ethical divergences, they still conceive distributive justice as a 'mastergoal' or 'supergoal' to be achieved or realised.[6] For example, they may be convinced that, under impartiality, justice requires shaping the rules that govern their social relations and their cooperation in order to maximise the total sum (or the average) of people's well-being; or they may believe that justice requires strict equality, or as much as equality as possible. In either case, they are moral beings, ready for sacrifice, if necessary, in the pursuit of their individual comprehensive doctrine of the good and to accept the social position and the amount of 'goods' that results from the just distribution. Since they are virtuous people with respect to justice, the question of distribution is again resolved.

However, what if they disagree about what distributive justice is? What if some are classical utilitarians, others egalitarians, and still others purely meritocratic? Although all these views of distributive justice are logical, coherent, and plausible, the fact is that these people experience what we can call a radical pluralism. Rawls warns us that this could be the inevitable result of the exercise of reason under free conditions that leads to a diversity in views on philosophy, religion, the good, and even justice. In other words, we can say that this group of people experience the condition of the subjective circumstances of justice: conflicts and disagreements about norms and principles that govern their social relations cannot be reconciled by appealing to their social virtues. However, they still may have a solution: why do those who persist in disagreeing not look elsewhere for the means of subsistence and for pursuing what they consider most valuable? If this is possible, the problem is solved again.

But the social reality can be very frustrating, and they may realise that they cannot physically go anywhere else, or that doing so is objectively highly costly and risky. Thus, on the other hand, they are also involved in the objective circumstances of justice; i.e., the social relations in which they are involved cannot be considered 'voluntary' and in which, by contrast, they are, to some degree, forced to share. As Rawls puts it, they are members of a 'society' in which 'its members enter it only by birth and leave it only by death' (Rawls 2005: xlvi, 12, 68). In other words, there is only one game in town, and they are obliged to play by the rules of this game; or what I call the primary rules (political, legal, socioeconomic etc.).[7]

Here I cannot enter into a discussion of all possible examples of subjective and objective circumstances of justice. For sure, the 'global society' is characterised by these circumstances and our global social relations are governed by a set of political, legal, socioeconomic rules. For this reason I think it is correct to argue about 'primary rules' and justice also in a global context. Nonetheless, I still agree with Rawls that the domestic context should be treated as a specific case of justice, but for the simple fact that what makes the difference is the degree of intensity and pervasiveness of domestic primary rules (political, legal, socioeconomic etc.).[8] Here, I will focus exclusively on domestic concerns of distributive justice.

In the literature, what I call primary rules are usually identified as 'social structures' or in Rawls' words 'the basic structure of society' (or background justice):

> The basic structure of society is the way in which the main political and social institutions of society fit together into one system of social cooperation, and the way they assign basic rights and duties and regulate the division of advantages that arise from social cooperation over time.
>
> (Rawls 2001: 10)[9]

According to Rawls (2005: 258), the basic structure is composed of all major social institutions: 'the political constitution, the legally recognized forms of property, and the organization of the economy, and the nature of the family'. Rawls' description explains why an explicit reference to these institutions is an essential component of any compelling account of social justice; as Rawls (1971: 7) puts it, the basic structure 'define[s] men's rights and duties and influence[s] their life prospects, what they can expect to be and how well they can hope to do [...] because its effects are so profound and present from the start'.

However, I prefer to opt for the notion of 'primary rules'. The intent is to avoid a rigid separation between public and private spheres (a problem Rawls is at risk of running into) and a common, unproductive opposition between those who advocate that justice is primarily concerned with individual actions and interactions, and those like Rawls (1971: 3) for whom 'justice is the first virtue of social institutions', or, in other words, the background conditions within which those actions and interactions take place.[10] In the first case, the notion of primary rules allows me, for example, to say that firms (at least those of a certain size) cannot be considered as merely private associations where the principles of justice cannot be applied in their internal rules and procedures.[11] In the second case, primary rules make explicit that what we commonly call the basic structure of society is, or should be, concerned with 'the ground [primary, in my view] rules that shape a society, or of the terms of social interaction that significantly involve or at least affect all its participants' (Pogge 1989: 22). In this sense, primary rules are potentially present, such as in Nozickean 'micro-cases' like a closed and self-contained group of persons sharing a small isolated island,[12] as well as in social relations at a global level.

I believe that the idea of primary rules avoids the risk of being depicted as a black box, something that very often occurs with the notion of a basic structure of society, or generally 'social structures'. By primary rules I mean a complex network of basic or ground rules – understood in broad terms as political, legal, socioeconomic, epistemic, and cultural – that govern the social relations in which individuals are involved. These rules find their codification on a spectrum that goes from the political constitution and the juridical system to regulations of schools and runs up to everyday practices.[13]

Thus, on the one hand, the notion of primary rules better expresses the idea that the object of social justice are those social rules that govern our social relations; meanwhile, on the other hand, primary rules do not include all kinds of social relations. Given that citizens have to live with an irreconcilable disagreement, the principles of justice cannot extend their scope and validity to all areas of social life. This makes room for a class of merely ethical duties whose compliance should not be coercively enforced. For example, in a liberal democratic society, social relations that usually remain excluded are how parents should educate their children or allocate resources towards the education of their children, how partners treat each other in a private and intimate relationship, how members of a private association should distribute their own resources, etc. This distinction is imperative to deal with the pluralism of comprehensive doctrines, of the radical yet reasonable kind that Rawls takes very seriously from *Political Liberalism* (2005) onwards. It means that a society characterised by subjective and objective circumstances should be organised in such a way that leaves room for forms of 'association' and 'community' within a 'political' society (Rawls 2005: 40–43), but, I add, once we are sure that these social relations are free from the risk of domination.[14]

Thus, to go back to our hypothetical case of a group of individuals who are tasked with dividing a certain limited or scarce material resource, we can assume that the members of this group share a politically unified entity; say, a liberal democracy. Now, under the subjective and objective circumstances of justice, they have learnt a fundamental lesson: the most common manner to indirectly cause harm or injury to others is by means of primary rules. It means that primary rules should be arranged in a way to ensure that citizens do not suffer systematic or gratuitous violence, coercion, and domination.[15] Once *the primary object of distributive justice is inevitably translated into* the primary rules of society, the question of 'authority' is inescapable. Given that primary rules (legal, political and socioeconomic) determine what people can legitimately claim according to their contribution and participation in social interactions and cooperation, they should not be taken as a natural fact or as a given. On the contrary, the main question becomes: who has the power to establish, shape and stabilise primary rules over the time? Thus, a just distribution should be assessed taking into account the fundamental question of whether people have the power to be co-authors of the primary rules that govern the 'social relations' in which they are involved.

This chapter proceeds as follows. The first section takes into account the three main normative ideas – impartiality, reciprocity and co-authorship – employed, in the current debate, to justify the terms of material distribution. In my view, the idea of co-authorship is best equipped to provide the most compelling moral and political reason – material domination – that we have to reject those material distributive principles insensitive to the inequality of outcome. In the second section, I explore the several mechanisms that affect how money is translated into political leverage, making the risk of material domination a condition that affects our liberal democratic societies. In the third section, I argue that all strategies so far constructed to avoid this outcome, including the so-called insulation strategy ('keep money out of politics'), fail. Thus, if we want to avoid the risk of material domination, the only adequate remedy is to ensure that the gap between the best-off and worst-off in a society never becomes so wide that the former have the opportunity to dominate the latter. Finally, in the fourth section, I outline how the idea that inequality in material resources should be contained within some ratio is not a new one. However, in the contemporary debate, the idea that proportional justice concerns inequality between the most and the least advantaged is quite lost. I argue that it is time to rescue this old as well as new form of employing proportional justice.

1.1 How to Justify the Terms of Material Distribution? Taking Primary Rules Seriously

Once the normative boundaries of my purpose has been clarified, it is appropriate to say that distribute justice demands a system or an order of social relations (or social cooperation as broadly understood) *free from arbitrary rules* (Rawls 1971: §1; Forst 2007). For me, primary rules. This means that the source of validity of these rules can be neither an external authority, like God's will, nor can it disregard individuals' own perceived interests, ideas and values.[16] Therefore, primary rules are non-arbitrary if, and only if, they can be reasonably accepted by all individuals who are affected by them or, better, rules that cannot be reasonably rejected by those people. Given that primary rules provide a way of assigning rights and duties and that they define the appropriate distribution of the benefits and burdens of a social order, in light of the profound and unavoidable disagreement and conflict among individuals, the main question becomes: what are the most appropriate principles of justice to set these rules?[17]

In the current literature,[18] to make this tremendous normative task simpler, at least for those who aim to provide a non-partial account of justice, a division of labour is often employed between those principles conceived to assign basic liberties and political and socioeconomic rights in order to enable and empower citizens to participate in social and political life as free and equal persons, and those principles that define the terms of material distribution.

To avoid undue misunderstandings, I am aware that those principles which do not directly concern material distribution also have distributive implications; for instance, they might require a social minimum to allow citizens' effective exercise of individual rights, or some more substantive distributive requirements to ensure the fair value of political liberties. But, these distributive implications are derivative and almost never prescribe a specific material distributive principle.

It is well-known that in Rawls' justice as fairness this division of labour is expressed by the two principles of justice.[19] Of course, not all current conceptions of social justice adopt Rawls' precise strategy and even less his two principles of justice.

However, this sort of division of labour theory is the most common way to deal with material distribution in liberal democratic societies. In a nutshell, we should assign individual, unequal rewards and compensations that are, *first*, the result of an equal system of individual rights and basic liberties and, *second*, a fair distribution of income and wealth that includes, at least, a substantive version of equality of opportunity (what Rawls calls 'liberal equality') and a further distributive principle to deal with what Rawls calls the lottery of natural endowments (in which the main controversy is whether this distributive principle should be expressed by Rawls' difference principle, a principle that simply guarantees 'enough' for all, or by one that compensates for outcomes that are independent of individual voluntary choices).

By keeping the question of political and socioeconomic liberties 'separate' from the question of material distribution, a division of labour theory seems to provide a great advantage. Indeed, once we fixed (*ex ante*) the institutional background, the advantage seems to be that we can easily choose, *all these things being equal*, the most efficient material distribution, regardless of the inequality of outcome – here understood as that outcome which is insensitive to the size of inequality between the best-off and the worst-off. By contrast, I argue that even applying a division of labour theory of this kind, this result does not follow. To find the reason for this, we can take into account the three main normative ideas – impartiality, reciprocity and co-authorship – employed, in the current debate, to justify the terms of material distribution. In my view, the idea of co-authorship is best equipped to provide the most compelling moral and political reason – material domination – that we have to reject those material distributive principles insensitive to the inequality of outcome.[20] Allow me to explain. I will start with the idea of moral impartiality.

In the current debate the predominant argument employed to show why the terms of material distribution taken alone cannot be established only by the fair equality of opportunity[21] is related to two main objections: first, it is extremely demanding in relation to the sphere of the family and it suffers the epistemological problem[22] insomuch as it can be imperfectly carried out; second, its distributive result is conditioned by the arbitrariness of natural circumstances.

The fair system of equality of opportunity requires that people who are similarly talented and earnest have similar prospects for attaining their material rewards 'regardless of people's racial, ethnic, or gender group, religious or philosophical views, or social or economic position' (Freeman 2007: 88). It is an essential *ex ante* concept: everyone should have an equal starting point.[23] From this perspective, inequality of outcome is a serious problem if formal and substantive equal opportunity cannot be perfectly implemented.

However, even if the problem of impracticability would be overcome, the second objection remains valid because an arbitrary moral factor is still at stake. This is what Rawls calls the natural lottery, stating that 'there is no more reason to permit the distribution of income and wealth to be settled by the distribution of natural assets than by historical and social fortune' (Rawls 1971: 74). In other words, people's native talent is arbitrarily distributed from an impartial moral point of view. So, Rawls' difference principle might be understood as a 'compensation' of the arbitrariness of the natural lottery. Similarly, others might endorse alternative distributive principles, such as prioritarianism or sufficientarianism, to provide a specific justification acceptable to all because they could ensure that material distribution would not be driven by arbitrary moral (not impartial) factors.[24] From this perspective, the most common proposal is the so-called luck-egalitarianism, under which we should compensate for natural arbitrary circumstances (brute luck) while distinguishing them from adult voluntary choices.[25]

In any case, the terms of economic distribution shaped according to the idea of an impartial moral point of view provides distributive orientations that are concerned only with people's absolute levels, rather than inequality between people. Most importantly, it does not address another moral and political reason why natural 'distribution' of individual endowments can be considered arbitrary – a reason usually associated with the idea of reciprocity.

The idea of reciprocity captures the most adequate explanation of the arbitrariness of natural endowments according to Rawls; that is, 'what is just and unjust [in the natural lottery] is the way that institutions deal with these facts' (Rawls 1971: 102). From this perspective, what matters is that individual endowments, such as abilities and talents, are institution-dependent in the sense that they depend in large part on existing social arrangements.[26] It means that whichever individual talents and abilities are the most economically valuable depends on the goals of the social institutions and on the way in which these institutions are organised. For example, as Scanlon puts it:

> [...] If a position requires lifting heavy objects, then physical strength is an important form of ability. But if the job is done with a fork-lift truck then it is not. If succeeding in a particular job, or in a university course of study, requires one to understand French, then knowledge of French is a relevant ability. If everything is done in English, then it is not. This dependence on the goals that justify an institution and on the way it is organized to promote these goals are what I mean by saying that the idea of talent, or ability, that is relevant to procedural fairness is "institution-dependent."
>
> (Scanlon 2018: 45)

According to Scanlon, this is the essential reason that forces us to offer a 'special' justification for economic inequality. Here, the point is not that the individuals' share of economic resources depend on a 'distribution' of individual endowments that is not impartial from a moral point of view (regardless how we understand this moral impartiality), rather that individuals receive unequal economic rewards according to how the rules of the game, so to speak, are set. We can establish them to favour the rewards of certain individuals' abilities, talents, and attitudes over others. Thus, according to the idea of reciprocity, the terms of distribution of the benefits and burdens of social cooperation must allow only reciprocal advantages.

Von Platz (2020a: 10–11) re-enacts Rawls' four requirements of democratic reciprocity: 1) as mutual advantage (everyone as a citizen should gain), 2) as reasonability (the fair terms of cooperation are those that everyone could reasonably accept as a free and equal person; that is, a person who is not dominated, manipulated, or inferior in terms of political and social status), 3) as no one benefitting at the expense of others, 4) as the requirement that inequalities are (maximally) to the advantage of the least well-off. According to Rawls, the first three requirements of reciprocity imply the last one; i.e. the difference principle. Any economic inequality that benefits the most advantaged without maximising (under any feasible alternative) the absolute share of the worst-off is a violation of reciprocity because it allows the best-off to benefit at the expense of others, or in other words to sacrifice the interests of the worst-off for the gains of others. Likewise, it would be unreasonable to discard a distribution, *other things being equal*, which maximises the economic resources of the worst-off simply because it generates an increase in inequality with respect to the best-off's resources.

However, as von Platz observes, the requirements of democratic reciprocity define an eligible set of principles to choose from, in which the difference principle is just one among them. According to him, assuming that basic liberties and rights and the fair equality of opportunity are secured (so that the requirement as reasonability would be satisfied), this eligible set of principles is limited only to those that secure a social minimum in order to avoid exploitation of economic systems and therefore to respect the requirement (3) as no one benefitting at the expense of others. But, combined with this sufficientarian guarantee, the eligible set includes principles compatible with democratic reciprocity in which virtually any level of inequality between the best-off and the worst-off may end up being justified.

Besides the question of how the idea of reciprocity should be interpreted, whether by maximising the expectations of the less advantaged or simply allowing mutual advantages, the basic assumption is the same: economic inequality is justified if, and only if, it benefits those who have less. Although the idea of reciprocity, much better than that of impartiality, inevitably binds economic inequality to the improvement of the share income and wealth of the worst-off, leaving open how great it should be, this improvement is concerned only with the worst-off's absolute levels. In other words, even in case (like Rawls' difference principle) this absolute improvement should be maximised, the idea of reciprocity applied to the terms of material distribution permits, in principle, indefinitely large inequalities in return for small gains to the less favoured (see Rawls 1971: 536). The idea of reciprocity applied to the terms of material distribution is, in principle, insensitive to the gap of the economic inequality between the best-off and worst-off. Is a material distributive principle of this sort satisfactory? No, it isn't.

The point is that when the width of the gap is not perceived as a normative problem, we risk embracing the dangerous illusion that in no case in a liberal democracy can we be forced to opt for a less-efficient society, say society Y, once we have a more efficient alternative, say society Z, in which the worst-off would be better-off in absolute terms, no matter how large the gap would be. By contrast, I assume that in a liberal democracy we *may* be forced to opt for the less-efficient society Y in which the gap of economic inequality is more narrow, even if in society Z the worst-off would be better-off in absolute terms.[27] This price may be paid, not because democratic citizens should share an egalitarian ethos, but to ensure all things are taken as equal in the division of labour theory: the equal system of political and socioeconomic liberties (or, better, the value of these liberties). Indeed, *other things being equal* are not so at all, if economic inequality between the best-off and the worst-off gives leverage to the former that can be easily converted into control over the economic system as well as into political power. As a result, the best-off might have the power to establish and shape the primary rules.

From this perspective, the moral and political reasons we have to reject a potentially unlimited size of economic inequality among citizens does not concern the question of maldistribution, whether from an impartial moral point of view or a reciprocity view, rather the main reason is related to a specific form of domination, one that violates individual 'deliberative autonomy'. Here, the idea that I advance to justify the terms of material distribution is that of co-authorship.[28] Therefore, a just distribution should be assessed by taking into account the fundamental question of whether people have the power to be co-authors of the primary rules. Domination occurs when a person or a group does not have the adequate power to be co-authors of these rules.

Obviously, domination is not caused only by material factors. The most evident form of domination occurs in a society in which a group is formally excluded from certain positions in government or denied equal political rights. This form of domination occurs even in a society with perfect material equality.[29] My focus, however, is on the form of domination caused by material resources; i.e. by owning material goods that can easily be converted into socioeconomic and political influence and power. In our modern free market societies, money is the best example of a material good with this potential. From this view, a potentially unlimited gap of economic inequality among citizens allows the best-off to have a *disproportionate* economic and political power in establishing and shaping primary rules, and, in doing so, the best-off might dominate other citizens. If this is true, a compelling conception of social justice is necessary to provide a material distributive principle that *explicitly* prescribes that economic inequality must not exceed a certain range. In other words, what I call the principle of proportionality.

I see two main objections to the normative requirement that prescribes *in principle* a limit range of economic inequality, regardless of what the absolute share destined to the worst-off would be. The first objection denies that the economic and political power and influence that the best-off would enjoy as result of an excessive economic inequality is of normative significance. On the second objection, albeit while accepting that material domination is a seriously normative problem, it states that the degree to which economic inequality is translated into economic and political power is an empirical question, and therefore justice does not require a distributive principle that prescribes *a priori* the limit range. I will start with the first.

The first objection may be put in the terms that no matter how much political and socioeconomic power the best-off might obtain as result of greater economic inequality, they must not, in any case, shape socioeconomic arrangements at their will; for instance, to lower people's absolute levels above a certain threshold or not benefiting those who have less as much as possible. From this perspective, strictly speaking, the most advantaged would have no power over socioeconomic arrangements, because everything that matters regarding political morality is decided beforehand. Although this objection seems to have a certain strength, it has three main flaws.

A. Even in the best scenario where those who stand to receive less would be better-off in absolute terms and any further increasing of inequality should entail an improvement for them (think of the most egalitarian interpretation of the prioritarian principle), the best-off still might have the power to determine the structures of production, organisation, and distribution. There are many different social schemes that can equally realise a certain justifiable distribution, and why should citizens renounce having their own voice about this? So, if all that matters are the people's absolute shares, we run the risk of conceiving citizens as passive recipients of goods, rather than as active subjects of justice.[30] In other words, as Forst (2014: 34) points out, distributive justice does not concern itself simply with the question of what amounts of goods should legitimately be allocated to whom, rather with the question of 'how these goods come into the world in the first place and of who decides on their allocation and how this allocation is made'. However, someone might reply that in a liberal democracy this second question stressed by Forst already has a 'definitive' answer: the free market. Some scholars argue that, in a liberal democracy, this choice would be mandatory because the free market is the best (or even the only) social scheme to ensure, not only economic growth and well-being of modern societies, but also and above all, to respect individual properties, the exercise of economic liberties, and the individual right to pursue their own life plans.[31] In this case, the state's function is simply to make the free market work properly, for example, by avoiding monopolies or correcting externalities (for this end Pigovian taxes and subsidies are acceptable). From this perspective, nobody has the power to establish and shape socioeconomic arrangements, because the latter are guided by the pure and perfect law of marginal productivity. On this theory of marginal productivity, for example, CEOs' astronomical earnings depend on the objective value of their contribution. Not surprising, this is the common way to defend the top 1% (Mankiw 2013). But, first of all, the idea that there exists an 'economic' law as such is an illusion, and empirically false. For example, Piketty's data of historical analysis of economic inequality (Piketty 2014: 332–334) shows that the theory of marginal productivity fails to explain the diversity of the wage distributions we observe in different countries at different times. However, although some might contest these empirical data, even in the best ideal hypothesis that a free market is able to compensate individuals exactly according to their own marginal product, a free market, unlike Hayek (2012) says, is not a natural and spontaneous order with no will and no designs, rather it is a social construct. Individuals' marginal product is simply the result of the specific rules and compromises of a certain free market, one among many. The market does not operate in a vacuum; instead, it is a complex set of institutions that are dependent 'on a system of laws, which could be structured in many – if not an infinite number – of different ways' (Widerquist 2015: 87). The free market is not a solution in itself, and again, what matters are legal, political, and socioeconomic rules, and who has the power to decide them.

B. Moreover, citizens can soon realise that many basic liberties are competitive in their use. This means that effective ways to exercise these liberties do not depend on citizens' absolute level of resources, rather on the quantity of resources one has compared to others. In other words, if formal liberty is the same for all, the worth of liberty is a function of an individual's relative position in relation to the distribution of resources (Daniels 1975). Not all liberties are competitive in their use, usually not civil liberties, for example, but political liberties are often considered as a paradigmatic case. This explains why Rawls (1982, 2005) had included the worth of political liberties (although only these liberties) in the first principle of justice.

C. Even in the very implausible case in which liberal democratic citizens would have blind faith in the free market and prefer to receive the most generous absolute share of economic resources, even at the cost of losing their voice on the question of how socioeconomic arrangements should be shaped, very few would argue that this trade-off might be achieved at the cost of political participation itself. In fact, citizens' political liberties and political power are essential, not only so that they have a say about the rules that determine economic production and distribution, but also about a set of fundamental aspects of citizens' lives other than those that are strictly economic. Liberal societies leave as much room as possible for individuals to pursue their life plans, but made possible only within a public framework that requires collective management. Furthermore, many problems whose solution is crucial for citizens' improved quality of life (and in some cases for the survival of the entire human species; think of the challenges imposed by climate change,) cannot be left to individual actions and preferences, but they can be addressed only collectively by public decision and deliberation. So, political power matters on its own.

Thus, if all these arguments are valid, we can unequivocally affirm that the risk of material domination is a serious normative problem of justice. To be clear, I do not want to assert that the only way to censor the causal relation between wealth inequality and unequal economic and political power is to endorse the idea of co-authorship and my own conception of material domination. Indeed, this normative assumption can be directly extrapolated, for example, from the general idea of democratic equality itself, in which a limit on economic inequality is necessary to ensure the fair value of political liberty.[32] In this sense, I do not deny that other relational egalitarian, contractualist and liberal democratic accounts of social justice have some valid normative resources to address the problem of an excessive gap between the top and bottom of the distribution chain (indeed, I believe and hope that they may accept and endorse my principle of proportionality). But, unlike all major orientations in normative theory, I defend that justice requires a distributive principle that rules out *a priori* as unjust a society with a potentially unlimited economic inequality and, therefore, prescribes that a just (liberal democratic) society should establish the permissible size of economic inequality that excludes the risk of material domination.

Hence, I think we have valid arguments to reject also the second objection according to which this question should be only left to empirical investigations. This objection can be formulated from two different perspectives. From the first perspective, some accept that economic inequality cannot be potentially unlimited but that the question of the limits should be left to the result of procedural justice, whatever it would be. From the second perspective, instead, some deny the need, *a priori*, to limit economic inequality because material domination can be avoided by means of the 'insulation strategy'.

Rawls and Scanlon, for example, follow the first perspective. For Rawls (2001: 68), 'the difference principle specifies no definite limits within which the ratio of the shares of the more and less advantaged is to fall'. So that 'we want to leave this ratio to fall where it may, as the outcome of pure background procedural justice'. Similarly, Scanlon argues that

> the problem does not lie in the ratios themselves, and that the explanation for why they are troubling does not rest on any particular view of what the ratios should be. The problem lies rather with the lack of justification for the factors that give rise to these disparate income levels.
>
> (Scanlon 2018: 150)

Here they want to make it clear that inequality of outcome should not be sanctioned from a consequentialist view, and I share this normative perspective with them.

The approach of proportional justice is also a procedural conception. Indeed, in my view, the size of economic inequality matters only because we should avoid the risk of material domination, likewise what matters for Rawls and Scanlon respectively might be to ensure the value of political liberty or political fairness. But if it is true, these reasons should constrain the choice of principle of justice so that the material distributive principle should be sensitive to the magnitude of the gap of economic inequality. Differently, our conception of social justice is exposed to a schizophrenic and puzzling normative prescription: our material distributive principle seems to collide with, or at least not realise, the fair value of political liberties and the constraints that the institutional background should impose on unbounded inequality. Of course, how to determine the permissible range is also an empirical question, but we must offer a normative guidance regarding the acceptable size of the gap.

At the same time, another empirical question is how to shape the political, economic, and social institutions in a way that prevents excessive material inequalities, or, in my view, to respect the permissible range. But again, this question should be evaluated by the light of an independent principle of justice that can orient our deliberative choice among all feasible social schemes. On this point, although I share Edmundson's assumption (2017) that 'the fact of domination' alongside the fact of reasonable pluralism should constrain the choice of principles of justice, I believe, unlike him, that this means endorsing a distributive principle which prescribes a limit of permissible economic inequality rather than a specific ideal social scheme, such as his democratic socialism with its public ownership of the means of large-scale production (Edmundson 2017: 39).[33] Even if, as Edmundson seems to believe, the only institutional setting that can avoid the risk of material domination is a setting that forbids the private means of large-scale production (something about which I remain sceptical), this is so only in case it would disallow excessive (disproportionate) economic inequalities. A public ownership of the means of large-scale production is not a guarantee in itself of material non-domination.[34]

Finally, in the absence of a distributive principle with this normative sensitivity for the size of material inequality, the option remains open that material domination can be avoided by means of institutional policies and devices, whatever the gap of economic inequality would be. The most common option in this sense is the so-called 'insulation strategy' which aims to insulate the political democratic process from the power of money. And it is the second perspective to appeal to the same objection.

As von Platz (2020a: 24–25) puts it: 'whether the political process can be adequately insulated is an empirical question, not a matter that can be settled a priori, and to establish that it is impossible to insulate requires showing that no feasible insulation scheme would work'. And according to him, proving it carries a heavy burden of proof.[35] Beyond the fact that, as I will try to demonstrate, it is possible to overcome the burden of proof, the main arguments, *pace* von Platz, are genuinely normative rather than empirical.[36]

First of all, the insulation strategy might be a valid alternative to limit economic inequality if, and only if, it is a sufficient strategy alone. But this is possible solely within the hypothesis that political power has quasi-total control, formally and informally, over the socioeconomic sphere. This is a scenario that those like von Platz and other social and liberal democratic scholars (including myself) put off the table because a political society as such (for example, a commanded economy) is not able to leave enough room for the reasonable pluralism in pursuing individuals' own life plans and exercising economic liberties.

Secondly, a conception of social justice that aspires to a certain universality, at least in its more general normative prescriptions, should not find its own justification in a specific form of social and political organisation; for instance, the modern state. For some, the contemporary scenario of a society without a modern state, or with a Nozickean minimal state, might seem an implausible ideal. However, it can be useful to explain how material domination cannot be reduced to a normative problem that arises only in the presence of a special kind of actor, such as a government or other political authority. In this sense, political domination (as a result of violating equal political status and basic democratic procedures) and material domination, albeit closely linked in the context of a liberal democracy, are two analytically distinct and irreducible forms of domination. In other words, material domination is a moral problem that cannot be ignored even in a libertarian ideal world. Van Parijs' example is instructive in this respect.

Nozick (1974: 52–53), it will be recalled, thinks that 'whether a distribution is just depends upon how it came about'. Thus, Van Parijs notices that it is easy to imagine a society that would strike us (libertarians included?) as unjust, in which property has moved from one individual to another with no breach of the three principles specified by Nozick (1974: 150–153):

> Just think of an island which happens to be owned, for whatever reason fully consistent with the libertarian characterization of a free society given above, by one of its inhabitants. Providing it is difficult or expensive enough to leave the island, the owner can impose on the other inhabitants any condition she fancies. If they are to be allowed to earn their livelihood, they may have to work abysmally long hours, for example, or give up their religion, or wear scarlet underwear. On a libertarian account, as presented above, such a society would not cease to be free.
>
> (Van Parijs 1995: 14)[37]

This imaginary scenario intuitively explains the notion of material domination. Clearly, the inhabitants are materially dominated by the owner. On any reasonable account, they live under the owner's arbitrary will. The idea of material domination adds a further specification that remains at best implicit in Van Parijs' example. We can say that the inhabitants are dominated because they do not have material power to shape primary rules (social and economic rules in this case, assuming that there are no formal political decisions to be taken on the island). From my view, therefore, I do not need to reject this scenario because libertarianism endorses an implausible idea of liberty or denies the value of equality, but simply because a compelling conception of social justice requires that individuals have the (material) power to be co-authors of the primary rules that govern the social relations in which they are involved.

Of course, Van Parijs' island appears as too distant from reality and the risk of domination accordingly quite remote. However, the point is that this risk does not disappear even if all individuals are extended equal political status through the democratic procedures of the rule of law – formal political equality, voting rights, constitutional provisions or specific forums for public contestation – neither if some version of the insulation strategy is enforced. Therefore, to borrow Frederick Neuhouser's words, speaking of material domination I want to 'detect and criticize forms of domination that are not encoded in legal statuses such as "slave" or "serf" but that arise out of conditions of dependence and inequality among individuals who are legally recognized as free and equal persons' (Neuhouser 2013: 203).

A group of citizens is materially dominated when the distribution of wealth and income in the society assigns to other, more affluent groups a significantly bigger share of economic and political influence on legislation and, in particular, on the shaping of primary rules.

1.2 Oligarchy, Material Domination and How Money Influences Politics

In this section, I will explore the several mechanisms that make the risk of material domination a condition that affects our liberal democratic societies. Many scholars from different scientific fields have forcefully and convincingly argued that excessive economic inequality gives leverage to the best-off that can be easily converted into political power.[38] In the literature this phenomenon is usually linked with that of an oligarchy.

Winters (2011) defines oligarchy as a specific empowered minority of individuals who draw their power from an extreme concentration of material power in the form of wealth.[39] Specifically, for Winters, oligarchs are individuals who have a 'personal' disposal of their material resources that allows them to produce extreme political inequality in their favour. Unequal political power that, in turn, reinforces their socioeconomic position through mechanisms of 'wealth defence' and creation of a 'civil' oligarchic system.[40] Although Winters' civil oligarchy captures the problem of economic inequality converted into political power in a liberal democracy, I prefer to deal with this phenomenon by means of the conception of material domination.[41]

The first reason is that Winters almost exclusively focuses on those mechanisms of 'wealth defence' that allow the super-rich to employ 'rent-seeking' practises, to influence politics for obtaining anti-egalitarian policies, and to pay experts to find legal instruments to pay less taxes by taking advantage of all fiscal rules (Stiglitz 2012; Saez and Zucman 2019). By contrast, we should also expand our investigation to those mechanisms that, by influencing public opinion and civil society, create a favourable (for the rich) socio-political and cultural hegemony.[42] In this sense, it is a possible scenario that a certain stable long-run hegemony, which is a result of a very unequal economic distribution, decisively collaborates to influence people's ideas and preferences to favour the best-off's interests; in this case, the best-off might not even need to spend their economic resources to protect their wealth (Dowding 2017). Secondly, excessive material inequality is still politically problematic, even in the case where oligarchs 'engage their material resources across a range of political issues and battles about which they care deeply and yet have nothing to do with wealth defense and oligarchy' (Winters 2011: 8). This kind of political inequality is clearly beyond Winters' civil oligarchy account, but I believe that it should also be included into the risk of material domination (see point c in the previous section).

One of the most solid (and impactful) studies on the relation between money and political influence has been the 2014 paper by Martin Gilens and Benjamin Page, 'Testing Theories of American Politics: Elites, Interest Groups, and Average Citizens' (Gilens and Page 2014). The authors show that economic elites (identified with the top 10%)

have a predominant impact on the public policies of the United States. In the book *Democracy in America?* (2017) Gilens and Page offered a more articulated and detailed version of the argument in which the oligarchic degeneration of the American political system is exposed even more forcefully. Other studies have confirmed their empirical analysis, while refining and expanding the conclusions to be drawn from it.[43]

To be sure, some critical views have cast doubt on these findings. For example, Branham, Soroka and Wlezien (2017) make two main points: 1) Gilens and Page's own data show there is a high correlation between the preference of the middle class and that of the rich and 2) the rich's success rates in having their preferred policies approved (and that the middle class opposes) is not much higher than the inverse success rate of when the middle class obtains policies it favours against the will of the elite, respectively 37% and 26%. Two major counterarguments, however, are possible. Firstly, if one looks not only at how many times the two groups have their preferred policy approved, but also at how many times they succeed in blocking policies they do not want, the rich manage to block these 74% of the time, while the middle class only 63% of the time.[44] The difference of eleven points is thus confirmed. Secondly, and more directly to the point concerning the size of the difference, the rich exercise their influence not only in shutting down unfavourable policies but also, and perhaps most importantly, in making sure that unfavourable policies do not even make it into the public debate. Influence on agenda-setting is known to be a phenomenon both powerful and (for its very nature) difficult to detect. It follows that the difference in influence that emerges from data would probably widen if one could refine and include the measure of policies clearly favourable to the middle class and clearly opposed to by the very affluent that hardly ever surfaced and touched public opinion.

However, despite the relevance of the empirical data, my argument is a normative and theoretical one. For example, in order to condemn slavery societies, all we need to know is the normative model of slave societies was such that slaves were denied, in principle, a fundamental resource of power – the political and civil status of citizenship – and this is enough basis to refuse slavery. In the same way, and first and foremost, everything we need to know about material distributive inequalities is whether we have normative reasons to be worried about material domination. Secondly, we need to know whether we have theoretical arguments to sustain that this risk is plausible and feasible in a liberal democracy. Whereas the previous section was designed to address the first task, the current section provides an answer to the second one, by providing a theoretical analysis of how money translates into political leverage.

To discuss this key issue, I will borrow the four mechanisms described by Thomas Christiano (2012) to identify the ways in which money influences politics. Christiano (2012) distinguishes four basic mechanisms through which economic power is converted into political influence: 1) money for votes, 2) money as gatekeeper, 3) money as means for influencing public and legislative opinion, and 4) money as independent political power.[45]

1. The first mechanism concerns the way rich people fund electoral campaigns of politicians in exchange for policies that benefit them. This mechanism is the most direct manner in which money influences politics. This mechanism presents a clear *quid pro quo*; the donors ask the politicians for something in return for their financial support (Christiano 2012: 244).
2. The distinctive characteristic of the second mechanism – money as gatekeeper – is that money is converted into political influence and power to set the agenda for collective decision-making (no direct *quid pro quo* mechanism). The distortion of the deliberative process in the agenda-setting occurs because 'the interests and points of view of the affluent segments of society will be better represented in political campaigns than those of the less well-off' (Christiano 2012: 246).
3. Money can also be used to influence public opinion, as happens with the third mechanism. The addressees are not politicians or candidates, but citizens. Money can influence politics by highlighting and boosting (through advertising for example) a selection of specific messages. Moreover, rich people can also influence public and legislative opinion by financing the activities of lobbyists, *think tanks* and intellectual activity in general (Christiano 2012: 250).[46] Some famous examples are those of Charles and David Koch, the brothers who spend millions on ultraconservative *think tanks* (Mayer 2016), or George Soros who usually finances left-wing parties and candidates. However, the third mechanism is more complex than Christiano addresses, and must be understood as functioning far beyond the obvious channels of material influence that can buy direct political messaging. Indeed, the way they can influence public opinion, and precisely, citizens' political and social values, preferences, desires and normative judgments is more pervasive than we can imagine at first sight. In this sense, the process of collective decision making and public opinion can be indirectly influenced. Indeed, a certain political hegemony can also be reached by not only investing money through political foundations, but also cultural and philanthropic non-profit foundations and activities.[47] These foundations are not only tools for obtaining extensive tax relief (Saez and Zucman 2019) but can also function as a way to shape (at least, partially) some spheres of social life according to an investor's or donor's own ideas and interests. As Rob Reich (2018) has demonstrated, philanthropic and charitable initiatives are also instruments to pursue personalistic projects.[48] The scope and the ways in which all these non-political *prima facie* activities (even the most eccentric like Elon Musk's project to colonise Mars) are organised and performed is not 'neutral'; rather they inevitably embody a specific set of cultural, political, social and normative values (or in broader terms a particular worldview) that influence citizens and the public opinion. The case of the *Chan Zuckerberg Initiative* is very significant here because it has the explicit scope of seeking to influence public policy debates by its philanthropic initiatives, and in this way it purports to embody a new model of philanthropy which demands more control over where the money is spent.[49] Another way to influence public opinion is by funding scientific dissemination of research on impactful issues

like climate change or health.[50] We do not need to assume (and I don't) that all these activities are morally or politically problematic or to establish a good way to carry them out. Here, the point is simply to take into account that they can significantly influence public opinion and the political agenda, and the impact of these activities is clearly *proportional* to their size and breadth, and therefore to the money that every citizen can legitimately decide to invest in them.

4. Finally, through the fourth mechanism money does not operate directly on the process of collective decision-making, but as an independent constraint (Christiano 2010, 2012). Imagine a government does something to pursue a democratically chosen aim, e.g. to impose costly environmental regulation, and big corporations subvert the aim by maneuvering the economic forces they control. They can, for example, decrease (or threaten to decrease) investments in that country, thereby increasing unemployment and popular discontent towards the government itself (Christiano 2012: 250). At the same time, firms' investments, disinvestments or production reallocations can be used, not only as a sort of countervailing power against a specific law that may affect their profits, but also as an advance means to obtain favourable regulations such as reducing taxation over profits, loosen labour laws, special subsidies, etc. These maneuvers amount to an independent exercise of political power, able to influence political actions and behaviours of those citizens, politicians and local and national governments involved and affected.

Even if these mechanisms do not capture all the ways in which money translates into political influence, they are enough to give an idea of how material domination unfolds. Now, given the pervasiveness of these mechanisms, the further question becomes what could be done to counter them?

1.3 'Keeping Money Out of Politics': An Insufficient Strategy

The 'insulation strategy' is the most common strategy that is taken to be a sufficient remedy for the influence of money on politics. It can be resumed in the lemma: 'keeping money out of politics' (Thomas 2017: xix).[51] This strategy foresees a set of methods to cap private contributions to candidates and parties and severely curtail television and radio advertising during campaigns. In addition, the government may guarantee public slots in the media devoted to equally representing the views of all different candidates.[52]

In the current debate, *The Price of Democracy: How Money Shapes Politics and What to Do about It* (2020) by Julia Cagé is the most comprehensive and remarkable empirical work on the insulation strategy that for her purposes should end the current 'logic of one dollar, one vote' in our liberal democracies. She proposes radical institutional reforms based on three main pillars: a) strict limits on private funding and electoral spending; b) a public voucher system (Democratic Equality Vouchers); c) a Mixed Assembly in which a fraction of seats in a parliamentary assembly is representative of social-occupational groups.

This proposal comes, first of all, from an empirical investigation to provide further empirical evidence of how private money plays such a central role in politics, specifically in the cases of France and the United Kingdom. These databases show a causal effect, statistically speaking,[53] of election spending: 'the candidate who spends the most will on average, other things being equal, obtain the largest number of votes' (Cagé 2020: 26). Moreover, the France and the United Kingdom cases are also interesting because both countries adopt a relatively low ceiling on campaign funding and candidates' expenses,[54] but even so, money *has a direct* impact on political equality.[55] Cagé's empirical analysis shows that the amounts of private donations are extremely unequal along the measure of bottom-up income and wealth distribution. In other words, it is only the very rich among the rich who contribute financially to political life. The reason for this is soon to be addressed. Indeed, even in the case of France's ceiling on private donations, we can realise that EUR 4,000, which corresponds to the average size of donations for the 0.01 percent of French people with the top incomes, is more than a third of the average annual gross income of the poorest 50 percent of French people (Cagé 2020: 101). To drive in the point: 'who could earmark a third of their annual income to the funding of political parties?' (Cagé 2020: 101).

Most important, Cagé's empirical investigation is also extended to current and past experiences, in the United States and European countries, in developing legislation to cap private donations and to develop public systems to fund campaigns and parties. In this case, she demonstrates that these attempts have been incoherent and ineffective. The most perverse aspect is that the current public system to fund electoral campaigns and parties in many liberal democracies (France, Italy, Germany, Spain, Canada, and Brazil) has a regressive character. Indeed, since in these countries donations and membership fees to political parties bring an entitlement to tax relief, least advantaged citizens literally pay, by the state, for the political preferences of the very rich (Cagé 2020: 77–80, 104–108). Moreover, the current model of public funding of parties is also obsolete because it does not allow new political forces, unless they are capable of raising enough private money, to emerge between two elections for lack of public funds that are assigned based on the results of the previous election (Cagé 2020: 203–204).

Given this broad picture, Cagé proposes a radical transformation of the current model based on: an annual ceiling of EUR 200 for individual private donations; a ban on corporate donations as well as strict limits on electoral spending, and the introduction of a system for the public funding of political movements based on Democratic Equality Vouchers (DEVs) which gives each voter an equal amount (seven euros, in a French setting) to spend in support of political movements (Cagé 2020: 335–336).

Additionally, along with severely curtailing television and radio advertising, Cagé (2016) proposes to extend her previous proposal applied to media companies to include political foundations. In the case of a media company, she suggests a new model of media business based on a 'nonprofit media organisation' (NMO) which combines features of both foundations and joint-stock companies.

The main innovation would be that profit taking is not allowed and capital invested to the media is irrevocable (like a donation for a foundation), in addition, the decision-making power of outside investors is also limited, but in exchange for which investors receive certain tax breaks (Cagé 2016: 83). The proposal aims to reformulate the model of Media capitalised ownership towards the so-called co-management in order to cap the voting rights of the biggest shareholders, and conversely to increase the weight of voting rights of the small shareholders (journalists and employees but also readers through crowdfunding).[56] In other words, beyond a certain threshold of participation, voting rights would cease to be proportional to shares owned. It can be considered an attempt to 'isolate' the large ownership from decision-making processes within Media companies and political foundations.

However, according to Cagé, this is not enough to realise the idea of democracy as 'one person, one vote', if we do not also solve the problem of representation in the current liberal democracies where some social classes are almost entirely excluded from the ranks of those elected in the parliament, with the result that their preferences are ignored by elected politicians. Hence, Cagé's solution is to reserve a significant proportion of the national assembly' seats (a third or even a half) for

> members elected by proportional representation on lists that are genuinely *representative* of the social-occupational reality of the population. In France, for example, this could mean that at least 50 percent of the lists would have to be made up of blue collar workers, employees, and workers in new forms of insecure employment.
>
> (Cagé 2020: 366)

To sum up, I believe that Cagé's proposal represents the most comprehensive and ambitious example of the insulation strategy, but while these regulations are not pointless, they are seriously insufficient. Although she also sustains policies of wealth taxation (Cagé 2020: 173), I argue that only a radical limitation of economic inequality can avoid the risk of material domination.

The main reason is that Cagé's proposal seems to be effective only against the first two of Christiano's mechanisms. Indeed, a very low ceiling of private domination to political parties and movements as well as the ban on corporate donations and strict limits put on electoral spending might avoid economic power being converted into political influence by mechanisms such as: 1) money for votes and 2) money as gatekeeper.

However, the problem with these restrictions is that they are difficult to implement because they often enter into conflict with freedom of expression. Not accidentally, supreme courts are inclined to accept contribution or expenditure limits with the aim of limiting the first mechanism: money for votes. But they are less inclined to counter the second mechanism.[57] When money supports candidates or parties without a *quid pro quo*, it is hard not to construe any contribution and expenditure as a non-problematic exercise of freedom of expression. Someone (for example, J. Cohen 2001) might sustain that a trade-off between political equality and freedom of expression is acceptable because money as gatekeeper would take place only during electoral campaigns. However, there are good reasons to remain sceptical. Contributions to politics do not *only* happen before elections. For this reason, Cagé proposes permanent limits on private donations and expenditures. She (Cagé 2020: 344) argues that supreme courts' decisions commit a mistake by equating money with political discourse, and the ceiling introduced in a consolidated liberal democracy like France seems to support her argument. But, although not unreasonable to imagine certain limits or more stringent regulations for very large private political donations – for example, those coming from Super PACs – a yearly ceiling of EUR 200 per head may be too rigorous.

Most important, supreme courts' decisions appear to appeal to a fundamental constitutional tenet that states in a liberal democracy the state should not limit or restrict citizens' political activities and participation carried out with any legitimately owned resources, whether individual charisma, free time, or wealth. In this sense, contribution limits are an inadequate and surrogate solution to the extreme level of economic inequality in our liberal democracies. But, even if we accepted Cagé's proposal for strict limits on private political donations and expenditures, is her premise able to deal with the other two mechanisms? Unfortunately, the answer is no.

Regarding the third mechanism, we have seen that it concerns the formation of public opinion and hegemonic steering, things that usually happen not only by means that can be considered 'political', such as activities of lobbyists and *think tanks*, but also through intellectual activity in general, such as cultural, scientific, and philanthropic channels. In these fields of social life, the implementation of certain 'isolation' policies (if feasible) as suggested by Cagé would have an unbearable cost on freedom of expression and individual liberties. For example, in order for her proposal of co-management to work, it should be extended to all modes of intellectual activity.

I do not know if Cagé's 'nonprofit media organisation' model might save the media from the current crisis, as she believes, but I have serious doubts about it: first, the possibility to forbid any other forms of profitable investments in the media business; second, the effectiveness in terms of separation between financial resources and decision-making power, and lastly in defusing Christiano's third mechanism.

About the first point, Cagé (2016) sustains that news, like education, is a public good and for this reason the media are vital for a healthy functioning of our democracy. Although she is right to give this centrality to the media, the same can be said for many other intellectual and productive activities, and it seems unviable to forbid profitable activities in all these fields in the context of a liberal democracy that assigns a central role to the free market (albeit regulated) through which citizens can pursue their own worldviews. In fact we don't even do this in regards to education.

On the second point, I am not sure that Cagé's proposal of co-management will be able to reduce the decision-making power of investors in any drastic way, for the simple reason that it works both indirectly and more pervasively. She herself acknowledges this when she mentions how 'outside investors' who have no seat on the board can still have influence, nonetheless, on the editorial line. To mention only two such cases: (1) prominent French advertiser Bernard Arnault deprived *Le Monde* of publicity revenue for being unhappy with *Le Monde*'s publication of the case *Paradise Papers*[58] (Cagé 2020: 166, 399 note 41), and (2) *Meredith group* provoked scepticism about their capacity to avoid undue influence on the editorial line of *Time* coming from the Koch brothers' investment fund (*Koch Equity Development*) who gave financial support to buy *Time Magazine* but without holding seats on the board of the company (Cagé 2020: 166).

Most important, by extending this co-management model to political foundations and other intellectual activities, I do not see how we might avoid the problem of unequal influence on public opinion that the rich enjoy through these activities and, at the same time, to maintain the attractiveness of these tools for those who are willing to invest their money. Indeed, these activities are not only perceived as ways to obtain economic profit or tax breaks, but are also explicit means to pursue personal and legitimate forms of life, including the aim to influence and orient public opinion and political agendas (a legitimate purpose in a liberal democracy). A foundation (political or otherwise) is created for a specific aim and with a particular worldview that is usually binding by statute, and if we impose Cagé's NMO model two simple things might occur.

First of all, if the disproportional mechanism of countervailing power is particularly strong, the original founders might lose control of the foundation (to the extent that new large investors would not have the leverage to gain control) in favour of a more 'democratic' management among many small investors. Secondly, and on the contrary, the disproportional voting rights acquired by small investors may not affect the dominant control of large investors for three main reasons: a) the management is in any case bound to the statutory mission of the foundation; b) it is very unlikely that small donors would start a massive investment into a foundation or another organisation in which they do not share similar cultural and political orientations, and, the most important; and c) the balance of power within the foundation would be far more 'democratic' if, and only if, wealth concentration and economic distribution in the society are not extremely unequal. Otherwise, we would not find this collection of small investors and donors who are compensating for the power of large investors – where the eventual countervailing power can favour the rich over the super-rich while the middle and lower classes would be excluded from this possibility.

In the first case, it is obvious that the tool will lose its attractiveness and the super-rich might follow Chan Zuckerberg Initiative's strategy to maintain ultimate control of the organisation (even at the cost of losing more generous tax benefits) or find other legal instruments; while in the second case, Cagé's NMO model may simply be a further gift to the richest in terms of tax deductions.[59]

However, and in any case, all these regulations and Cagé's NMO model remain fully ineffective in dealing with Christiano's fourth mechanism. First, the set of strict limits on private funding and electoral spending are ineffective because, as we have seen, wealthy individuals and corporations are able to undermine and subvert public policies while giving the impression of remaining fully within the exercise of their prerogatives and liberties, with no need to 'buy' consent directly among legislators or citizens. Second, Cagé's NMO model is unfit because we cannot convert all productive activities in a non-profit business, and in particular a financial investment, into a 'gift'; that is, into an irrevocable donation for the firm. Thus, the main weapon for increasing and decreasing investments as well as making decisions on production reallocations remains in the hands of large investors. This does not mean that we cannot pursue some forms of co-management (at least, in major corporations) like in the famous examples of German and Swedish systems for sharing voting rights within firms (see Piketty 2020); however, this tool is thought to pursue two different aims: workplace democracy and long-term redistributive effects.[60] Of course, in the case that forms of co-management are highly effective means to achieve a significant dispersion of wealth and property, we could enjoy a positive corollary effect of a depletion of political influence of the best-off; albeit this would be the result of economic inequality reduction rather than of regulations and barriers instated to control the power of money.

Perhaps I am ignoring the effectiveness that Cagé's proposal for a mixed assembly could have in defusing Christiano's third and fourth mechanisms? But no, that's not the case. Indeed, if the best-off are able to profoundly influence public opinion and the political agenda through the third mechanism, the idea of creating a proportional representation of all social occupations in a parliament would not change the picture at all. Even the representatives of the most disadvantaged social groups, now better and fairly represented, would participate in the decision-making process that takes place within a certain political and cultural hegemony where unfavourable policies for the rich do not even appear in the public debate. And a mixed assembly is even more inefficacious against Christiano's fourth mechanism because in this case money does not operate directly within the process of collective decision making.

Moreover, besides the fact of being fully ineffective, Cagé's mixed assembly severely risks violating formal political equality. Although I agree with Cagé that preferences and interests of those who occupy social occupations at the bottom of distribution seem to be underrepresented and misrepresented in many liberal democracies, we still need to find the adequate institutional devices and rules to address this problem. But granting a 'privilege' of representation in democratic assemblies does not seem such a solution. Indeed, many other social categories as important and worthy of equal representation as that of social occupation could claim the same form of 'representation'. Why not institute mixed assemblies according to gender, identity, religion, etc.? Any attempt would involve undeniable arbitrary choices, as well as be destined for impracticality. I think we have very good reasons to keep the form of our representative democracies away from that of the corporate type.

To summarise, in no way do I think that Cagé's several proposals are useless. On the contrary, her Democratic Equality Vouchers proposal is an ingenious model of public funding capable of overcoming many shortcomings of the actual one, and it can serve as a valid model even in the best case scenario of a society in which economic inequalities are not wide enough to upset political equality. In addition, in contemporary societies that present extreme levels of wealth inequality (while we do everything possible to reduce it), I believe that we ought to find the way to implement some limits on electoral spending, place a ban on corporate donations and also a cap on very large private political donations in respect to the tenets of a constitutional democracy.

Nonetheless, I hope to have offered some decisive arguments to show how even the most ambitious of the insulation strategies is not only insufficient but also fully ineffective in dealing with mechanisms through which money indirectly influences the political system.[61] Moreover, Cagé's attempts to defuse these indirect mechanisms inevitably expose themselves to the risk of violating freedom of expression and individual liberties, and also formal political equality. In this respect, the insulation strategy seems to work only in the implausible (and undesirable) hypothesis that political power has quasi-total control, formally and informally, over the social and economic spheres. By contrast, in mixed economies in which the regulatory role of the state over the free market and material distribution is combined with private ownership of the means of production, even if barriers meant to insulate the political dimension from external influences worked effectively, a big 'if' indeed, economic inequality and its corresponding economic power would still continue to offer wealthy people a significantly bigger share of political influence (broadly understood) than the one left to the worst-off.

In this respect, some might object that I am unjustifiably excluding the exact possibility of opting for a form of commanded economy that abolishes private ownership of the means of production as a remedy to material domination. After all, if the ownership of the means of production are not in private hands, we might easily maintain very low material inequality and therefore avoid unequal political influence in advance. But, unfortunately, this is not a viable alternative. Here, I will not focus on the well-known and discussed problem of lack of economic efficiency, even if it is a big problem; rather, I mobilise a normative reason to reject a command economy: the fact of reasonable pluralism.

As Piketty (2014: 531–532) observes, the point is that private property and the free market economy do not have the sole problematic effect of exposing the risk of domination of capital, but they also play an indispensable role in coordinating the actions of millions of individuals. Given the complexity of our modern society and the need for high levels of coordination, it is impossible for everyone, even for a central political authority, to collect and manage all information in the social order in terms of individual preferences and needs. Only if we posit that human needs, preferences, and aspirations are relatively simple and very few in number, could we believe that a centrally planned society and economy is able to satisfy them without disrespecting legitimate differences among individuals (Piketty 2020: 666–668). Most importantly, although some currently believe that new Big Data technology can provide these powerful and almost magical tools, the technical challenge is not the main obstacle.[62] What normatively matters is that 'the mere attempt to do so would negatively affect the social process through which individuals come to know themselves' (Piketty 2020: 668). In other words, the way in which individuals can try to satisfy their ideas, preferences and needs has an essential role in the development and the exercise of what Rawls calls the two moral powers of democratic citizenship: the capacity for a conception of the good and the capacity for a sense of justice.[63]

Even if a centrally planned society and economy is based on equal political and civil rights and democratic procedures, unless all individuals share the same comprehensive view (an implausible society with no kinds of pluralism), political authority and those who are temporarily (four years?) in charge would have the power to shape the entire social order. The various minorities could do nothing but follow the life plan of the majority. In this sense, economic liberties and rights are indispensable power resources for citizens to be co-authors of primary rules.[64]

It is easy to envisage a reply by those who defend the abolition of private ownership of the means of production. It sounds as if, in these terms, although we may reject a commanded economy for normative reasons, a mixed economy is not a valid alternative because it is inevitably condemned to fail in maintaining economic inequality within an acceptable (non-domination) range. According to a central claim of Marxist political theory, by opting for a mixed economy we are *inevitably* caught in the trap of the structural dependence of the state on capital (see Przeworski and Wallerstein 1988). In short, the theory is based on the assumption that no government can simultaneously reduce profits and increase investment since investment decisions are private; hence, governments face a trade-off between distribution and growth as well as between equality and efficiency. The result would be that all governments will pursue policies with limited redistributive effects in exchange for economic growth. However, there is a decisive reason to consider this empirical assumption as false.

Indeed, this inverse inference between investment and income distribution in capitalistic society is true only if governments' policy instruments are restricted to those on income tax (Przeworski and Wallerstein 1988). By contrast, governments can choose different effective policies concerning distribution and growth, not only by differentiating tax rates according to the sources of income inequality (income from labour, capital ownership and income from capital), but also, and above all, endorsing a distributive pluralistic approach involving a wide set of policies and institutional devices combining progressive taxation, predistribution of both public and private forms of capital (for example, state investment funds and a universal capital endowment), as well as forms of workplace democracy and efficient educational and social security systems (Atkinson 2015; O'Neill 2017). For example, Piketty's most recent proposal of 'Participatory Socialism' (2020) seems to be characterised by a similar pluralistic approach.[65] We can be confident enough about the empirical possibility, also learning from past experiences, to 'imagine a society that allows privately owned firms of reasonable size while preventing excessive concentration of wealth' (Piketty 2020: 666). This means that, although Christiano's fourth mechanism seriously exposes liberal and social democracies to the risk of material domination, we are not inexorably condemned to this risk in a mixed economy.

Of course, what form this society should take is another issue that demands not only empirical but also normative investigations. From this perspective, it is not surprising that the current egalitarian debate focuses a lot on the question of which ideal social system is the most effective to prevent wealth and property concentration. Although this kind of discussion is welcome and necessary, I want to clarify that this debate should not overlook (as often happens) the fact that pre-distributive social systems should be evaluated by the light of some independent criterion or principle of justice. Rawls, for example, has this logical priority clear. He assesses his five ideal models of social systems taking the two principles of justice as a benchmark, and not *vice versa*. Similarly, my principle of proportional justice is meant to justify a preference for one social system over possible others. For instance, a libertarian system is clearly ruled out, because its very essence is to reject any *a priori* limit to economic inequality. At the same time, the principle does not force us to choose a specific social system because it is compatible with many of those defended by current theories of justice, provided that they incorporate the requirement to contain economic inequality within well-specified limits.

To conclude, what is the crucial lesson to learn? I hope by now it is clear. If we want to avoid material domination, we should ensure that the gap between the best-off and worst-off in a society never becomes so wide that the former have the opportunity to dominate the latter. The solution can neither be that the worst-off are guaranteed to stay above a decent threshold of material wealth, nor that they maximise their absolute shares, nor that their co-authorship is ensured alone by an insulation strategy. Given the competitive and relational nature of economic and political powers, the significance of power ensuing from wealth depends not simply on how much one has in absolute terms, but on the comparative difference between what some have and what others do not.[66] Nothing in the fact that average citizens of a Western society today have more material resources and better living conditions than mediaeval kings make them less exposed to the risk of material domination. Therefore, the worst-off in a society could and should reasonably reject social arrangements that leave them so *distant* from the best-off that they risk domination, regardless of their absolute shares of economic resources.

Note that this does not mean that we should make each citizen perfectly equal in terms of political power. Differences in political power and influence, even considering only economic factors, will likely remain in any just society. The only way to eliminate these would be to opt for perfect equality in material resources among citizens, a solution hardly compatible with many of the basic liberties people should not renounce.[67] If this is the case, then the normative priority should be to ensure that the difference in question never becomes wide enough to be reasonably construed as a form of domination. In other words, social justice needs what I call a distributive 'principle of proportionality', understood as a commitment to set a limit range on economic inequality between the best-off and the worst-off.

1.4 Rescuing Proportional Justice: Back to the Future

This idea that inequality in material resources between the best-off and the worst-off should be contained within a limit range is not new. Indeed, its origin can be traced back to Plato and Aristotle. In *The Laws* (1960), Plato argued that no one should be more than four times richer than the poorest member of the society while Aristotle in the *Politics* (1998) favoured 'proportional equality', thereby condemning extreme material inequalities because they produce a situation in which the poor and the rich are not able to establish a just constitution and government.[68] In modern times, the most authoritative proponent of proportional justice is likely Rousseau. In a famous passage of *The Social Contract* (1997) he holds that 'no citizen be so very rich that he can buy another, and none so poor that he is compelled to sell himself'.[69] However, in the contemporary debate, the idea that proportional justice concerns inequality between the most and the least advantaged is quite lost.[70]

The idea of proportionality is, nowadays, employed to assign a certain good, reward, punishment or blame in *proportion* to the strength of each individual's claim or due, regardless of inequality of outcome among individuals (see Temkin 1993, 2000; Reiff 2009; Brighouse and Fleurbaey 2010; Kagan 2015).[71] To be sure, the idea of proportionality as directly applied to what individuals deserve or are due is also an old one. Indeed, Aristotle in the *Nicomachean Ethics* (2004) also endorsed proportional equality or proportional justice (we can consider them as equivalent concepts here) in this second sense. Thus, we can see that there are two different and opposite ways to lead with proportional justice: (a) one that prescribes that the inequality should be contained within some limit range, and (b) the other that is insensitive to inequality of outcome. Nonetheless, there is no reason to see these two different forms of treating proportional justice as contradictory; rather they simply concern two different domains, that of political and social justice and that of ethics or specific issues of redistributive justice that are not concerned with the question of primary rules. Let me briefly explain this distinction.

Proportional justice can be considered the method of distribution that justice *prima facie* requires (Reiff 2009: 8). First of all, it implies the principle of formal equality. Indeed, as Gosepath observes (2021: 3), the assumption that 'unequal claims to treatment or distribution must be considered proportionally [implies] the prerequisite for persons being considered equally'.[72] Although nowadays nobody accepts Plato and Aristotle's ideas that human beings are unequal in certain relevant moral senses, it is still indispensable to understand in which cases or contexts individuals can be considered as equal claimants; for instance, equal simply because they are human beings, contribute to the social product, share the citizenship of the same political authority, or, as in my view, they are involved in certain social relations governed by primary rules. Secondly, once we have circumscribed the proper case in which individuals should be considered as equal claimants, proportional justice provides a substantive method of distribution of rewards or punishments. Thus, we need to pursue two further steps: 1) identify the relevant moral or political claims there might be for distributing a certain 'good' to one claimant rather than another, and 2) assess the moral weight of each individual's claim, so that the distribution should be *proportional* to the latter. There are two different ways to satisfy both steps that carry out two opposing forms – (a) sensitive and (b) insensitive to inequality – to express proportional justice.

In the literature, for example, pure desert-based theories (like perfectionists and meritocrats) usually endorse proportional justice in the second form (b): they assign economic rewards and remuneration gained by individuals in *proportion* to their individual desert, regardless of what is up to others. Although there are various pure desert-based theories (Sher 1989; Olsaretti 2003; Kagan 2015), all of them satisfy the two aforementioned steps in the same way. The first step is satisfied by identify a certain moral value or concept (i.e. enforcement, entitlement, responsibility, etc.) which is logically prior to and independent of public institutions and their rules for assigning individuals gains (Feinberg 1970: 240; Scanlon 2018: 119); while the second step is accomplished by exactly identifying the weight of each individual's desert.

At this point in my discussion, it should be clear enough why a pure desert-based theory (or other similar ways to deal with proportional justice) is not adequate when justice concerns the question of primary rules and the material distribution of a society as a whole. Besides the epistemological problem that represents a severe, and maybe undefeatable, obstacle to exactly identifying individuals' meritorious motives, here I recall the two normative reasons that make pure desert-based theories politically, if not morally, unworkable. First, they are intrinsically teleological and, therefore, fail to provide a justification that does justice to reasonable pluralism. In other words, it is not clear why a desert-based distribution favouring one moral value over another would be accepted by those who are less advantaged within this distribution (Scheffler 2000). Second and most important, moral values such as individual ability, effort, and responsibility are institution dependent in the sense that they depend, at least partly, on existing social arrangements (Rawls 1971: 104; Daniels 1978; Scanlon 2018: 120–124).[73] For this reason, the question of who has the power to establish and shape these political and socioeconomic arrangements is, in any case, inescapable.

The lesson is simple. Not only is it quite impossible to overcome the epistemological problem, but also and mainly to identify a relevant moral value in such a way as to have absolute priority in establishing and shaping the entire material distribution. In the circumstances of justice (subjective and objective) we cannot find this kind of 'consensus' without disregarding reasonable pluralism and exposing individuals to the risk of (material) domination.

To be clear, this does not mean that we cannot identify an overwhelming claim or moral value when we focus on some specific moral and ethical domains, such as retributive justice (praise, admiration, gratitude, blame or condemnation), or some distributive issues that are not concerned with the question of primary rules; for example, internal rules for admission to college, or intermediate socioeconomic positions along the top and bottom of distribution, assuming that economic inequality between the extremes of distribution is contained within a certain limit range to avoid material domination. Indeed, in a liberal democracy that ensures its citizens are not exposed to the risk of domination (or other fundamental dimensions of social injustice) we have no reasons to exclude that individual responsibility or merit might have a certain place in specific distributive issues.[74] From this perspective, the two forms (both presented in Aristotle) to employ proportional justice are not in contradiction, but simply concern different moral and political circumstances and domains.

In summary, when proportional justice concerns the question of primary rules, it prescribes that individuals should have a *proportional* amount of key power resources with respect to others in order to avoid the risk of domination (in all its different forms). And specifically, when we focus on material power, proportional justice requires what I call the principle of proportionality which prescribes that material resources (in terms of income and wealth) between the best-off and the worst-off should be contained within a limited range (to avoid material domination). It is time to rescue this old as well as new form of employing proportional justice.

Notes

1 Indeed, the subjective and objective circumstances of justice give rise to what others call the facts of pluralism and domination, see Edmundson (2017).

2 Here, I do not enter into the question of the 'ultimate' ground of moral obligations and the source of moral motivations; or in other words, the question of why be moral? Although this issue is one of the most fundamental and controversial matters in moral philosophy (see Parfit 2011a, 2011b), I believe that for my investigation I can assume as an axiomatic point of view that human beings are able to be reasonable persons.

3 From this perspective, the reasonable is defined as an alternative to the rational (see Sibley 1953). As Scanlon (1998: 191–192) observes, the rational (or rationality) can be understood in a number of different ways, but recently the notion has most commonly been taken to mean 'what most conduces to the fulfilment of the agent's aims.' Thus, a rational agent lacks 'the particular form of moral sensibility that underlies the desire to engage in fair cooperation as such, and to do so on terms that others as equals might reasonably be expected to endorse' (Rawls 2005: 51). By contrast, this sensibility is characteristic of a reasonable person. Put in these terms, according to Rawls (2005: 48), the distinction between the reasonable and the rational goes back to Kant: 'it is expressed in his distinction between the categorical and the hypothetical imperative.'

4 Rawls seems to be quite ambiguous about this point. And for this reason, many authors argue that Rawls' notion of reasonableness is obscure and unclear, and therefore risks to be arbitrary and ultimately indefensible (see Rorty 1991; Mouffe 1994; Gaus 1999; Habermas 1995); for Rawls' own defence see: Rawls (2005) reply to Habermas. Other authors tried to clarify and defend Rawls' notion of reasonableness (see Boettcher 2004; Maffettone 2004; Rasmussen 2004). Here I do not have to enter this debate, however, I have already argued elsewhere: see Alì (2018).

5 In a Kantian spirit, we can identify the first case with our perfect duties, while in the second we have imperfect duties (Kant 1996: 64–67, [239]–[242]). More precisely, here I follow Onora O'Neill's distinction (1996) between perfect and imperfect obligations.

6 For a discussion on this view, see Pogge (2000).

7 About the metaphor of the game, see Edmundson (2021: 9–11), Pogge (1989: 26), Wright (2019: 77–84). I borrow the term 'primary rules' from Shklar (1990: 18). Similarly, Pogge (1989: 22) refers to Rawls' notion of basic structure as 'ground rules.'

8 Thus, although we can agree that the existence of a politically unified entity matters, we can avoid two unsatisfactory alternatives: the strong 'statism' (Nagel 2005) and the strong cosmopolitan 'globalism' (Cohen and Sabel 2006). According to the strong 'statism' our duties of distributive justice (or socioeconomic rights) emerge only with the state; meanwhile, the strong cosmopolitan globalism claims that the demands of distributive justice should be wholly insensitive to facts about existing social and political institutions such as a national state, or about human relations and practises between them. A middle position between them might be the right way to proceed, see Pogge (1989, 2008) and M. O'Neill (2008).

9 See also Rawls 1971: §2, 7–11; 2005: 258.

10 For the debate, see Murphy (1998, 2000), G. A. Cohen (2000), Pogge (2000), and Young (2006, 2011).

11 Note that the rules enforced in organisations in which people have to work to earn a living (e.g. those concerning hiring and promotions) can hardly be left to the fully unchecked liberty of owners without generating a specific risk of domination, see E. Anderson (2017). Rawls' own thinking (2005: 468) seems to go in the opposite direction about firms. For a forceful reading that makes firms part of the basic structure, see Celentano (2019). A notion of the basic structure that makes a rigid separation between public and private spheres also runs the risk of being insensitive to some significant forms of injustice that fall within the dimension of misrecognition. Rawls was criticised in this respect, see Okin (1989), Fraser and Honneth (2003: 34), Fraser (1996: 27–28), and Abbey (2013). For Rawls' reply, see Rawls (2005: 466–474; 2001: 167) or for some Rawlsian defences, see Barry (2001), Lægaard (2005), Caranti and Alì (2021), and Piroli (2021).

12 This is the exact objection that Nozick (1974) raises to Rawls. The island case is used by Pogge (1989) and also Van Parijs (1995) to reject right-libertarian objection. In Section 1.1, I will return to this peculiar case.

13 Here for rules I appeal specifically to Rawls' understanding (1955).

14 For example, in the case of marriage, primary rules include all gender biassed circumstances that surround marriage, no matter how equally and fairly the law treats the spouses and even if the legal system provides some particular juridical protection for women, as in the case of Brazilian legislation (see Instituto Maria da Penha 2018). Thus, it means to evaluate whether women have a fair opportunity to enter in the labour market and receive adequate payment, whether they have the same chances as men to get out of marriage or other kinds of familial relationships and so on. I will return to this point in Chapter 2.

15 It does not mean that individuals are exempt from complying with their obligations not to directly cause harm or injury to others – for instance, kill, torture or threaten someone – even in the extreme case in which the primary rules of society do not sanction these actions and conduct. In a slave society, however, individuals have the obligation of justice not to have slaves, beyond the obligation to abolish the legal institution of slavery.

16 In this sense, I do appeal to a substantive interpretation of arbitrariness, as alternative to a formal one for which 'arbitrary' simply means rules that are unpredictable or are not enforced by an independent third-party authority (the rule of law). About a formal procedural or a substantive interpretation of arbitrariness, see Lovett 2012.

17 In the literature there is a wide debate about the 'ultimate' moral ground of these principles and the kind of normative device or procedures employed to justify and eventually choose them. Some can advocate natural rights, others a contractualist foundation based on Rawls' original position (1971) or Dworkin's envy test (2000), still others on Habermas' discourse principle (1990), Forst's principle of justification (2012) or Benhabib's discourse-theoretic account of human rights (2012).

18 I do not feign to offer a complete overview of theories of distributive justice. For a recent attempt, see von Platz (2020c).

19 For more broad discussions on the division of labor between the two principles of justice in Rawls' theory, see von Platz (2016, 2020a, 2020b, 2020c).

20 Although the idea of co-authorship as deliberative autonomy that I defend here is clearly indebted to many scholars – like Habermas (1990), Benhabib (2012), Forst (2014), Scheffler (2015), and Azmanova (2016) – I derive from this idea a material distributive principle that I do not find in them.
21 It includes formal and substantive equality of opportunity, or in Scanlon's terms (2018), procedural fairness and substantive opportunity.
22 According to the epistemological problem (Rawls 1971; Fishkin 2014: 56–65), it is very difficult, or even impossible, to isolate what is an exclusive reflection of individuals' preferences and actions from social circumstances. In the debate, there are some attempts to overcome the epistemological problem, see Roemer (1998), Moriarty (2005, 2018) and for a rejection of these attempts, see Wolff (2003), Fishkin (2014) and Baiasu (2021).
23 For a general debate about the principle of equality of opportunity, see Fishkin (1983, 2014), Freeman (2007), Brighouse and Swift (2014), and Arneson (2015). From a strong egalitarian interpretation, Freeman (2013) sustains that a broader interpretation of fair equality of opportunity also requires concern with inequalities of outcome.
24 For instance, Parfit (1997) and Frankfurt (2015) defend their respectively prioritarian and sufficientarian views from an impartial moral point of view.
25 Luck egalitarianism has been initially formulated as an extension and generalisation of a fundamental insight in Rawls' conception of justice: the issue of individual responsibility; but this assumption is hardly contested, see Scheffler (2003) and Daniels (2003). However, luck egalitarianism is currently presented as the conception of justice or idea of equality on its own. Also in this case, it has received serious objections, see E. Anderson (1999), Scheffler (2003) and Forst (2020).
26 For a similar reading, see Freeman (2007, 2013, 2018), Scheffler (2000, 2003), Daniels (2003), and Forst (2020).
27 However, although in this sense my proportional justice account holds (like Rawls' justice as fairness) the normative priority of justice over efficiency, it does not risk being incompatible with efficiency. On this point, see Chapter 4, Section 4.1.
28 Here, I put at a distance those accounts of social justice that endorse the idea of self-authorship, see Tomasi (2012), Brennan and Tomasi (2012) and Claassen and Herzog (2019). The simple idea of self-authorship applied to the primary rules is unsatisfactory because it is not able to deal with collective political decisions.
29 Indeed, the approach of proportional justice should be applied to all those key power resources that allow citizens to be co-authors of primary rules, see Chapter 2.
30 See Forst (2014: 18–19). This point was raised before by Young (1990), E. Anderson (1999) and Scheffler (2003).
31 This view is usually identified with Classical Liberalism including authors such Smith, Hayek and Friedman, see Freeman (2011), Brennan and Tomasi (2012) and von Platz and Tomasi (2015).
32 This normative position is usually called political egalitarianism, and the literature on it is very rich, see Sunstein (1994), Brighouse (1996), Bohman and Rehg (1997), Christiano (1999), Rawls (2005), M. O'Neill (2017), Freeman (2018), Scanlon (2018).
33 Edmundson (2019) understands 'means of production' as only those basic resources that belong to society's basic structure.
34 For example, if in a democratic system of public ownership of the means of production excessive economic rewards are assigned to citizens, the most advantaged might have disproportionate economic resources with respect to others for influencing public and legislative opinion and debate through other mechanisms (about these mechanisms, see Section 1.3). Indeed, Edmundson (2021) himself also agrees that the public ownership of the means of large-scale production is not itself sufficient to avoid excessive economic inequality. Thus, I believe that the ultimate aims of Edmundson's proposal (2021) is to defend the public ownership of the means of large-scale production not as the best or most unique effective tool to prevent excessive economic inequalities, rather as the only institutional setting in industrialised societies that can ensure a fair exercise of productive life and the participation of productive activities for all. However, this is a separate issue.

35 For a similar point, see Gaus (2010).
36 For other accounts that reject the insulation strategy from a normative point of view, see Thomas (2017), Robeyns (2017), Edmundson (2017), Schemmel (2021). On the insulation strategy, see Section 1.3.
37 The island is a perfect example of objective and subjective circumstances of justice: the 'costs' to leave the island are extremely high and we are also in the presence of pluralism.
38 Empirical research (in particular in the USA) provides overwhelming evidence of this process. I argued about and listed them in the introduction.
39 In this way, material power is that kind of power resource that distinguishes oligarchs from elites, where the latter are considered other empowered minorities characterised by having a concentration or an exclusionary disposal of other kinds of resource power; such as power based on *political rights*, the power of *official positions* in government or of being at the helm of organisations, *coercive* power, or *mobilisational* power (Winters 2011: 12).
40 According to Winters (2011: 32), all oligarchies can be categorised according to four types of regimes that determine the different ways in which oligarchs are able to defend their property and wealth: warring, ruling, sultanistic, and civil oligarchies. Civil oligarchy is a phenomenon that can be present in a modern state based on the rule of law.
41 For other accounts that opt for the notion of domination in identifying this phenomenon, see Przeworski (1998), Shapiro (2003) and Edmundson (2017).
42 Winters (2011: 13, note 17) recognizes that cultural power is important but he believes that its character is systemic, and therefore is not something that can be held or wielded as a power resource by individuals as such. Although it is true that no one alone is capable of creating a cultural hegemony, Winters misleads the normative point. Indeed, what matters is the share of material power by which each citizen can contribute to create a certain cultural hegemony with respect to others. Note that although my notion of hegemony is in debt to that of Gramsci (2011), here what I mean by hegemony is 'neutral'. A hegemonic idea is simply one that provides a kind of selective (moral or political) justification or representation about a certain social and political reality, but is not intrinsically a result of, or a justification for, a process of exploration or domination. However, also in my view, a certain hegemony might represent a form of injustice if it is the result of a disproportionate distribution of power as well as if it claims to justify such a disproportionate distribution of power. Recently, Piketty (2020) seems to adopt a similar 'neutral' notion of ideology.
43 See Rosset and Stecker (2019), Grossmann and Isaac (2017), Rhodes and Schaffner (2017), and Schäfer and Schwander (2019). A comparative study argues that there is no clear evidence that poor citizens are under-represented *in government formation* (Guntermann 2021). However, the study admits that low-income citizens are disadvantaged by other processes, such as the influence of money on policy-makers, and the scant attention parties pay to issues that would be in the objective interest of these citizens.
44 This point was made by Gilens in an informal reply cited by a newspaper article (Matthews 2016).
45 In a previous analysis of the different ways in which money can influence politics, Winters and Page (2009: 740–743) distinguished between lobbying, electoral impact, and opinion shaping. Similar mechanisms are extensively discussed in deliberative democracy debate, see Bohman and Rehg (1997), Elster (1998), Shapiro (2003), and Przeworski (1990, 2003).
46 On this specific phenomenon, see West and Loomis (1998), Jacobs and Shapiro (2000), and Graetz and Shapiro (2005). Nowadays, an effective tool is used by social media platforms, such as WhatsApp and Facebook, which targets voters with personalised political advertisements. See the famous scandal with *Cambridge Analytica*, a company owned by the hedge fund billionaire Robert Mercer (Cadwalladr 2017).
47 This context concerns what Habermas (1996) calls the 'informal public sphere' and Rawls (2005) calls the 'background culture'.

48 Indeed, it is not surprising that sometimes these philanthropic activities are contested by those citizens and communities that would be the beneficiaries; for example, the Chan Zuckerberg Initiative's USD 100 million donation to improve the public schools in Newark that encountered fierce resistance from many parents, community activists, and unions (Goel and Wingfield 2015)

49 It is a limited liability company founded by Mark Zuckerberg and his wife Priscilla Chan that should receive (at least according to what they announced) 99 percent of their Facebook shares (during their lives). Although it is not a non-profit foundation, this unusual corporate structure allows enjoyment of major tax breaks in relation to profits and inheritance duty, while leaving Zuckerberg and his wife with ultimate control of the organisation (Goel and Wingfield 2015).

50 In some cases, these scientific disseminations have the not-so-hidden aim of discrediting or spreading doubts about established scientific data rather than contributing to the scientific debate itself, see Oreskes and Conway (2010), Farrell (2016) and Cagé (2020).

51 The insulation strategy can be the main pillar of a theory of justice, like in the case of Walzer's complex equality (1983), in which the different 'spheres of justice' are rigorously separated in order to avoid what he called the risk of domination of one sphere over others.

52 An alternative manner to implement the insulation strategy is one based on an egalitarian culture in which people renounce use of money as the medium in the spheres of life that are not intrinsically economic. Kaus (1995) relies on a strategy as such. In this case, public policies should seek to instil, for example, in school and through the media, this practical egalitarian culture. However, as Schemmel (2021: 242) observes, the insulation strategy based on this sort of 'socio-psychological protection' of the political sphere involves heavy interference with individual liberty to pursue their own conception of good and comprehensive doctrine.

53 It means that this phenomenon does not happen in every election.

54 In France the permissible amount that anyone may donate to a candidate is low (EUR 4,600 per campaign) and since 1995 no direct corporate donations have been allowed (Cagé 2020: 265). The United Kingdom also imposes expenditure limits but it has rejected contribution limits. In both cases, the differences between the hundreds of millions of dollars available in American campaigns is great.

55 These data led Cagé to advance an approximate estimation on 'the price of a vote' in France which 'is roughly six euros for legislative elections and thirty-two euros for municipal elections' (Cagé 2020: 281). For example, the average of EUR 8,000 extra in private donations received by candidates gives them an advantage of 1,367 to 2,734 votes over their rivals in legislative elections.

56 For example, she suggests that company investments above 10 percent may obtain voting rights corresponding to one third of the amount invested, meanwhile those that contribute less than 10 percent (but above the 1 percent) would receive a proportionate boost in their voting rights so that the total is always 100 percent (Cagé 2016: 100; 2020: 169–170).

57 For the case of the Supreme Court of The United States, see *Buckley v. Valeo* decision 424 US 1 (1976) and *McCutcheon v. Federal Election Commission*, 572 US 185 (2014). About the debate on these decisions, see Rosenkranz (2000), A. Anderson (2000), Kuhner (2014), Post (2014), and Hasen (2016). European courts also shared the content of the Supreme Court's decisions, see 1998 judgement of the European Court of Human Rights (ECHR) in the *Bowman v. United Kingdom* case.

58 See the report of the International Consortium of Investigative Journalists (2017).

59 I would like to be clear on a fundamental point here. All these private initiatives (political, cultural and philanthropic) that have direct and indirect consequences on influencing public opinion and the political agenda are not themselves incompatible with liberal democracy; on the contrary, they can be considered necessary for its healthy functioning.

60 Workplace democracy aims to counterbalance managerial and owners' power of control and authority over the conditions of employment within firms: duration, intensity, and performance. Recently, Piketty (2020: 1094) proposes to extend Cagé's proposal of a vote rights ceiling to profit-making sectors in order to reinforce the weight of workers' decision-making within firms above a certain size (>100 employees). However, the exact aim seems to be that of pursuing workplace democracy and long-term distributive effects for a reduction of economic inequality.

61 Marquez's (2015) proposal to design the electoral system so that voting power is inversely *proportional* to income is, for the same reasons, insufficient.

62 See Thornhill (2017).

63 See Rawls (2001: 18–24; 2005: 18–20, 73–75, 81–82, 302).

64 I will go back to this point in Chapter 4, Section 4.2.

65 I will argue more about this strategy and the debate about ideal types of social systems in Chapter 4, Section 4.3.

66 For the same reason, the solution is not that the rich do not surpass an upper limit, as proposed by Robeyns' limitarianism. I will go back to the limits of Robeyns' limitarianism in Chapter 3, Section 3.4.

67 Estlund (2000: 127; 2008: 196) has a similar ambition to find an acceptable point between merely formal political equality and perfect (substantive) political equality of influence. But, I think that in this regard, the principle of proportionality fares better than his moderate formalism.

68 See Plato (1960: V.744e, 127) and Aristotle (1998: Book IV, xi 1296a, 28–32, 121).

69 See Rousseau (1997: Book II, chapter XI, ii, 78).

70 As far as I know, the only proposal to explicitly apply the idea of proportionality to power is that of Harry Brighouse and Marc Fleurbaey (2010). However, what they call 'the proportionality principle' simply applies to formal power. However, beyond any apparent similarity, the approach of proportional justice that I defend is profoundly different. First, I extend the idea of proportionality to material power (in terms of income and wealth). Second, and most important, the cornerstone of my proposal is that power resources (material and immaterial) should be distributed among individuals not exceeding a certain permissible range. This fundamental egalitarian feature is fully absent (maybe unintentionally) in Brighouse and Fleurbaey's approach to proportionality.

71 The contemporary literature on proportionality mainly focuses on war, individual self-defence and, in general, theories of law, see Uniacke (1994), Hurka (2005), Alexy (2010), Huscroft, Miller and Webber (2014), McMahan (2015), and Ripstein (2017). Although in many cases these approaches advocate the idea of proportionality in a way that makes comparative judgments about the balance of good results and bad side effects that occur while carrying out a certain action or procedure, the inequality of outcome among individuals is not the normative issue of these proportional approaches. On the contrary, they often appeal to an aggregative utilitarian conception of proportionality (for a critical discussion on this utilitarian view, see Ripstein (2017) and Letsas (2018). In this respect, I agree with Lever (2020) that, in the current debate, 'proportionality' can often end up concealing people's egalitarian claims. However, this only depends on the way we advocate the idea of proportionality.

72 In this sense, Reiff (2009: 11) sustains that 'the principle of equality is just a special case of the principle of proportionality, for it applies when the moral weights of the competing claims are equally balanced, while the principle of proportionality applies in all cases.' Although Reiff (2009) does not discuss political and deontological justice, I believe that there may be some analogies between my approach of proportional justice and Reiff's account. In any case, in my account, the principle of proportionality has a specific aim, one that only concerns the distribution of material resources. Gibson (2016) instead borrows Reiff's principle of proportionality to solve the problem of moral priority between domestic inequality and global poverty.

73 Note that in light of this second reason, nothing changes for those who abandon the idea of desert as having moral value (see Friedman 2002 [1962]; Hayek 2012; Mankiw 2013), and alternatively, they advocate the view that the free market is, in a liberal society, the only means to assign the social product among participants as result of their individual liberties; Olsaretti (2004) calls this approach entitlement-based theories to distinguish it from moral desert-based theories. As I said, the free market and individuals' productivity depends, *at least partially*, on social and political institutional settings as well as on the relative bargaining power of the individuals involved. Lister (2017) sustains that, by reason of the fact that the dependence of individual market contribution on institutional setup is not total, we cannot completely discard desert-based theories, rather desert needs to be balanced against the goal of raising the lowest social position (for example, providing an unconditional basic income). He calls this account a reciprocity-based conception of desert. However, his account is insensitive with respect to the size of economic inequality and, therefore, it is not able to deal with the question of material domination.

74 Similarly Baiasu (2021) suggests that desert-sensitive theories should be used only where the goods to be distributed are not crucial for our lives. However, I think that the question of primary rules better determines this limitation of scope.

Bibliography

Abbey, Ruth. 2013. 'Introduction: Biography of a Bibliography: Three Decades of Feminist Response to Rawls', in Ruth Abbey (ed.), *Feminist Interpretations of John Rawls*, pp. 1–23. Pennsylvania: Pennsylvania State University Press.

Alexy, Robert. 2010. *A Theory of Constitutional Rights*. Oxford: Oxford University Press.

Alì, Nunzio. 2018. 'Economic Inequality and Proportionality: How rich should the 1% be?' Ph.D. dissertation, Federal University of Santa Catarina, https://repositorio.ufsc.br/handle/123456789/191680, (accessed on 11 August 2022).

Anderson, Annelise (ed). 2000. *Political Money: Deregulating American Politics. Selected Essays on Campaign Finance Reform*. Stanford: Hoover Institution Press.

Anderson, Elizabeth. 2017. *Private Government: How Employers Rule Our Lives (And Why We Don't Talk About It)*. Princeton: Princeton University Press.

Anderson, Elizabeth. 1999. 'What Is the Point of Equality?' *Ethics*, 109(2): 287–337.

Aristotle. 2004. *Nicomachean Ethics*. Trans. and ed. by Roger Crisp. Cambridge: Cambridge University Press.

Aristotle. 1998. *Politics*. Trans. by C. D. C. Reeve. Cambridge: Hackett Publishing Company.

Arneson, Richard. 2015. 'Equality of Opportunity', *The Stanford Encyclopedia of Philosophy*, Edward N. Zalta (ed.), https://plato.stanford.edu/archives/sum2015/entries/equal-opportunity/. (accessed on 26 January 2022).

Atkinson, Anthony B. 2015. *Inequality: What Can Be Done?* Cambridge: Harvard University Press.

Azmanova, Albena. 2016. 'The Right to Politics and Republican Non-Domination', *Philosophy and Social Criticism*, 42: 465–475.

Baiasu, Sorin. 2021. 'Distributive Justice and the Epistemological Argument Against Desert', *Academia Letters*, 127: 1–7.

Barry, Brian. 2001. *Culture and Equality: An Egalitarian Critique of Multiculturalism*. Cambridge: Polity Press.

Benhabib, Seyla. 2012. 'Is There a Human Right to Democracy?' in Claudio Corradetti (ed.), *Philosophical Dimensions of Human Rights*, pp. 191–213. Heidelberg, London and New York: Springer.

Boettcher, James W. 2004. 'What is Reasonableness?' *Philosophy & Social Criticism*, 30(5–6): 597–621.

Bohman, James and William Rehg (eds.). 1997. *Deliberative Democracy: Essays on Reason and Politics*. Cambridge: MIT Press.

Branham, J. Alexander, Stuart Soroka and Christopher Wlezien. 2017. 'When Do the Rich Win?' *Political Science Quarterly*, 132: 43–62.

Brennan, Jason and John Tomasi. 2012. 'Classical Liberalism', in David Estlund (ed.), *The Oxford Handbook of Political Philosophy*, pp. 115–132. Oxford: Oxford University Press.

Brighouse, Harry. 1996. 'Egalitarianism and Equal Availability of Political Influence', *Journal of Political Philosophy*, 4(2): 118–141.

Brighouse, Harry and Adam Swift. 2014. *Family Values: The Ethics of Parent-child Relationships*. Princeton: Princeton University Press.

Brighouse, Harry and Marc Fleurbaey. 2010. 'Democracy and Proportionality', *The Journal of Political Philosophy*, 18(2): 137–155.

Cadwalladr, Carol. 2017. 'The Great Brexit Robbery: How Our Democracy Was Hijacked.' *The Guardian*, 7 May 2017, https://www.theguardian.com/technology/2017/may/07/the-great-british-brexit-robbery-hijacked-democracy (accessed on 7 February 2022).

Cagé, Julia. 2020. *The Price of Democracy: How Money Shapes Politics and What to Do About It*. Trans. Patrick Camiller. Cambridge: Harvard University Press.

Cagé, Julia. 2016. *Saving the Media*. Trans. by Arthur Goldhammer. Cambridge: Harvard University Press.

Caranti, Luigi and Nunzio Alì. 2021. 'Redistribution, Recognition, and Pluralism: A Rawlsian Criticism of Fraser', in Denise Celentano and Luigi Caranti (eds.), *Paradigms of Justice: Redistribution, Recognition, and Beyond*, pp. 163–183. London: Routledge.

Celentano, Denise. 2019. 'Cooperating as Peers: Labor Justice Between Distributive and Relational Equality'. Unpublished Ph.D. dissertation, UNICT/EHESS.

Christiano, Thomas. 2012. 'Money in Politics', in David Estlund (ed.), *The Oxford Handbook of Political Philosophy*, pp. 241–257. Oxford: Oxford University Press.

Christiano, Thomas. 2010. 'The Uneasy Relationship between Democracy and Capital', *Social Philosophy and Policy*, 27(1): 195–217.

Christiano, Thomas. 1999. *The Rule of the Many*. Boulder: Westview Press.

Claassen, Rutger and Lisa Herzog. 2019. 'Why Economic Agency Matters: An Account of Structural Domination in the Economic Realm', *European Journal of Political Theory*, 20(3): 465–485.

Cohen, Gerald A. 2008. *Rescuing Justice and Equality*. Cambridge: Harvard University Press.

Cohen, Gerald A. 2000. *If You're an Egalitarian, How Come You're So Rich?* Cambridge: Harvard University Press.

Cohen, Joshua. 2001. 'Money, Politics and Political Equality', in Alex Byrne, Robert Stalnaker and Ralph Wedgwood (eds.), *Fact and Value: Essays on Ethics and Metaphysics for Judith Jarvis Thomson*, pp. 47–80. Cambridge: MIT Press.

Cohen, Joshua and Charles Sabel. 2006. 'Extra Rempublicam Nulla Justicia?' *Philosophy & Public Affairs*, 34(2): 147–175.

Daniels, Norman. 2003. 'Democratic Equality: Rawls's Complex Egalitarianism', in Samuel Freeman (ed.), *The Cambridge Companion to Rawls*, pp. 241–276. Cambridge: Cambridge University Press.

Daniels, Norman. 1978. 'Merit and Meritocracy', *Philosophy & Public Affairs*, 7(3): 206–223.

Daniels, Norman. 1975. 'Equal Liberty and Unequal Worth of Liberty', in Norman Daniels (ed.), *Reading Rawls*, pp. 253–281. New York: Basic Books.

Dowding, Keith. 2017. *Power, Luck and Freedom: Collected Essays*. Manchester: Manchester University Press.

Dworkin, Ronald. 2000. *Sovereign Virtue: The Theory and Practice of Equality*. Cambridge: Harvard University Press.

Edmundson, William A. 2021. *Socialism for Soloists: Spelling Out the Social Contract*. Cambridge: Polity Press.

Edmundson, William A. 2019. 'What Are "The Means of Production"?' *The Journal of Political Philosophy*, 28(4): 421–437.

Edmundson, William A. 2017. *John Rawls: Reticent Socialist*. Cambridge: Cambridge University Press.

Elster, Jon (ed.). 1998. *Deliberative Democracy*. Cambridge: Cambridge University Press.

Estlund, David. 2008. *Democratic Authority: A Philosophical Framework*. Princeton: Princeton University Press.

Estlund, David. 2000. 'Political Quality', *Social Philosophy and Policy*, 17(1): 127–160.

Farrell, Justin. 2016. 'Corporate Funding and Ideological Polarization about Climate Change', *Proceedings of the National Academy of Sciences of the United States of America*, 113(1): 92–97.

Feinberg, Joel. 1970. 'The Nature and Value of Rights', *The Journal of Value Inquiry*, 4(4): 243–257.

Fishkin, Joseph. 2014. *Bottlenecks: A New Theory of Equal Opportunity*. Oxford: Oxford University Press.

Fishkin, Joseph. 1983. *Justice, Equality Opportunity and the Family*. New Haven and London: Yale University Press.

Forst, Rainer. 2020. 'The Point of Justice: On the Paradigmatic Incompatibility between Rawlsian "Justice as Fairness" and Luck Egalitarianism', in John Mandle and Sarah Roberts-Cady (eds.), *John Rawls: Debating the Major Questions*, pp. 148–160. Oxford: Oxford University Press.

Forst, Rainer. 2014. *Justification and Critique: Towards a Critical Theory of Politics*. Trans. by Ciaran Cronin. Cambridge: Polity Press.

Forst, Rainer. 2012. *The Right to Justification*. Trans. by Jeffrey Flynn. New York: Columbia University Press.

Forst, Rainer. 2007. 'Radical Justice: On Iris Marion Young's Critique of the "Distributive Paradigm"', *Constellations: An International Journal of Critical and Democratic Theory*, 14(2): 260–265.

Frankfurt, Harry. 2015. *On Inequality*. Princeton: Princeton University Press.

Fraser, Nancy. 1996. 'Social Justice in the Age of Identity Politics: Redistribution, Recognition, and Participation', *The Tanner Lectures on Human Values*, Delivered at Stanford University, 30 April and 2 May 1996, https://tannerlectures.utah.edu/_resources/documents/a-to-z/f/Fraser98.pdf, (accessed on 2 February 2022).

Fraser, Nancy and Axel Honneth. 2003. *Redistribution or Recognition? A Political-Philosophical Exchange*. London: Verso.

Freeman, Samuel. 2018. 'Rawls on Distributive Justice and the Difference Principle', in Serena Olsaretti (ed.), *The Oxford Handbook of Distributive Justice*, pp. 1–33. Oxford: Oxford University Press.

Freeman, Samuel. 2013. 'Property-Owning Democracy and the Difference Principle', *Analyse & Kritik*, 35(1): 9–36.

Freeman, Samuel. 2011. 'Capitalism in the Classical and High Liberal Traditions", *Social Philosophy and Policy*, 28: 19–55.

Freeman, Samuel. 2007. *Rawls*. New York: Routledge.

Friedman, Milton. 2002 [1962]. *Capitalism and Freedom. 40th Anniversary Edition*. Chicago: University of Chicago Press.

Gaus, Gerald. 2010. 'Coercion, Ownership, and the Redistributive State: Justificatory Liberalism's Classical Tilt', *Social Philosophy and Policy*, 27(1): 233–275.

Gaus, Gerald. 1999. 'Reasonable Pluralism and the Domain of the Political: How the Weakness of John Rawls's Political Liberalism Can Be Overcome by Justificatory Liberalism', *Inquiry*, 42(2): 259–284.

Gibson, Francisco García. 2016. 'Conflicts Between Domestic Inequality and Global Poverty: Lexicality Versus Proportionality', *Ethics & Global Politics*, 9(1): 1–16.

Gilens, Martin and Benjamin I. Page. 2017. *Democracy in America? What Has Gone Wrong and What We Can Do About It*. Chicago: University of Chicago Press.

Gilens, Martin and Benjamin I. Page 2014. 'Testing Theories of American Politics: Elites, Interest Groups, and Average Citizens', *Perspectives on Politics*, 12(3): 564–581.

Goel, Vindu and Nick Wingfield. 2015. 'Mark Zuckerberg Vows to Donate 99% of His Facebook Shares for Charity', *The New York Times*, 2 December 2015, https://www.nytimes.com/2015/12/02/technology/mark-zuckerberg-facebook-charity.html (accessed on 7 February 2022).

Gosepath, Stefan. 2021. 'Equality', *The Stanford Encyclopedia of Philosophy*, Edward N. Zalta (ed.), https://plato.stanford.edu/archives/sum2021/entries/equality/ (accessed on 25 January 2022).

Graetz, Michael J. and Ian Shapiro. 2005. *Death by a Thousand Cuts: The Fight over Taxing Inherited Wealth*. Princeton: Princeton University Press.

Grossmann, Matt and William Isaac. 2017. 'Oligarchy or Class War? Political Parties and Interest Groups in Unequal Public Influence on Policy Adoption', *Tumblr*, 22 December 2017, http://matthewg.org/Gilens-Parties4.pdf (accessed on 7 February 2022).

Guntermann, Eric. 2021. 'Does Economic Inequality Undermine Political Equality? Testing Two Common Assumptions', *Electoral Studies*, 69(102202), https://doi.org/10.1016/j.electstud.2020.102202.

Habermas, Jürgen. 1996. *Between Facts and Norms: Contributions to a Discourse Theory of Law and Democracy*. Trans. by William Regh. Cambridge: MIT Press.

Habermas, Jürgen. 1995. 'Reconciliation Through the Public Use of Reason: Remarks on John Rawls's Political Liberalism', *The Journal of Philosophy*, 92(3): 109–131.

Habermas, Jürgen. 1990. *Moral Consciousness and Communicative Action*. Trans. by Christian Lenhardt. Cambridge: MIT Press.

Hasen, Richard L. 2016. *Plutocrats United: Campaign Money, the Supreme Court, and the Distortion of American Elections*. New Haven & London: Yale University Press.

Hayek, Friedrich August von. 2012. *Law, Legislation and Liberty: A New Statement of the Liberal Principles of Justice and Political Economy*. London: Routledge.

Hurka, Thomas. 2005. 'Proportionality in the Morality of War', *Philosophy & Public Affairs*, 33(1): 34–66.

Huscroft, Grant, Bradley W. Miller and Grégoire Webber (eds.). 2014. *Proportionality and the Rule of Law: Rights, Justification and Reasoning*. New York: Cambridge University Press.

Instituto Maria da Penha (IMP). 2018. 'A lei na íntegra e comentada', *Instituto Maria da Penha*, https://www.institutomariadapenha.org.br/lei-11340/lei-maria-da-penha-na-integra-e-comentada.html#:~:text=11.340%2F2006%20pune%20os%20agressores,combate%20%C3%A0%20viol%C3%AAncia%20de%20g%C3%AAnero, (accessed on 2 February 2022).

International Consortium of Investigative Journalists (ICIJ). 2017. 'About the Paradise Papers Investigation: The Paradise Papers is a global investigation into the offshore activities of some of the world's most powerful people and companies', *ICIJ*, 5 November 2017, https://www.icij.org/investigations/paradise-papers/about/ (accessed on 7 February 2022).

Jacobs, Lawrence R. and Robert Y. Shapiro. 2000. *Politicians Don't Pander: Political Manipulation and the Loss of Democratic Responsiveness*. Chicago: University of Chicago Press.

Kagan, Shelly. 2015. *The Geometry of Desert*. Oxford: Oxford University Press.
Kant, Immanuel. 1996. *The Metaphysics of Morals*. Trans. by Mary Gregor. Cambridge: Cambridge University Press.
Kaus, Mickey. 1995. *The End of Equality. Second Edition*. New York: Basic Books.
Kuhner, Timothy. 2014. *Capitalism vs. Democracy: Money in Politics and the Free Market Constitution*. California: Stanford Law & Politics.
Lægaard, Sune. 2005. 'On the Prospects for a Liberal Theory of Recognition', *Res Publica*, 11: 325–348.
Letsas, George. 2018. 'Proportionality as Fittingness: The Moral Dimension of Proportionality', *Current Legal Problems*, 71(1): 53–86.
Lever, Annabelle. 2020. 'A Sense of Proportion: Some Thoughts on Equality, Security and Justice', *Res Publica*, 26(3): 357–371.
Lister, Andrew. 2017. 'Markets, Desert, and Reciprocity', *Politics, Philosophy & Economics*, 16(1): 47–69.
Lovett, Frank. 2012. 'What Counts as Arbitrary Power?' *Journal of Political Power*, 5(1): 137–152.
Maffettone, Sebastiano. 2004. 'Political Liberalism: Reasonableness and Democratic Practice', *Philosophy & Social Criticism*, 30(5–6): 541–577.
Mankiw, Gregory. 2013. 'Defending the One Percent', *Journal of Economic Perspectives*, 27(3): 21–34.
Marquez, Xavier. 2015. 'Maximizing Accountability to the Least Privileged: The Difference Principle, the Fair Value of the Political Liberties, and the Design of Democratic Institutions', *Polity*, 47(4): 484–507.
Matthews, Dylan. 2016. 'Remember that Study Saying America is an Oligarchy? 3 Rebuttals Say It's Wrong', *Vox*, 9 May 2016, https://www.vox.com/2016/5/9/11502464/gilens-page-oligarchy-study (accessed on 7 February 2022).
Mayer, Jane. 2016. *Dark Money: The Hidden History of the Billionaires Behind the Rise of the Radical Right*. New York: Doubleday.
McMahan, Jeff. 2015. 'Proportionality and Time', *Ethics*, 125(3): 696–719.
Moriarty, Jeffrey. 2018. 'Desert-Based Justice', in Serena Olsaretti (ed.), *The Oxford Handbook of Distributive Justice*, pp. 1–24. Oxford: Oxford University Press.
Moriarty, Jeffrey. 2005. 'The Epistemological Argument Against Desert', *Utilitas*, 17(2): 205–221.
Mouffe, Chantal. 1994. 'Political Liberalism: Neutrality and the Political', *Ratio Juris*, 7(3): 314–324.
Murphy, Liam B. 2000. *Moral Demands in Nonideal Theory*. Oxford: Oxford University Press.
Murphy, Liam B. 1998. 'Institutions and the Demands of Justice', *Philosophy & Public Affairs*, 27(4): 251–291.
Nagel, Thomas. 2005. 'The Problem of Global Justice', *Philosophy & Public Affairs*, 33(2): 113–147.
Neuhouser, Frederick. 2013. 'Rousseau's Critique of Economic Inequality', *Philosophy & Public Affairs*, 41(3): 193–225.
Nozick, Robert. 1974. *Anarchy, State, and Utopia*. Oxford: Blackwell Publishers.
Okin, Susan Moller. 1989. *Justice, Gender, and Family*. New York: Basic Books.
Olsaretti, Serena. 2004. *Liberty, Desert and the Market*. Cambridge: Cambridge University Press.
Olsaretti, Serena (ed.). 2003. *Desert and Justice*. Oxford: Oxford University Press.
O'Neill, Martin. 2017. 'Survey Article: Philosophy and Public Policy After Piketty', *The Journal of Political Philosophy*, 25(3): 343–375.

O'Neill, Martin. 2008. 'What Should Egalitarians Believe?' *Philosophy & Public Affairs*, 36(2): 119–156.

O'Neill, Onora. 1996. *Towards Justice and Virtue: A Constructive Account of Practical Reasoning*. Cambridge: Cambridge University Press.

Oreskes, Naomi and Erik M. Conway. 2010. *Merchants of Doubt: How a Handful of Scientists Obscured the Truth on Issues from Tobacco Smoke to Global Warming*. New York: Bloomsbury Press.

Parfit, Derek. 2011a. *On What Matters. Volume One*. Oxford: Oxford Scholarship.

Parfit, Derek. 2011b. *On What Matters. Volume Two*. Oxford: Oxford Scholarship.

Parfit, Derek. 2000. 'Equality or Priority?' in Matthew Clayton and Andrew Williams (eds.), *The Ideal of Equality*, pp. 81–125. New York: St. Martin's Press.

Parfit, Derek. 1997. 'Equality and Priority', *Ratio* 10(3): 202–221.

Piketty, Thomas. 2020. *Capital and Ideology*. Trans. by Arthur Goldhammer. Cambridge: Harvard University Press.

Piketty, Thomas. 2014. *Capital in the Twenty-First Century*. Trans. by Arthur Goldhammer. Cambridge: Harvard University Press.

Piroli, Diana. 2021. 'Justiça e reconhecimento: uma interpretação das bases sociais do autorrespeito de John Rawls a partir do debate redistribuição e reconhecimento'. Ph.D. dissertation, Federal University of Santa Catarina, https://repositorio.ufsc.br/handle/123456789/229097, (accessed on 11 August 2022).

Plato. 1960. *The Laws*. New York: E.P. Dutton and Co.

Pogge, Thomas W. 2008. *World Poverty and Human Rights. Second Edition*. Cambridge: Polity Press.

Pogge, Thomas W. 2000. 'On the Site of Distributive Justice', *Philosophy & Public Affairs*, 29(2): 137–169.

Pogge, Thomas W. 1989. *Realizing Rawls*. Ithaca: Cornell University Press.

Post, Robert C. 2014. *Citizens Divided: Campaign Finance Reform and the Constitution*. Cambridge: Harvard University Press.

Przeworski, Adam. 2003. *States and Markets: A Primer in Political Economy*. Cambridge: Cambridge University Press.

Przeworski, Adam. 1998. 'Deliberation and Ideological Domination', in Jon Elster (ed.), *Deliberative Democracy*, pp. 140–160. Cambridge: Cambridge University Press.

Przeworski, Adam. 1990. *The State and the Economy Under Capitalism*. London: Routledge.

Przeworski, Adam and Michael Wallerstein. 1988. 'Structural Dependence of the State on Capital', *The American Political Science Review*, 82(1): 11–29.

Rasmussen, David M. 2004. 'Defending Reasonability: The Centrality of Reasonability in the Later Rawls', *Philosophy & Social Criticism*, 30(5–6): 525–540.

Rawls, John. 2005. *Political Liberalism. Expanded Edition*. New York: Columbia University Press.

Rawls, John. 2001. *Justice as Fairness: A Restatement*. Cambridge: Harvard University Press.

Rawls, John. 1982. *The Basic Liberties and Their Priority. The Tanner Lectures on Human Values. Volume III*. Salt Lake City: University of Utah Press.

Rawls, John. 1971. *A Theory of Justice. Original Edition*. Cambridge: Harvard University Press.

Rawls, John. 1955. 'Two Concepts of Rules', *The Philosophical Review*, 64(1): 3–32.

Reich, Rob. 2018. *Just Giving: Why Philanthropy Is Failing Democracy and How It Can Do Better*. Princeton: Princeton University Press.

Reiff, Mark. 2009. 'Proportionality, Winner-take-all, and Distributive Justice', *Politics, Philosophy & Economics*, 8(1): 5–42.

Rhodes, Jesse H. and Brian F. Schaffner. 2017. 'Testing Models of Unequal Representation: Democratic Populists and Republican Oligarchs?' *Quarterly Journal of Political Science*, 12(2): 185–204.

Ripstein, Arthur. 2017. 'Reclaiming Proportionality', *Journal of Applied Philosophy*, 34(1): 1–18.

Robeyns, Ingrid. 2017. 'Having Too Much', in Jack Knight and Melissa Schwartzberg (eds.), *NOMOS LVI: Wealth. Yearbook of the American Society for Political and Legal Philosophy*, pp. 1–44. New York: New York University Press.

Roemer, John E. 1998. *Equality of Opportunity*. Cambridge: Harvard University Press.

Rorty, Richard. 1991. 'Priority of Democracy to Philosophy', in Richard Rorty (ed.), *Objectivity, Relativism, and Truth*, pp. 175–196. Cambridge: Cambridge University Press.

Rosenkranz, E. Joshua (ed.). 2000. *If Buckley Fell: A First Amendment Blueprint for Regulating Money in Politics*. New York: Century Foundation Press.

Rosset, Jan and Christian Stecker. 2019. 'How Well Are Citizens Represented by Their Governments? Issue Congruence and Inequality in Europe', *European Political Science Review*, 11(2): 145–160.

Rousseau, Jean-Jacques. 1997. 'The Social Contract', in Victor Gourevitch (ed. and trans.), *The Social Contract, and Other Later Political Writings*, pp. 39–152. Cambridge: Cambridge University Press.

Saez, Emmanuel and Gabriel Zucman. 2019. *The Triumph of Injustice: How the Rich Dodge Taxes and How to Make Them Pay*. New York: W. W. Norton & Company.

Scanlon, Thomas M. 2018. *Why Does Inequality Matter?* Oxford: Oxford University Press.

Scanlon, Thomas M. 1998. *What We Owe to Each Other*. Cambridge: Harvard University Press.

Scanlon, Thomas M. 1982. 'Contractualism and Utilitarianism', in Amartya Sen and Bernard Williams (eds.), *Utilitarianism and Beyond*, pp. 103–128. Cambridge: Cambridge University Press.

Schäfer, Armin and Hanna Schwander. 2019. '"Don't Play If You Can't Win": Does Economic Inequality Undermine Political Equality?' *European Political Science Review*, 11(3): 395–413.

Scheffler, Samuel. 2015. 'The Practice of Equality', in Carina Fourie, Fabien Schuppert and Ivo Wallimann-Helmer (eds.), *Social Equality: On What It Means to Be Equals*, pp. 21–44. Oxford: Oxford University Press.

Scheffler, Samuel. 2003. 'What Is Egalitarianism?' *Philosophy & Public Affairs*, 31(1): 5–39.

Scheffler, Samuel. 2000. 'Justice and Desert in Liberal Theory', *California Law Review*, 88(3): 965–990.

Schemmel, Christian. 2021. *Justice and Egalitarian Relations*. Oxford: Oxford University Press.

Shapiro, Ian. 2003. *The State of Democratic Theory*. Princeton: Princeton University Press.

Sher, George. 1989. *Desert*. Princeton: Princeton University Press.

Shklar, Judith N. 1990. *The Faces of Injustice*. New Haven: Yale University Press.

Sibley, W. M. 1953. 'The Rational Versus the Reasonable', *The Philosophical Review*, 62(4): 554–560.

Stiglitz, Joseph. 2012. *The Price of Inequality: How Today's Divided Society Endangers Our Future*. New York & London: W. W. Norton & Company.

Sunstein, Cass R. 1994. 'Political Equality and Unintended Consequences', *Columbia Law Review*, 94: 1390–1414.

Temkin, Larry. 2000. 'Equality, Priority, and the Levelling Down Objection', in Matthew Clayton and Andrew Williams (eds.), *The Ideal of Equality*, pp. 126–161. New York: St. Martin's Press.

Temkin, Larry. 2017. 'Equality as Comparative Fairness', *Journal of Applied Philosophy*, 34(1): 43–60.

Temkin, Larry. 1993. *Inequality*. Oxford: Oxford University Press.

Thomas, Alan. 2017. *Republic of Equals: Predistribution and Property-Owning Democracy*. Oxford: Oxford University Press.

Thornhill, John. 2017. 'The Big Data Revolution Can Revive the Planned Economy', *Financial Times*, 4 September 2017, https://www.ft.com/content/6250e4ec-8e68-11e7-9084-d0c17942ba93 (accessed on 7 February 2022).

Tomasi, John. 2012. *Free Market Fairness*. Princeton: Princeton University Press.

Uniacke, Suzanne. 1994. *Permissible Killing: The Self-defence Justification of Homicide*. Cambridge: Cambridge University Press.

Van Parijs, Philippe. 1995. *Real Freedom for All: What (If Anything) Can Justify Capitalism?* Oxford: Oxford University Press.

von Platz, Jeppe. 2020a. 'Democratic Equality and the Justification of Welfare-State Capitalism', *Ethics*, 131: 4–33.

von Platz, Jeppe. 2020b. 'Rawls's Underestimation of the Importance of Economic Agency and Economic Rights', in John Mandle and Sarah Roberts-Cady (eds.), *John Rawls: Debating the Major Questions*, pp. 95–108. Oxford: Oxford University Press.

von Platz, Jeppe. 2020c. *Theories of Distributive Justice: Who Gets What and Why*. New York: Routledge.

von Platz, Jeppe. 2016. 'Social Cooperation and Basic Economic Rights: A Rawlsian Route to Social Democracy', *Journal of Social Philosophy*, 47(3): 288–308.

von Platz, Jeppe and John Tomasi. 2015. 'Liberalism and Economic Liberty', in Steven Wall (ed.), *The Cambridge Companion to Liberalism*, pp. 261–281. Cambridge: Cambridge University Press.

Walzer, Michael. 1983. *Spheres of Justice: A Defense of Pluralism and Equality*. New York: Basic Books.

West, Darrell M. and Burdett A. Loomis. 1998. *The Sound of Money: How Political Interests Get What They Want*. New York: W. W. Norton & Company.

Widerquist, Karl. 2015. 'The Piketty Observation Against the Institutional Background: How Natural is this Natural Tendency and What Can We Do About It?', *Basic Income Studies*, 10(1): 83–90.

Winters, Jeffrey A. 2011. *Oligarchy*. Cambridge: Cambridge University Press.

Winters, Jeffrey A., and Benjamin I. Page. 2009. 'Oligarchy in the United States?' *Perspectives on Politics*, 7(4): 731–751.

Wolff, Jonathan. 2003. 'The Dilemma of Desert', in Serena Olsaretti (ed.), *Desert and Justice*, pp. 219–232. Oxford: Oxford University Press.

Wright, Erik O. 2019. *How to Be an Anticapitalist in the Twenty-first Century*. London: Verso.

Young, Iris M. 2011. *Responsibility for Justice*. Oxford: Oxford University Press.

Young, Iris M. 2006. 'Taking the Basic Structure Seriously', *Perspectives on Politics*, 4(1): 91–97.

Young, Iris M. 1990. *Justice and the Politics of Difference*. Princeton: Princeton University Press.

2

WHAT DOES IT MEAN TO BE DOMINATED?

In the literature, domination is usually characterised by specific asymmetrical relations of power that (a) are stable over a long period and (b) exhibit a certain need for 'cooperation'[1] by those in a more disadvantaged position (Wartenberg 1990; Lovett 2010; Neuhouser 2013). By this first broad formulation, it seems that an agent involved in an asymmetrical relation of power as such is dominated. In this sense, domination and power over another might be treated as synonymous. However, in the literature there has been an effort to normatively distinguish the two concepts, opting for a 'neutral' conceptualisation of power (neither good nor bad in itself),[2] whereas the concept of domination is employed in situations where someone falls under an arbitrary power. The normative challenge, then, is to understand what an arbitrary power consists of. The debate on domination has run along two related lines of investigation.

A first question concerns understanding how power is exercised. Scholars usually conceive the exercise of power in two different manners: relational as interagentive and structural as impersonal. For some scholars, power is always and exclusively understood as interagentive; i.e. between identifiable agents: A has the capacity to interfere and alter (intentionally, or at least with foreseeable effects) the free actions, choices and ideas of B.[3] What is more, this interagentive dimension is the object of relational domination also when A's capacity is dependent and inscribed within social structures. In this sense, although these scholars do not overlook the existence and impact of social structures, they argue that 'structures do not "exercise" power as persons do; rather, they rely on and provide opportunities for exercising it' (Forst 2017: 45). Thus, if we can speak about power only between identifiable agents (an agent-centred notion), domination is also, and always, relational as interagentive.

The main divergence on this point lies with those structural theorists who assert that power is not exclusively located in agents; rather it is also and mainly exercised

DOI: 10.4324/9781003189428-3

by structures themselves without identifiable agents, insofar as these structures operate with several *impersonal* mechanisms.[4] These scholars argue that it is not that a 'powerful' agent (individual or collective) that imposes structural constraints over other agents, but rather that structural power is 'the result of multiple, large-scale social processes, which interact to create relational and structural inequalities and power subordination that no identifiable agent directs or controls or intends' (Young 2011: 52; see also Hayward (2018: 64)). From this perspective, the interagentive dimension of power might determine only a form of domination: relational domination. By contrast, structural power as impersonal generates the most significant and impactful form of domination in modern societies: structural domination. An important consequence of conceiving structural power as impersonal is that *all agents* (both the powerful and the powerless) are considered as 'relatively' constrained by social structures in their free actions as well as by their own perception of interests and ideas. This means that it is impossible to fully identify and separate an agent's (B) actions and interests from the power of interference or influence of another agent (A). The outcome is that the way in which we believe that power is essentially exercised – whether relational (interagentive) or structural (impersonal) – determines the way in which we identify the corresponding form of domination: relational or structural.

The second line of investigation consists, then, of identifying the arbitrary exercise of power. Hence, for relational theorists, domination occurs when power is exercised to alter the free actions of others in a manner contrary to a power-subject's interests – 'manifest' (Dahl 1957) or 'real' (Lukes 2005) – or when an agent possesses the capacity to interfere, intentionally and at their pleasure, in certain choices that the other is in a position to make (Pettit 1997: 52; Lovett 2010) or when this power is not reciprocally and generally justified (Forst 2017). On the contrary, according to those who advocate structural domination, we need to see how a society as a whole, by its own social structures, constrains free actions and choices of all individuals producing 'patterned asymmetries' of social freedom among individuals (Hayward 1998), or how diminishing the 'common interest and good' towards 'elite interests and benefits' (Thompson 2018), or how diminishing the capacity of 'actors to control the institutions through which the operative logic of the social system is enacted, which translates as their impotency to affect the "rules of the game."' (Azmanova 2020: 181).

The aim of this chapter is to explain how my conception of domination differs and complements the major contemporary theories of power and domination. As I said, domination occurs when a person does not have adequate key power resources with respect to others to be co-author of the primary rules that govern the social relations in which they are involved. In this sense, domination means to violate or disrespect our 'deliberative autonomy'. I believe this conception to be the best way to realise the classical idea of domination, that is, obedience to the foreign wills of others as opposed to 'obeying only oneself' (Rousseau 1997) or 'being his own master' (Kant 1996).

This definition implies two main points. First, social power implies a strict interweave between key power resources that social actors have with respect to others and primary rules that govern social relations in which they are involved.[5] The result is that domination occurs when social actors are 'relatively' or 'proportionally' deprived of those key power resources that establish, shape and stabilise primary rules. Second, and as a consequence, domination might assume different forms according to the kind of key power resource we take into account; for instance, in the case of material resources I refer to material domination.

From this perspective, we might obtain two fundamental steps forward in respect to the current debate. First of all, the common distinction between interagentive and structural domination is misleading. On the one hand, interagentive theorists risk taking for granted the primary question of how primary rules are established and shaped. They overlook that both A and B agents' actions, interests and ideas are not only influenced but also *partially* formed by primary rules. Thus, the point is who has power with respect to others to set otherwise primary rules. On the other hand, I disagree with structural theorists about the idea that individuals might be dominated by an impersonal form of power. It is possible to avoid the unproductive contraposition between interagentive and structural power, if we realise that social power is located in agents, but it is attributed to them only through their '*relative*' capacity, by mobilising key power resources, to establish, shape, and stabilise primary rules. My own conception of social power embodies this essential feature. Secondly, we can rescue the centrality of asymmetrical 'distribution' of key power resources into the concept of domination. In this way, we might be able to adequately rescue the spirit of Rousseau's conception of domination. According to him, indeed, what matters is the 'degree of power and riches' that should not 'be absolutely identical for everybody', but rather 'that power shall never be great enough for violence, and [...] in respect of riches, no citizen shall ever be wealthy enough to buy another, and none poor enough to be forced to sell himself' (Rousseau 1997: 78). Let me show how the most relevant current theories conceive the notion of domination and why they miss this point or do not adequately address it.

The first section begins with neo- or civic republicanism as a perfect representation of an interagentive account of power and domination; while in the second section, I focus on the structural account. Then, in the third section, I provide a specific and narrow conceptualisation of power, that I call expressly 'social power'. The purpose is, first of all, to overcome the unproductive dualism between interagentive and structural models and provide a better explanation of the strict intertwine between agency and structure, and secondly, to provide a concept of power capable of passing the test of 'publicity'. In the fourth section, contrary to what most scholars seem to assume, I show how the concept of non-domination cannot be, in principle, insensitive to the scale of inequality of power resources between citizens. I contend that what should be avoided is the 'risk of domination'; that is, those primary rules that allow, in principle, an unbounded inequality in the 'distribution' of key power resources should be judged as unjust. This forces us to theoretically and empirically establish a certain 'limit' range or a 'proportion' for each of these key power resources.

2.1 Relational Domination: An Interagentive Notion of Power

The agent-centred notion of power and domination is surely central to the Anglo-American debate in which the main question has focussed on how power is exercised between identifiable agents and how broadly the notion of agency should be conceived. Dahl's work (1957; 1958; 1961) on power was a benchmark of this debate. He defines social power (or power over) in the following way: 'A has power over B to the extent that he can get B to do something that B would not otherwise do' (Dahl 1957: 202–203). Dahl's main goal was to test elite theories of community power (Hunter 1953; Mills 1956) measuring who effectively has *more power in social life*, or better *Who Governs?* Contrary to elite theories, Dahl (1961) inferred from his analysis that power was distributed pluralistically. However, Dahl's analysis is considered a one-dimensional view of power. He measured power among citizens and groups (using a certain 'base' of power, such as institutional positions or resources as a means of exercising power) only in terms of who prevails in community decision-making in case of manifest and observable conflicts between citizens' preferences. Preferences 'that are assumed to be consciously made, exhibited in actions, and thus to be discovered by observing people's behaviour' (Lukes 2005: 19).

The debate grew out from this work trying to expand its narrow notion of agency, and consequently the way in which power is exercised by means of other dimensions. For example, for Bachrach and Baratz (1962), the study of power cannot be limited to the inquiry of concrete decision-making analysis about political issues. By contrast, a powerful agent has power over others not only by prevailing in manifest conflicts, but also by hindering the participation in politics to express their preferences or imposing an agenda on them. Thus, according to Bachrach and Baratz (1962), power has 'two faces': prevailing in conflict and 'forcibly' suppressing conflict. Lukes (1974, 2005) has gone further in this debate including a third dimensional view, where power consists in influencing, shaping or determining power-subjects' desires, beliefs and judgments; for instance, the control of information, through the mass media and through the processes of socialisation (Lukes 2005: 27).

However, we can observe an essential point of convergence in all of these three 'faces' or dimensional views: power is always and exclusively understood as interagentive; i.e. between identifiable agents. What is more, the interagentive perspective is also considered valid when A's power to interfere or alter B's free and authentic actions and ideas is inscribed within social structures. For example, a teacher's power over her students derives not only from her personal abilities and motives, but above all from her position within a certain educational structure that gives her a certain authority and power over a student (for example, to assign grades and to sanction students' behaviours). In this sense, interagentive theorists are aware that a teacher's power over students would disappear without an educational structure and 'peripheral' social agents involved in this structure (Isaac 1987a, 1987b). Nonetheless, what matters is the causal relation (structural or not) between identifiable agents. In other words, how a teacher exercises the power, which educational structure allows for, over her students (for example, if she assigns grades in arbitrary or discriminatory manners).

This power relation between identifiable agents is usually associated with the classical master–slave relationship. In this respect, into the interagentive paradigm, neo- (or civic) republicanism represents the most relevant position.[6] For neo-republicanism, power is exercised on arbitrary bases when an agent possesses the capacity to interfere, intentionally and at their pleasure, in certain 'choices that the other is in a position to make' (Pettit 1997: 52).[7] Here interference itself is conceived negatively; that is, 'interference cannot take the form of a bribe or a reward; when I interfere I make things worse for you, not better' (Pettit 1997: 52). To avoid domination, the exercise of power-holders should be specifically constrained in a way that compels them to track persons' *own perceived* interests, ideas and welfare of those who are subjects to that power (Pettit 1997: 55; 1999: 165; Lovett 2012: 139). However, the main normative challenge lies in how to identify the power-subject's own interests. Neo-republicanism rejects both objective and subjective conceptions of interest. An objective interest account would generate a 'moralised' conception of domination (Lovett 2012: 142); meanwhile, a subjective account faces the serious normative problem of interpersonal comparisons and adaptive preferences. For this reason, scholars of neo-republicanism endorse some version of the procedural deliberative account to deal with the question of how to take into consideration the 'idea', 'interest' or 'worldview' of power-subjects. In other words, it is only possible to be free in a free state which entails some forms of self-government (Skinner 2012: 60); not coincidentally indeed a republican state. As Pettit says,

> the only possible means is by recourse to public discussion in which people may speak for themselves and for the groups to which they belong. Every interest and every idea that guides the action of a state must be open to challenge from every corner of the society.
>
> (Pettit 1997: 56)

Therefore, the key element is 'contestatory' mechanisms at work.

At this point, two different paths can be followed. According to the first one, non-domination coincides exactly with whatever outcome comes from tracking the interests of those who might be potentially dominated through 'the processes and institutions of democratic contestation' (Maynor 2006: 137). But this means that non-domination is not an independent criterion, and it collapses the distinction between non-domination and democracy. To say something about when a person or group is dominated we should expect the process of public deliberation, and in the meantime we can merely discuss 'what would count as a sufficiently democratic mechanism of contestation, which may not be easy to do' (Lovett 2012: 144). An alternative path is to maintain an independent criterion to assess or guide the deliberative result. This is what Pettit (2001, 2004) suggests when he identifies in the fund of 'shared reasons' of a certain group (for example, citizens) the framework for the deliberation of their members. In this case, Lovett (2012: 145) is right to define Pettit's republican account as deliberative-communitarian. Pettit's fund of shared reasons seems to give a substantive formulation to another very familiar and crucial republican concept: the common interest or good of the community as a whole. However, although in this way non-domination is distinguished from democracy itself, Pettit's account faces the same problem of other communitarian accounts that appeal to 'our shared understandings' (for example, Walzer 1983). But, the main concern of non-domination regards precisely the kinds of conflict around meanings and interpretations of 'our understandings of social goods'. Again, this puts us back to the centrality of the mechanisms and channels for public contestation to give hope that the exercise of power-holders will truly track or power-subjects' own interests.

Of course, for Pettit (1997: 171–205) and other neo-republicans, 'contestatory' practices go well beyond simply voting, but even in the best scenario the neo-republicanism account is able to detect only the kind of domination that is encoded in legal statuses such as 'slave' or 'serf'. It means that only those conditions of dependence and inequality that arise out of unequal political status can count as domination. In this sense, when it comes to material inequality, neo-republicanism overlooks the inequality of outcome. Indeed, wealth inequality as a result of free market activities is not considered a tool of domination. First, the market economy is not seen as a source of domination itself insofar as 'it is the cumulative, unintended effect of people's mutual adjustments, where that history of adjustment may or may not have begun in government initiatives' (Pettit 2006: 139). Second, in a free labour market 'no one would depend on any particular master and so no one would be at the mercy of a master: he or she could move on to employment elsewhere in the event of suffering arbitrary interference' (Pettit 2006: 142). Third, the market economy can and should be regulated by the state, for example, to prohibit slave contracts and to guard against other abuses of the market (predatory pricing, insider trading, market manipulation, and so on). Clearly, some distributive requirements also fall under these regulations, for example, when citizens are so poor that they have difficulty participating in the labour market and risk being dominated by the wealthy. In this line of reasoning, Pettit and others[8] maintain that universal basic income (albeit with some forms of conditionality) is the best way of guaranteeing economic independence and free labour. But, beyond this, it seems that material inequality, regardless of how vast it would be, does not matter.

However, there is one case, at least, which should seriously alert the sensitivity of neo-republicanism; that is, when economic inequality is translated into unequal political power, giving to the rich greater chances to advance and protect their own interests. Although the neo-republicans are absolutely aware of this problem, surprisingly they do not provide an inherent normative prescription to deal with it. Lovett (2012) reformulates his account of domination to opt for a 'pure procedural' interpretation of arbitrariness without any additional substantive requirements, in order to avoid whatever attempt to track power-subjects' own perceived ideas and interests. Thus, from his normative perspective, the problem does not rise, either. Pettit (1997: 194) suggests nothing else than a classical insulation strategy in order to identify 'measures for effectively separating the worlds of government and business'. Dagger (2006) goes further, taking into account the strategy to limit the disparities in wealth that flow from markets, designing what he defines as the 'neo-republican civic economy' in the form of a property-owning democracy. But, in his proposal, the main and only instrument to deal with economic inequality capable of upsetting political equality seems to be an inheritance tax.[9] Moreover, Dagger is aware that his proposal is affected by a high level of normative indeterminacy in terms of substantive principles or policies (Dagger 2006: 167). For example, he admits that by his neo-republican civic economy, we might have great difficulty justifying the loss of efficiency, and establishing how much efficiency can be sacrificed. Again, from the neo-republican perspective, these substantive issues should be purely the subject of public debate and discussion (Dagger 2006: 168), although this comes close to a declaration of surrender.

In summary, what unequivocally emerges is that neo-republicanism treats material inequality as derivative from equal political status, and as one facet among many empirical contingencies (Pettit 1997: 119). Therefore, in spite of how it may appear at first glance, this frugality (or even absence) of normative arguments regarding the fundamental question of how economic inequality might offer the rich more political influence than others is not surprising. Indeed, unequal political influence that comes from material resources does not seem, in principle, to upset neo-republican political status. For neo-republicanism, what political status requires in terms of individual power resources is unclear. In other words, how should republican citizens be politically empowered? Certainly they should enjoy formal political and legal equality, voting rights, constitutional provisions and the existence of channels for public contestation, such as 'suitable forums' (Pettit 1997: 195–200), but nothing in this list counts as suitable 'individual' power that comes from individual material resources or other kinds of resource power (for example, basic individual liberties). Thus, the neo-republicanism theory of domination carries two main flaws.

First of all, it downgrades the primary question of asymmetrical power among two or more agents. Although Pettit (1997: 113) acknowledges that individual power is a function of the powers at the disposal of others ('in the land of the blind, the one-eyed man is king'), no normative requirement follows from this consideration. Rather, Pettit (1997: 67, 114) considers as insufficient the strategy of equalising (or reducing as much as possible) 'reciprocal power' or 'power-ratio' resource of agents to avoid domination. Only more recently, Pettit (2012) seems to be aware of the normative relevance of the relative inequality of individual power resources. He (Pettit 2012: 87–90) opts for a sufficientarian strategy based on the capability approach in which the sufficient threshold identified by the eyeball test seems to be sensitive to what other citizens have.

Unfortunately, the problem is that Pettit's consequentialist approach assigns a normative priority of political legitimacy over social and distributive justice. The result is that distributive requirements of justice are seriously weakened, and above all, as Pansardi (2015) observes, Pettit misses the point that social justice, on the contrary, should be considered as a necessary condition and a prior requirement for political legitimacy. More precisely, according to Pettit (2012: 136), political legitimacy is a matter of vertical relations between citizens and the state that rules over them, while the issue of social justice is a matter of horizontal relations between citizens themselves. Hence, on the one hand, political legitimacy is achieved when republican citizens have control over government decisions and thus over how the state can or cannot interfere (interference without domination). On the other hand, by a republican theory of social justice, the government provides 'substantive' means and resources for ensuring those range of choices that allow citizens to realise a meaningful life (note it is only at this point that a list of basic liberties is provided), see Pettit (2012: 103). However, both this analytical distinction and the lexicographical order between vertical and horizontal relations are misleading. Indeed, political legitimacy understood as a full control over the government decision-making power and interference is achieved only if all citizens are empowered by key power resources at the horizontal level. Indeed, if I am (relatively) disempowered with respect to others in some key power resources (material and immaterial), political freedom of non-domination that I would enjoy, at best, does not go beyond a kind of benevolent paternalism: the track of a person's own perceived ideas and interests ultimately stand on the goodwill of the others (or those who occupy the official positions of the state). In the best possible scenario, I may live under 'non-arbitrary rules', but I will not identify myself as a co-author of these rules.[10] To be clear, I am not claiming that being paternalistic in any kind of situation automatically entails domination, but on the contrary that a compelling conception of non-domination cannot coincide with paternalism.[11]

This serious shortcoming might partially depend on the second main flaw of neo-republicanism theory: its inadequacy to deal with social structures. This deficit is usually identified in the exclusive emphasis on 'the master–slave relationship'. This problem does not include only neo-republicanism, but also the interagentive paradigm in general. Indeed, even Lukes' (2005) interagentive account of power and domination is exposed to the same deficit. For example, in the dialogue between Hayward and Lukes (2008) on the question of 'who did it?' or 'whom to shoot?', Lukes (Hayward and Lukes 2008: 7) suggests that 'we need to know whom to hold responsible for outcomes that seriously affect the interests of others'. Thus, when a social problem, such as the lack of access to decent and affordable housing by the poor and racially oppressed, is 'due to the action or inaction of identifiable individuals or groups or institutions, that, by acting otherwise, could have made a difference, then it makes sense to see the latter as powerful because responsible'. And Lukes (Hayward and Lukes 2008: 12) acknowledges that the power of those who are powerful (in this case to remedy injustice) might be 'limited by the structures – the constraints and opportunities, roles and norms – within which they operate'. The problem is that this perspective is blind to the most critical aspect of power: the authority to set and define these structures (or primary rules, as I prefer to identify them). Lukes (2005) and Pettit (1997) also agree that the most severe form of domination occurs when some have the social power to define, at their will and pleasure, what counts as a 'social problem' and as 'interests of others'. But what they do not take into account is that both of these things are defined and shaped by primary rules that govern our social relations. By taking them for granted, we lose the most fundamental insight for those who study social power and domination.

2.2 Structural Domination: An Impersonal Notion of Power

As we have already seen, those who exclusively advocate the interagentive notion of power do not deny the relevance of social structures. However, they assert that moral and political responsibility can be proved only if we maintain that interference in choices or actions occurs between identifiable agents; therefore, given that, unlike with agents, it is impossible to assign intentions, ideas and interests to social structures themselves, they cannot be a source of domination. Social structures entail consequences for individuals, but these consequences are the aggregate result of unintentional and unforeseeable individual actions and choices. On this point lies the main divergence and contraposition with those who advocate a structural power model. Their reply is that structural interference and their negative consequences are not the aggregate result of unintentional individual actions and choices; on the contrary, this aggregate result is causally determined by social structures and systems. This is because agents' actions, interests and ideas are to a certain point determined by structures themselves that appear to agents as a 'second nature' objectified social order (Habermas 1987; Young 1990, 2009; Allen 1999; Azmanova 2014, 2018; Hayward 2018). From this point of view, 'power over' is not simply exercised by agents within structures, but by norms and mechanisms inscribed within those structures.

This line of thought has its genesis in Marxism, Foucault's genealogical work, and Bourdieu's theory.[12] Nowadays, very few scholars are ready to accept, at least explicitly, a strong determinist position according to which human agency is totally determined by social structures, or social praxis and habits. From a deterministic view, domination appears to be an escapable social phenomenon via human agency itself, or the only 'exit-strategy' for agents seems to be apolitical or libertarian in nature. By contrast, in contemporary debate there is a predominant tendency to sustain that, although agents are not fully autonomous and transparent in their judgments, they maintain some critical approaches towards social structures and everyday practises (Boltanski and Thévenot 2006), or their lack of self-reflection is only confined to certain specific sub-structures or sub-systems, and not to the entire society and lifeworld (Habermas 1987).[13]

However, those who defend structural power do not deny the interagentive form of power (and consequently relational domination), but they argue that in modern societies, the most pervasive and durable form of power is, instead, structural in nature. In other words, there are two distinct, and yet irreducible from each other, forms of power and domination: relational (or interagentive) and structural. In more explicit terms, even if we eliminated relational domination to include all members of a society and made their relations of power perfectly equal, they might still suffer a structural or systematic form of domination – a form that cannot be traced back to power asymmetries resulting from unequal distribution of resources like wealth, knowledge, and recognition (Azmanova 2016b, 2018, 2020). But how is this possible?

A good starting point is represented by Hayward's de-facing account of power (2000; 2006; 2011; 2018), which provides one of the most interesting and thoughtful reformulations of relational and structural forms of power and domination. Hayward's main objection moved against the classical form of conceiving power in interagentive terms is grounded on the impossibility to 'disentangle the role an actor's will plays in determining a given action from the role played by the institutionalised actions of other actors' (Hayward 2006: 161). This means that when we analyse an asymmetrical relation of power between agents A and B involved in certain social structures, it is misleading to define power 'as an instrument that a powerful "A" uses to constrain, to distort, or otherwise to alter the free action of a powerless "B"' (Hayward 1998: 3), where B's actions and choices are taken to be, at a certain point, authentic and independent from A's exercise of power. If we proceed in this way, we neglect that 'social actors [both A and B] never act in ways that are *wholly independent of* social constraint on action' (Hayward 2006: 161). Let me offer some examples.

In the case of a power relation between agents within a certain social structure and institution like school or university, for instance between teacher and students, interagentive theorists of power do not deny that the education system determines the intensity and modalities of the teacher's power over her students, but they also maintain that, within this structural 'space', teachers and students are 'free' to act and choose. So, the teacher's exercise of power over students is dependent on real-world dynamics, 'determined by the way particular individuals and groups choose to deal with their circumstances' (Isaac 1987a: 24). For example, the students may boycott class and conduct their own teach-in to contest some forms of authority exercised by the teacher. This framework is also considered true for other common social power relations, such as between bosses and employees or husbands and wives. Hayward contests this exact simplified picture of social relations of power.

According to her, within structures, free actions, choices, and ideas of both teachers and students or bosses and employees are shaped by social constraints in a way that it is impossible to isolate students' or employees' *authentic* choices, actions and ideas from the exercises of power of teachers and bosses. For instance, '[a] student's decision to participate in the hypothetical boycott [...] likely derives from and depends upon social influences that themselves are unchosen: her parents' child-rearing practises, for example, or norms prevailing among her peers at school' (Hayward 1998: 11). But the same is true for teachers, bosses, or politicians who are usually considered the most powerful agents. The social structures do not simply circumscribe and determine their 'space' of free authority, but impose certain mechanisms of incentives and disincentives (material and not) that although not fully determinate of all their actions, choices and ideas, they render some of them very costly and difficult, while rewarding or otherwise encouraging others (Hayward and Lukes 2008: 14–15; Hayward 2018: 64). For instance, the educational system might not forbid that a teacher could exert participatory and anti-hierarchical methods, but the code of conduct of his university, the conservative attitude of his colleagues and students' parents, or a productivist mechanism in assigning any extra-wage benefits, might make these methods highly costly for the teacher. The same applies to an employer who might want to increase their employees' wages and benefits, but for a very aggressive and competitive market system that negates this as an option. These structural and systematic mechanisms also seriously hinder a trade union initiative by workers. Finally, even politicians and officials might be constrained by imperatives of competition (domestic and global) and the interests of those who finance the costs of their election that enable them, against their genuine will, to increase the marginal top taxation.

In other words, structural power does not simply give the opportunity to social agents to exercise power over others, but it also influences and severely shapes the way in which the power would be *otherwise* exercised. Most pervasively, structural power can shape everyday practises and worldviews of all these social actors in a way that eliminates alternative choices and actions from the spectrum of their real possibilities. When all these things take place, social actors are not subordinated to power over other agents, but to the power of the rules, norms, values and everyday practises themselves inscribed into those social structures and systems.

Hayward (2000, 2013, 2018) identifies four mechanisms of the social process that generate what she intends to be structural power: a network of collective rules that are, to varying degrees, (1) institutionalised, (2) objectified, (3) internalised as motivational systems, and (4) embodied as enduring dispositions or habitus.

To explain these four mechanisms, Hayward uses the example of the racial genealogy of USA home ownership. It is a long-term phenomenon that began with a set of systematic laws and legal norms accomplished with racial ideologies and narratives. These laws and norms are progressively institutionalised by specific public policies; for instance, the Home Owners Loan Corporation (HOLC) and the Federal Housing Administration (FHA) policies which insured mortgages only in racially separated neighbourhoods. When this set of 'rules' are institutionalised, rewards and penalties are systematically distributed. These federal subsidies, which in turn include the private mortgage insurance market, made it a disadvantage for a white home buyer to move into an integrated neighbourhood rather than a racially exclusive white suburb. The historical wealth inequality between white and black social groups reinforced the set of rewards and penalties; for instance, schools and other public services in white suburbs have progressively performed significantly better than in other parts of the city. And this happened precisely by virtue of the 'exclusive' nature of its inhabitants. Thus, the result was the creation of a long process of objectification of these social norms and their corresponding rewards and penalties in a 'material' form, such as the physical spaces of the black ghetto and the racially exclusive white enclave. Finally, this network of collective norms is embodied and internalised by citizens in their everyday practises, forms of life, and social habits. This means that even when previous policies and norms are abolished, as seen now in the USA where neither the FHA nor any other American government agency discriminates in home mortgage lending or insurance, social actors who are not necessarily 'racists' still contribute to maintain racial segregation by simply pursuing their respective interests. For instance, when a middle-class citizen moves to one of the USA's racially exclusive white suburbs just because the schools and other public services are significantly better, while going against her preference to live in an integrated neighbourhood (Hayward and Lukes 2008; Hayward 2018).

The result of this process is that a white middle-class person

> is *privileged* by the racially inegalitarian structural context that she inhabits. She is also *complicit* in its reproduction, since her decision to move to the affluent, white suburb interacts with institutionalized and objectified norms in a way that helps reinforce structural racial injustice. But she is not *powerful* in the sense [that] she does not intentionally exercise power over others to create a desired effect.
>
> (Hayward 2018: 64)

From this perspective, according to Hayward, it is misleading to understand power in terms of absolutely powerful and powerless agents, when instead they are *relatively* powerful and powerless.

Accordingly, power's mechanisms are best conceived not as instruments that 'agents use to prevent the powerless from acting independently, but rather as social boundaries – such as laws, rules, norms, institutional arrangements, and social identities and exclusions – that constrain and enable action for all actors' (Hayward 1998: 2). For Hayward, only if we take into account this impersonal form of structural power do we pay attention to the necessity of structural change and transform the society as a whole. At this point, it should be clear why, according to structural theorists like Hayward, it is necessary to analytically distinguish relational domination and structural domination.[14] The result is that these two forms of domination do not covary. For example, structural or systematic domination can *equally* affect all participants in power relations, regardless of whether or not those power relations are characterised by relational domination. Hayward explicitly endorses this position.

> Systemic domination can *equally* affect all participants in a power relation, as when, for example, all believe and conform to a religious doctrine that, let us stipulate, is false. Systemic domination can *equally* affect all participants in a power relation characterized by inter-agentive domination, as well. Suppose, for example, all men and all women in a patriarchal society regard gender norms as natural, because biologically rooted, and as invulnerable to critique, challenge, and change. If so, men are dominated systemically, as participants in power relations defined by norms of femininity and masculinity.
>
> (Hayward 2011: 483)[15]

In this sense, even the advantaged and privileged agents in social relations of power can be dominated, when and if they 'fail to act to challenge and change particular norms, principles, and institutions because they regard them as natural, inevitable, or otherwise unalterable' (Hayward 2011: 483). Even more, put in these terms, not only is interagentive non-domination not a sufficient condition, but also 'in some cases, fostering one form of nondomination may militate against achieving the other' (Hayward 2011: 470). For example, the way we reduce social inequality and exclusion within certain social structures might reinforce the acceptance or even appreciation by those social actors who seek more inclusion or equality. In other words, it might undermine their capacity to question the social system itself.

This reading is common in the classical Marxist's concern that an improvement in the conditions of some categories of workers and their inclusion in the liberal political system could defeat the conquest of working-class consciousness. Or it could be mentioned as a feminist critique of capitalism which highlights how the struggle for women's parity with men in the labour market usually has come at the cost of exacerbating the dynamic of neoliberal capitalism by adding further legitimation to the current social system (Fraser 2009; Azmanova 2012a, 2016a, 2020). Thus, this interagentive inclusion undermines the capacity of social actors to change and challenge the system of rules that becomes even more 'naturalised' and 'objectified'.

Along the same line of thought, Azmanova's critical theory account (Marxian-inspired) is particularly interesting because she also distinguishes between inter-agentive and impersonal forms of power and domination, and, like Hayward, she sustains that these different forms do not covary and therefore a success in fighting one form of domination comes at the price of aggravating another form. Azmanova calls this phenomenon 'the paradox of emancipation'. For example, struggles against inequality and exclusion (relational domination) tend to enhance the value of the social system within which equality and inclusion are being sought, thus increasing the legitimacy of an unjust system (Azmanova 2020: 181). This is because, 'we have to value the world within which we seek inclusion and equality; the harder the struggle to achieve access and status within that world, the more we value it' (Azmanova 2020: 122). From this perspective, for Azmanova structural domination is also based on an impersonal form of power that gains its own force and legitimacy 'through actors' mundane interactions in the course of everyday social practices (such as working or paying the bills) and stabilised by the rules that regulate these practices' (Azmanova 2020: 16).

But the main difference with Hayward's account is that Azmanova (2018, 2020) explicitly endorses a (Marxian-inspired) functionalist approach for which systematic power is that phenomenon wherein social structures are determined by a certain, and maybe unique, functionalistic or operational logic. Much more, she distinguishes between systemic and structural dimensions in the sense that the same particular operative logic – for instance, the competitive profit production logic in capitalism – can persist in very different ways to set structures (for example, either in structures set by the private property of the means of production and management or in structures in which these means are in public hands). Therefore, Azmanova draws three different, linked and yet analytically separated forms of power and domination – relational, structural and systemic – each of which corresponds to its own type of injustice and remedy. Azmanova's account is detailed in the following terms.

What Azmanova calls relational domination is grounded on an interagentive form of power. Indeed, it consists in the subordination of one group of actors to another by force of the unequal distribution of material or ideational power resources in society (e.g., wealth, knowledge, recognition). Thus, inequality and exclusion are the corresponding forms of injustice (*relational injustice*) (Azmanova 2020: 180). It is worth emphasising that relational domination, according to Azmanova, is avoided by inclusion and equalisation of power (for example, expanding the electoral franchise or the redistribution of wealth). In other words, the remedy is to reduce the power ratio between agents (and not impose external constraints to exercise power over power-holders). In this, Azmanova follows Strange's (1988, 1989) conception of relational power that 'implies a comparison between the power two actors possess relative to each other' (Azmanova 2018: 3).[16] However, as I anticipated, for Azmanova (2020: 46), even in the case we eliminate relational domination, making all members of a society included and perfectly equal, they might still suffer structural and systematic forms of domination that represent forms of injustices which cannot be traced back to power asymmetries resulting from unequal distribution of resources (e.g., wealth, knowledge, recognition). This phenomenon is possible because, for Azmanova, structural and systematic powers are not agent-centred notions. As a consequence, both the most and the less advantaged in the asymmetrical distribution of power are subjected to structural and systemic domination.[17]

Structural domination 'concerns the constraints on judgement and action imposed on actors by the main structures of the social system'. As a result, structural injustice

> takes the form not of inequality and exclusion (the ambit of relational domination), but of the actors incapacity to control the institutions through which the constitutive dynamic of the social system is enacted. This translates as their impotency to affect the "rules of the game" or alter the systemic logic.
> (Azmanova 2020: 57)

For example, 'in the case of capitalism as a social system, this concerns the structures of private property and management of the means of production, as well as the market as a mechanism of economic governance' (Azmanova 2020: 57). Thus, the remedy is the abolishment of these structures. However, at this point, Azmanova's Marxian understating of capitalism as a social system diverges from that of Marx in that the abolition of capitalistic structures is equivalent to overcoming the operative logic of the capitalist system.

By contrast, the distinction between structural and systemic dimensions of capitalism allows Azmanova to say that

> even if we obtain a society in which the means of production and management are in public hands and all members are included and perfectly equal,

> this does not mean that the society would not be engaged in the competitive production of profit, with all the negative effect this has on human beings and their natural environment.
>
> (Azmanova 2020: 48)

For Azmanova an example of this is provided by communist dictatorships or others' experience of 'real socialism' that are perpetuated in the competitive production of profit in the clash with capitalist democracies during the Cold War. In this sense, 'it is the engagement of *all actors* in the process of competitive production of profit that establishes the nature of the social system as properly capitalistic' (Azmanova 2020: 48). From this perspective, China is a capitalistic society insofar as it acts with the state as an entrepreneur in the global economy.[18] Thus, systematic domination is eliminated only if we eradicate the operative logic of the system because it can be equally imposed on all social actors by different structural means.

> Systemic domination consists in the subjugation of all members of society to the operative logic of the social system, including the winners in the asymmetrical distribution of power. In capitalism, it is engendered by the imperative of competitive production of profit to which the owners and managers of capital, as well as workers, succumb. *Systemic injustice* has to do with social harm beyond the unequal distribution of social advantage and disadvantage; this is harm engendered by [...] the system-specific definition of social status.
>
> (Azmanova 2020: 180)

Here, the question is not 'who dominates?' but rather 'what dominates?', or, more clearly, not who establishes and shapes 'the rules of the game' but what operative logic allows these 'rules' to reproduce themselves. Again this occurs because the operative logic is enacted through everyday social practises and functions that orient individuals' worldviews, social common sense, and normative judgments, creating what Azmanova calls 'ethos'. According to Azmanova, in the 21st century, the competitive production of profit logic has created a condition of generalised social precarity, uncertainty and involuntary flexibility that affect almost all members of society, the famous 99% (even skilled workers with well-paying jobs as well as owners of capital). So, social grievances against the super-rich and the unfair distribution of wealth (and even demands against immigration and for more national integration) are just a vague epiphenomenon of a more acute dissatisfaction with capitalism which depends not on its poor economic performance, but, on the contrary, on 'its excellent economic performance, its intensity' (Azmanova 2020: 172). In this sense, systemic non-domination, for Azmanova, is understood as emancipation from the accelerating productivist imperatives of capitalism in order to avoid that the economic system itself creates needs and then pushes individuals to satisfy them.[19]

To summarise, those scholars who advocate a conception of structural or systemic power are able to grasp the main limit of the interagentive model; that is, it undertheorises the question of how social structures themselves are set and shaped. Unfortunately, structural or systemic power and domination understood as an impersonal (or free-agent) notion is not a valid alternative.

I agree with structural theorists that social actors' actions, choices and ideas are shaped and *partially* determined by social structures that might also appear to those actors as an objectified and naturalised social order. In this sense, and particularly in modern complex societies, the process of socialisation under these structures might lead to a vast reflective and unreflective 'consensus' over them. This is the reason why social power has pervasive effects and why what they call social structures or systems – and I call instead primary rules – should be the primary object of investigation for scholars who study social power and domination. But what I totally disagree on is that (a) these structural social and political phenomena can be considered as the result of an impersonal or free-agent power, and (b) the mere fact that social actors might not take, or just not think to take, actions to contest, challenge and change the 'social order' tells us absolutely nothing about whether they are dominated or not.

The point is that a conception of structural and systemic domination that is 'impersonal' and, as a consequence, might equally affect all participants in power relations, treats social power as if it were something either like a law of physics (such as that of gravity) or a pure psychological state of mind. This makes the conception of structural domination politically impracticable or potentially paternalistic and authoritarian. By contrast, in a complex stratified society, if we can speak about domination, we should identify some people who severely risk suffering the condition of domination, likely other people that do not incur this risk, and still others that might potentially be the dominants.

I suppose that contemporary scholars who advocate structural or systemic power also share with me the normative benchmark that individuals involved in social structures and systems are not fully determined by them. Here, there is no need to linger in explaining what the moral and political consequences are in taking a determinist position. We would have no opportunity to change these structures unless we hope for a random occurrence or we have faith in some iron laws of socioeconomics or, worse, in a revolutionary self-illumined vanguard. Thus, by excluding a deterministic view, two main things emerge about the question of structural power and domination. First, if these structures are created by the social coordinated action and activity of social actors, at least partially self-transparent and reflective, it means that we need to know who has the power and by which resources do they establish, shape and stabilise social structures over the time. In this respect, there is a strict intertwine between power resources in which social actors dispose of respect to others and social structures or systems that govern social relations in which they are involved. From this point of view, I defend (in the next section) the notion that the so-called interagentive and structural (or systematic) dimensions should be included in the same conception of social power and domination. Second, if people are not fully determined by structures it means that the mere fact people might see social structures or systems as legitimate or valid says nothing about their reasons to obey and follow structural constraints. Otherwise we would scrutinise their minds, a domain that is not fully accessible and self-evident for social actors themselves. Therefore, unless we assume that the ultimate source of structural or systemic domination is grounded on a state of mind of social actors, this form of domination cannot be assessed in terms of the degree of acceptance and legitimation that social actors might assign to structures or systems. Thus, to know if (structural) domination occurs, we should look elsewhere. Again, Jeff Bezos's case might be clarifying.

Indeed, I am unable to realise how, in the USA's liberal democracy, we may consider Jeff Bezos as being dominated in some 'politically' and 'publically' relevant forms, even if we suppose that Bezos regards, along with one of his low-skilled workers at Amazon, the actual USA's social norms, laws, and institutions to be 'natural', unalterable or simply valid. Both Bezos and his employee might not even consider contesting and challenging the USA's social structures, but this does not make both of them subjects of structural or systemic domination. Instead, we should specify what key power resources Bezos has in order to challenge and change the USA's social structures, and what 'structural' or 'systemic' costs he must afford in order to carry out such actions, choices, or to develop the mere idea of doing it. We can deduce from this that Bezos, compared to his employees and other citizens, does not run the risk of being dominated. He has enormous material power in terms of wealth that can also be easily converted into political power, and a powerful social position that he enjoys as the owner and CEO of Amazon, and owner of the *Washington Post*, and has social power based on political and civil rights (rights that as a white and super-rich citizen, he is able to fully enjoy and exercise, unlike many of the USA's poor and black citizens who face serious institutional obstacles to simply exercise their right to vote). On the contrary, the USA's citizens who do not have the same level of key power resources at their disposal in relation to Bezos might see themselves as potentially dominated by his position of power. They might be dominated in the sense that the possibility to change the 'rules of game' and improve their conditions or just make those rules more compatible with their own ideas and interests depends on the goodwill of Bezos and all other citizens who have similar *disproportionate* amounts of power. In other words, the disadvantaged citizens might have strong reasons to claim that they are not co-author of these rules. This means to fall under arbitrary power. And it is true regardless of whether these USA's least advantaged citizens regard this as 'natural', unalterable or valid social structures.

2.3 Social Power: Taking Key Power Resources Seriously

In the previous two sections, we have seen how both interagentive and 'impersonal' structural models focus on social structures (or social systems as some prefer) that set and define the terms of social relations in which social actors are involved, but from two very different perspectives. In my view, both of them deal with social structures in an unsatisfactory manner. I think that it is possible and necessary to provide a conception of social power that is able to overcome the dualism between agency and structures.[20]

Although up to this point I have kept, for the sake of simplicity, the classic terminology 'social structures' that is used in the debate. From now on I prefer to revert to my own terminology: 'primary rules'. In the debate, it is not clear how scholars fully define social structures, but they usually intend to include sets of procedures, laws, institutions, collective norms, and in some cases even everyday 'objectified' practices. As mentioned in Chapter 1, the term primary rules makes more clear, at least from my view, what is the main content of social (basic) structures: a complex network of 'rules', understood in broad terms as political, legal, socioeconomic, epistemic, and cultural norms that govern the social relations in which individuals are involved.[21] Rules that find their codification in a spectrum that goes from the political constitution and the juridical system, to regulations of schools, firms and order institutions, up to some everyday practises.

Given that I also believe that we have to avoid overlapping the notion of power and domination – in which the former is 'neutral' and the latter is normative – the purpose of this section will only focus on a specific conception of power. This conception that I call expressly 'social power' is a narrow conceptualisation of power.[22] I believe that this conceptual delimitation (empirically and normatively) of social power, first of all, overcomes the unproductive dualism between interagentive and structural models and provides a better explanation of the strict intertwine between agency and structure; and secondly it is able to pass the test of 'publicity'.[23] I maintain that the pivotal element is to rescue the normative relevance of asymmetrical 'distribution' of individual power resources (power to), but in a way that combines them with social relations of power (power over) and the rules that govern these relations (*structures*). From this perspective, when we realise the embedded relation between power resources that social actors have with respect to others and primary rules, two things clearly emerge: first, social power is a question of power-ratio or, as I prefer to say, a question of *proportionality*; second, social power can be deconstructed into subfields of power according to those key power resources that we take into account, such as political power, epistemic power, symbolic power (or status power), authority power (or power of official positions), and material power. The following three main features form what I call social power.

The first feature includes a specific form of power as an individual's capacity to act or as 'being able to' (Pitkin 1972; Allen 1999; Barry 2002; Morriss 2002). In the debate there is wide discussion about what is the most basic interpretation of power, whether it should be conceived without taking into account social causation or whether it is a notion that necessarily implies a social environmental contextualisation. In the first case, we have to distinguish between what we have the power 'to do' (power to) and 'over whom' we have power (power over) (Morriss 2002: 32), see also Pansardi (2012a: 74). It does not mean that power to is understood as a social or non-relational concept (power is itself a dispositional concept); rather it implies that if *power to* has consequences over others' actions, these consequences are a side-effect and not the means to obtain something (Dowding 1991). Instead, this last mechanism – to alter other's actions and choices – is what expressly characterises power over, usually identified as synonymous with social power. In the second case, on the contrary, power to and power over are two components of a single and unified concept of power (Oppenheim 1981). This means that what actors are actually 'able to do' (power to) inevitably depends on the social context in which they operate (Pansardi 2012a). Besides this *controversy* about the most basic interpretation of power itself, what matters is that in both perspectives scholars agree that power over necessarily includes a certain power to, otherwise it would be impossible for an agent to exercise power over someone (Dowding 1991).

However, there is still an important controversy about how we should understand an agent's abilities to act or to do. Certainly these abilities depend on some manner of resources, whether a person's own properties such as his body and intellectual faculties or external means such as a gun, wealth, or social position. We can define all of them as individual power resources.[24] The point is to know if we should measure an agent's power to just in terms of resources that she owns or instead in terms of her actual outcomes.

The first approach that identifies an agent's power with resources – a resource-based account of power – is usually accused of 'reductionism' by those who advocate the second one. This objection is commonly exemplified with what Morriss (2002) calls the 'vehicle fallacy metaphor'. The objection is grounded on the fact that 'even if we could accurately measure all actors' resources we could still not predict precisely what the outcomes of their interactions would be' (Dowding 2008a: 240). In other words, we cannot say that an actor has the 'actual' power to act on or do with it what she wants. The problem seems to be that two agents who have the same resources might achieve very different results, one obtains what they want while the other does not. At the same time, two agents might obtain the same result but by means of different resources. This is because the result depends not only on individuals' resources but also on their preferences and environmental circumstances. Morriss (2002: 81) provides the following explanation: the poor are not able to feed off caviar and champagne (unlike the rich) not due to their lack of masticatory ability, but because of the social and economic environment they inhabit. Thus, according to Morriss (2002: 80), power is a property of an individual agent that should be measured in terms of her 'ablenesses' to achieve actual outcomes. Other scholars instead rejected the vehicle fallacy for the reasons that it does not make sense to distinguish individuals' mere abilities or resources from an individual's ableness. As Pansardi (2012a) observes we can conceive of individuals' power resources (or mere abilities) only if we had already included in our measurements an analysis of external and social conditions in which an agent's action, along with those of the others, had taken place. Along the same line, Dowding (2008a: 246) says that 'the ability to read, only makes sense, in an environment (a culture) where reading exists' or

> how much we can buy with the money in our possession in part depends upon how much money is in the possession of others. The power of money is relative to its distribution. This means that strategic considerations must enter into the very essence of the concept of power.
>
> (Dowding 2008a: 255)

Here, it does not need to enter into the question of how we should define the notion of power itself, but less ambitiously I defend that in the conception of social power, an individual's capacity to act or to do (power to) should be measured in terms of power resources she owns or disposes, rather than in terms of actual outcomes. Otherwise, our measurement will lose whatever is normatively valuable from a political and public point of view of the idea of social power.[25] If we do match the social power of an actor with what she actually does or achieves, *firstly*, we are incapable of distinguishing when a certain result might be the product of an agent's power or a product of simple luck; *secondly*, we might uphold the undesirable cost of forcing the analysis of an actor's social power to their preferences. For these reasons, we should accept the 'reduction' approach that corresponds to agents' power with their 'relative' resources.

About the first point, we can quickly see how important it is to track the difference between someone who achieves a certain result by means of her power resources and another who actually achieves the same result due to some lucky circumstances. For example, today two people, A and B, have the same amount of wealth, one million dollars, but A was a homeless man who today won exactly one million dollars in the lottery by buying a one dollar ticket, while B today simply increased his wealth by USD100,000 from his USD900,000 financial investment. Today, taking into account only the economic resources, we could say that they are equally powerful (but obviously they are hardly so taking into account other resources), but was it the same yesterday when they invested respectively one dollar in a lottery ticket and USD900,000 in a fund of investment? A's ableness to achieve the outcome to have USD1 million in her account is the same as B's ableness, but this result itself says nothing about their economic power that generates it. Any useful account of social power should capture this distinction. I should not have to wait for the result of using their wealth resources to find out which of the two is more powerful (if of course we know that money is a key power resource in that society).[26]

About the second point, it is equally important to draw a conception of social power that can represent a metric of comparison between individuals that can be politically and publicly shareable. As Dowding (2008a: 244) observes, the only way to avoid resisting the reduction of power to resources is to pay the cost of taking into account social actors' preferences. Indeed, all outcomes are also the product of agents' different ideas, beliefs and desires, but if we include them in our measurement, our conception of power becomes simply an incommensurable metric of individual comparisons. Therefore, it might be useless for our social and political analysis (see also Pansardi 2012b).

The second feature means that social power not only includes a specific form of power to, but it is also primarily a form of power over: an individual's capacity to act over someone (a single actor or a group). The first question is to understand whether all kinds of acts over someone can be considered a form of power over. My point is that social power does not describe all forms of power over.

First of all, in the literature, there is a broad consensus to separate power from sheer violence.[27] Power is usually characterised by leaving room for a certain degree of a power-subject's acceptance or compliance. In this sense, power always seems to include a 'noumenal' dimension (Forst 2015), insofar as it comes together with all other things, with 'justifications' and 'motivations' to act and obey. Much of the debate regards how to conceive the nature of this 'acceptance', whether exclusively reflexive or non-reflexive or a compliance that implies legitimacy or validity. I will consider this question at the end of this section. Here what matters is that when power over is at stake, it should always be possible for the subject of power to disregard and not follow a power-holder's command or offer. Thus, power over someone might follow two forms: 'making the action one wishes the other to perform more attractive and making the alternatives to it less attractive' (Barry 2002: 161). However, it is open if we should exclude from the definition of power over, not only violence but also classical forms of coercion as physical or psychological threats; for example, holding a gun to someone's head to command: stand and deliver! Also in this case, a person who has the gun held to her head may refuse to execute that command. Power exercised by means of a gun might be able to change another party's incentives if, for example, the 'cost' to avoid the punishment (a bullet in the head) is just to give up the victim's wallet. But the threat of the gun might be ineffective if the 'cost' is to reveal the names of comrades in resistance to an authoritarian regime. In this case, the victim of the threat may prefer to die rather than betray her comrades. Forst (2017: 41), for instance, considers pointing a gun at someone as an exercise of power over; meanwhile libertarians exclude coercion from the notion of power.[28]

I leave the question open as to whether power over can be exercised also by coercion or not, but I believe that it is necessary to exclude coercion from the concept of social power. Although it is difficult to precisely define coercion, I think many could agree that coercion includes all kinds of actions or threats in order to 'punish' someone who refuses to execute a command or accept an offer – threats performed directly and indirectly by those who give or extend that command or offer; for instance, if they threaten to pull the trigger or to disseminate a victim's sensitive personal information. It does not mean that social power excludes any exertion of coercive power, but that a coercive power resource does not provide *prime facie* the justification/motivation to follow the command or offer.

To catch the difference, think of two different cases in which the power-subject 'accepts' giving away a part of her wealth: 'predation' and 'taxation'. Predation is performed by coercive power because the power-subject's motivation is exclusively to avoid penalties performed, directly or indirectly, by the power-holder. Taxation, instead, 'is one part of a complex structuring of everyday life by the state' (Haugaard 2012: 36). This means that in taxation, power over does not depend, at least intrinsically, on coercive power to be socially effective. The justification/motivation for taxation is that citizens have the right to enjoy the fruit of their social cooperation but this (final) fruit is determined, for example, by citizens' monetary contribution on collective services and expenses and the fair terms of our social cooperation (in this sense, taxation is also an instrument to satisfy moral and political requirements of distributive justice). Thus, for citizens, the incentive to pay taxes depends on their ability to fairly enjoy the benefits of social cooperation. In other words, taxation is a form of power over that is socially effective by means of the social rules that govern the complex network of political and economic activities and tax system. The point is that if I 'exercise' power over someone through taxation I should have the power to establish, shape, or give stability over time to these rules. Of course, the state uses coercive power to protect citizens and also to punish non-compliance actions, such as tax evasion, but in this sense coercive power is a 'second order' key resource of social power. And it is also undeniable that for some citizens the truthful motivation to pay taxes is to avoid the consequences of the use of coercive power, but again it is not the intrinsic mechanism of how normally (or statistically) taxation works as an instrument of social power.[29]

This distinction helps us to capture the clue element in the conception of social power: A's power over B is able to be (socially) effective only by means of establishing, shaping or stabilising primary rules that govern social relations in which they are involved. This means that we should also exclude from the definition of social power, besides sheer violence and coercion, those forms of power over that are 'exercised' by simple 'interactional' relations between actors. I think that much of the controversy between interagentive and structural power models might be overcome, or at least be mitigated, if we are able to explicitly mark the distinction between mere interactional forms of power over and what I mean by social power which is socially effective through primary rules. Unfortunately, in the debate the most relevant conceptions of power over, or social power, are unable to clearly track this distinction. Indeed, through Dahl's conception of power over (1957: 202–203) in which 'A has power over B to the extent that he can get B to do something that B would not otherwise do', up to Barry's (2002: 161) definition of social power, which 'has as its instrument the ability to change another party's incentives'; or, most recently, Forst's noumenal power as 'the capacity of A to influence the space of reasons for B and/ or C (etc.) such that they think and act in ways they would not have without the interference by A' (Forst 2017: 49), we find the identical limitation in all accounts.

As I said, A's capacity to act depends upon some power resources that that agent owns or disposes, but what makes the difference is the way she mobilises these resources to alter or distort B's actions, choices or ideas. An actor (A) might mobilise some power resources like wealth or her official position to get B to think or do something that B would not otherwise think or do; for instance, to perform a risky physical task or to read Leo Tolstoy's *War and Peace*. However, A's form of power over B, depending on the way in which it is 'exercised' or 'effective', might be considered as interactional or as social power. In case of interactional power, A as a rich person might offer a poor man a sum of money to lower himself into a well and retrieve the favourite ball of the rich man's son, or A as a professor might offer a student who hates Tolstoy to read *War and Peace* – a reading that is not required by the school program – as a compensation of an insufficient grade and thus to avoid repeating the course. In both cases what makes the difference is the degree of inequality of power resources, wealth, or position of authority, between rich and poor, or professor and student. However, these interactional forms of power over say nothing about social power.

Indeed, social power is at stake if the poor actor is a formal employee of a rich one, and that risky task is a work duty according to contractual rules, and if *War and Peace* is a mandatory reading of that school or the national educational system. If this is the case, the poor worker and the student will perform the risky task or read Tolstoy only because they follow certain social rules. In this sense, we need to make the relation more complex between power-holder (A), power-subject (B) and the *source* that leads B to think or act in a certain way. In interactional forms of power over, A's power resources perfectly coincide with the source of power over. It is the amount of money that A offers or her authority to offer an exchange between reading *War and Peace* and a bad note that leads B to act on or think something that B would not otherwise do or think. By contrast, in the case of social power, A's capacity over B is made effective by social rules that define the terms of the social relation with B, which assign a certain set of rewards or disadvantages rather than another.

I believe that what structural theorists correctly contest about the interagentive model is that the structural form of power is not exercised in an interactional manner between social actors (employer–employee or professor–student). Likewise, social power is not simply A's capacity to change another party's incentives (offering money or an advantageous trade-off), but A's capacity to change 'the incentive structure of another actor' (Dowding 1991: 48; 2016). In other words, the capacity to establish and shape primary rules where that risky task is envisaged as a job and under what conditions and remuneration, or the capacity to include *War and Peace* as a formal requirement to obtain an educational qualification.[30] However, recognising that primary rules have this essential function does not mean locating power in them (understood as impersonal). By contrast, when social power is at stake A needs to mobilise some key power resources to establish, shape or stabilise these rules.[31]

Returning to my example, to study social power means to know if that a wealthy actor has material power resources to establish a job relationship with the less advantaged actor (or more than one), to establish and shape job rules and compensation, and, above all, given that these rules are also legally codified, if she has sufficient material power to establish and shape them at the formal level (for example, financing political parties or political foundations). Or in the case of the professor, we want to know if she has the official authority to impose *War and Peace* as a formal requirement of her course, or to impose it as mandatory in her university or the national system of education. In both of these cases, social power is a question of degree or range between boss and worker or professor and student. Indeed, in a society with perfect material equality the boss does not have the material power to establish and shape the primary rules more than her employee does. Of course, she might have other key power resources to do it, for example, in terms of political status if her employee does not enjoy equal political rights. Similarly, the professor's authority to impose *War and Peace* as mandatory in her course might be none if this decision is taken at the national level where professors (and students) as such have no decision-making power. However, in this latter case, unlike students, the professor still enjoys social power in terms of a position of authority because she can use this power resource to give stability to educational rules. It is easy to observe how, regardless of social power that the professor may have, she could still exercise a form of interactional power over by proposing to one of her students to retake the exam as long as she reads a non-mandatory text that she would not have read otherwise. Interactional power over and social power do not coincide.

The question of social power makes evident a strict interplay between the distribution of individual power resources and primary rules. It is the latter that determines a certain asymmetrical distribution of power resources and, in turn, only through these resources can individuals establish, change, or stabilise those primary rules.[32]

However, a last point should be clarified about this interplay relation. What I call social power cannot be associated with all kinds of individual power resources, but only with those resources that are indispensable to establish and shape primary rules. Therefore, we speak about social power insofar as we identify key power resources that are 'socially generalisable' (in a certain society) and for which their asymmetrical 'distribution' can be a subject of mutual and public claim. This means to exclude those power resources that are effective only through a 'subjective' commitment of the others; for instance, personal qualities like beauty, intelligence, and charisma, or a piece of wood to which magical or religious qualities are attributed. These resources need to gain a personal and subjective commitment from the others in order to be converted into power resources in durable social relationships, like between lovers, a group of activists or a religious community.[33] This kind of 'subjective' disposition is not necessary with respect to other resources such as money or political status; although there will always be an ascetic over whom money or authority has no power whatsoever.

It is true that it is impossible to draw a list of socially generalisable power resources that is universal for each time and place and effective for each member of a certain society. However, given that each society needs to make social relations stable and ordered (otherwise it would be impossible to speak about a social order) it is possible to identify some key power resources that in a certain society have a high degree of generalisability (or universality) among its members. We can identify some categories of power resources that, with a certain degree of generalisability, are essential to establish and shape primary rules of every complex society; such as political power, material power, the power of official positions, epistemic power, symbolic power, etc. The point is that all of our social relationships, even the most intimate like family or friendship, are usually characterised as asymmetrical relations of power, but it is impossible to argue about social power unless we analyse these social relations as composed not of mere individuals but social actors; that is, in terms of gender, race, income and wealth class, employment, or citizenship. The case is different for a woman to get out of a marriage or other kinds of familial relationships that are 'costly' because she assigns a high 'subject' value to those relationships, or because these 'exit-costs' (see Lovett 2010) depend on a lack of some key power resources: the status of equal citizenship, material power, or epistemic power. In the case of marriage, the unfair chances to get out for women with respect to men (taking into account only a gender perspective) is affected by their unequal possibilities to occupy public offices (because they are socially and publically stigmatised in their social and sexual preferences), to enter in the labor market and receive equal payment to men or to access the same level of education.

The third feature concerns a wide discussion, in the debate, about how power over is 'exercised', whether intentionally (by action or inaction), or unintentionally and unreflectively. Concerning social power, once we have excluded mere interactional forms and defined it as a social actor's capacity to establish and shape primary rules, we can fully realise that social power is not 'exercised' (intentionally or not), but rather is socially 'effective'. In other words, social power should be understood as an 'opportunity concept' (Taylor 1979), see Pansardi (2012a, 2013).

In this sense, neo-republicans are right to associate power with 'capacity' to interfere rather than with actual interference. Indeed, a master's power over his slave is due to his capacity to establish and shape, at his own will, social rules that govern their relation. This 'capacity' produces effects in the way in which a slave acts or chooses even if the master might not interfere or 'exercise' his power because the slave should always take into account this possibility and try to forecast the master's will. It is possible because the slave is involved in a social relation (durable and stable) and he is absolutely disempowered by denial of two key resources: political and civil status. By contrast, the master's power resources are his political identity, racial identity (white), his money to buy a enslaved person, and mainly his position as master is made possible by a legal system of slavery. Thus, the master's power (at least, legal power) is extinct only if we abolish the institution of slavery; that is, if we cut off his exclusive key power resources – political and civil status – with respect to the slave.

However, social power is also an 'opportunity' concept in a liberal democracy. A significant asymmetry in a key power resource like wealth among citizens might make the actual primary rules stable over time by discouraging or inhibiting those attempts to modify them in a way that may affect the interests of the wealthy. The worst-off citizens may refrain from taking action to change the rules that favour the most advantaged simply by assuming, for example based on past experiences, that the best-off will use their resources to prevent such changes. It is the 'opportunity' or 'capacity' to mobilise a certain key power resource – in this case, wealth – with respect to others to establish, shape, or stabilise the primary rules that characterises social power, rather than its 'exercise'. But social power is socially effective in a more pervasive way (something that is overlooked by neo-republicanism) because primary rules shape and partially determine citizens' actions, choices and ideas. Thus, a certain stable long-run hegemony, which is a result of a very unequal economic distribution, may decisively collaborate to influence people's ideas and preferences to favour the realisation of the best-offs.[34] In this case, it is a possible scenario that, for instance, the best-off might not even need to spend their economic resources to achieve their goals and interests or protect their wealth.[35]

Finally, taking into account these three main features, we can advance the following definition of social power:

> Social power exists as the capacity of a social actor A, by mobilising certain 'key power resources', to make social actor B or C think and act in a certain way by establishing, shaping, and stabilising primary rules that govern 'social' relations in which both A and B or C are involved.

2.4 The Risk of Domination and Its Different Forms

In the previous section, I have drawn a conception of social power but I did not explain when exactly it entails domination. I agree with Haugaard (2012) and Forst (2017, 2018) that it is important to keep normative and empirical claims about power distinct. Thus, my definition of social power is a 'neutral' conception, and also for me, like Haugaard (2012: 51), 'both power as domination and emancipation presuppose the same process'. In this chapter, my effort has been to show that a social actor's capacity to establish and shape primary rules is directly 'proportional' to key power resources that they dispose of with respect to others.[36] My point here is to identify whether non-domination can be reached, whatever the range of the asymmetrical 'distribution' of key power resources between individuals would be. Contrary to what most scholars seem to assume, I do not believe that it can.[37] Nonetheless, this normative consideration does not condemn us to the indeterminacy of the concept. By contrast, this means that we should avoid the *risk of domination*; that is, we should judge as unjust those primary rules that allow, in principle, an unlimited inequality in the 'distribution' of key power resources. This forces us to theoretically and empirically establish a certain 'limit' range or a 'proportion' for each of these key power resources. Allow me to expound on this point.

For the vast majority of scholars in the contemporary debate, given that asymmetrical power relations are inevitable in a complex society, it appears unavoidable to adopt a conception of non-domination that is grounded on how power is 'exercised' or on what effects it produces, regardless of the size of the asymmetrical distribution of key power resources between citizens. In the debate, there are three main strategies to obtain this result: 1) to constrain arbitrary interference on free actions, choices, and ideas of others; 2) to guarantee that power will be mutually beneficial; 3) to ensure that the exercise of power follows certain reciprocal and mutual respect procedures.

As we have already seen, the first strategy is usually endorsed by a neo-republican interagentive model. The solution is to design primary rules in a way that externally constrain the most powerful in their exercise of power in order to track power-subjects' interests. But, put in these terms and as I have already shown, this is a result that, in principle, even a 'civil' oligarchy that shares a high level of political legitimacy might achieve. In other words, this kind of non-domination can be obtained regardless of the range of the asymmetrical 'distribution' of key resource powers between citizens. In this sense, Thompson's objection to the neo-republicanism paradigm (2013a: 279) is right to affirm that 'domination should be seen as the expression of oligarchic (and even tyrannical) concentrations of power within society as a whole, as pathological results of a badly arranged society', rather than as arbitrary interference on actions and choices of others. In other words, neo-republicanism takes the question of primary rules for granted. Even Lukes' (2005, 2018) account of domination that acknowledges that power over (his dimensional view) can be used, not only to interfere, but also to shape and control agents' *own perceived* interests and ideas in favour of the most powerful agents, is still exposed to the same deficit. Indeed, for his account of non-domination what matters is, 'how to devise and maintain institutional structures that restrain the powerful from harming others' interests and from limiting their freedoms [including their third-dimensional capacity to distort or suppress people's perceptions of their interests]' (Hayward and Lukes 2008: 7). But, this way to achieve non-domination is again possible only if we assume that we can know what B would otherwise do and think without A's exercise of power.

Thus, both Lukes and neo-republicans overlook the fact that *both* A's and B's actions, choices and ideas are not only influenced but also *partially* formed by the way primary rules are set. Dowding (2008b, 2016) describes this phenomenon as 'deep structuralism'. However, I agree with Dowding that being aware that primary rules (or social structures as others prefer to call them) have this deep effect does not mean to assume a fully deterministic position that leaves no room for agent autonomy or free will. Indeed, people who are subject to the same primary rules and social conditions are able to act and think in a remarkably different way. However, the deep effect of primary rules consists of a significant challenge by the manner in which we may conceive of agent autonomy or individual free will. The solution, at least when primary rules are at stake, is to move from the classical idea of 'self-authorship' towards the most adequate idea of co-authorship as 'deliberative' autonomy.[38] What we need to know is whether people's interests and ideas are partially determined by primary rules which they can reasonably consider themselves co-authors of. From this perspective, non-domination is reached only if social actors are not 'relatively' disempowered by the lack of those key power resources to establish, shape and stabilise primary rules that govern the social relations in which they are involved.

The second strategy to conceive non-domination is also drawn in a manner that remains insensitive to the range of asymmetrical 'distribution' of key power resources. In this case non-domination does not consist of restraining the exercise of power by the powerful; rather, it concerns the 'result' of power which should be of mutual advantage for all social actors involved. Furthermore, authors who usually endorse this 'mutually beneficial' approach focus on how a society is structured as a whole. For example, Haugaard (2012) suggests rethinking all dimensions of power over taking into account how structural constraints are arranged. Thus, power over is normatively commendable if these structural constraints make power into a positive-sum phenomenon; that is, 'power in which one party does not gain at the expense of the other' (Haugaard 2012: 35). Note that for Haugaard the same normative evaluation should include what he calls the four dimensions of power which is the equivalent of Foucault's 'constitutive' or disciplinary power (1979). This 'subject' dimension does not represent domination only if its long-run result is mutually beneficial. A similar approach is advocated by Thompson's radical republicanism for which domination includes two faces: 'extractive' and 'constitutive'. Extractive domination is a (structural) relation of power in which agents are able to 'take more than is sufficient for itself, to derive surplus benefit interests' (Thompson 2018: 49). According to Thompson, extractive domination can be stable and effective over time in modern societies only if it is combined with constitutive domination which occurs when those who are subordinated perceive surplus benefit in favour of the most advantaged as legitimate and valid. Thus, for Thompson (2018), non-domination is associated with a well-known republican idea: 'the common interest' or 'common good' which is achieved when 'private' *pleonexic* interests or goods are diminished in favour of public goods. The former is the opposite of the public good because they are obtained using 'capacity and resources that belong to individuals and the community as a whole toward elite interests and benefits' (Thompson 2018: 56).

However, although this approach of non-domination as 'mutually beneficial' is able to take into account the question of how primary rules are set, it is not able to fully satisfy the idea of co-authorship as deliberative autonomy. Indeed, the problem is that the 'mutual advantage' or 'common good' are, in principle, insensitive to the size of inequality of power resources between the most and the least advantaged. Indeed, 'positive-sum power' or 'common good' can be reached simply to maximise the absolute level of the worst-off's power resources (a sort of prioritarian principle).[39] This is an approach of non-domination that is, in principle, compatible with an unlimited inequality in the 'distribution' of key power resources.

Finally, those scholars who advocate the third strategy to conceive non-domination usually associate it with the idea of co-authorship as deliberative autonomy, for instance in the case of Forst (2014, 2015, 2017); Scheffler (2015); and Azmanova (2016b, 2020). From this perspective, non-domination relies neither on the protection of individual freedom of action and choice nor on the 'beneficial' result of power. However, the 'deliberative autonomy' is evaluated by means of certain procedures or criteria on the exercise of power. In other words, non-domination depends on how people treat or relate to each other in an asymmetrical (structural) relation of power; for instance, relations should be shaped by procedures of mutual respect and reciprocal authority (Scheffler 2015), or be grounded on reciprocal and general justifications (Forst 2017). However, in the debate, these normative criteria that assess the justified or legitimate uses of power can be satisfied, in principle, regardless of the size of the inequality between individual power resources owned by social actors involved in these (structural) social relations.[40]

This is particularly evident when these procedures or criteria are associated with communicative power based on argumentative discourse. Ideally, in asymmetrical relations of power between two or more actors, the most powerful actor (for instance, the leader) might 'convince' others to assign the fruit of their social cooperation by flipping a coin and the result, even if particularly unequal and not 'beneficial' for all, will be perfectly compatible with reciprocal and deliberative procedures. In this ideal example, the exercise of power does not incur domination because it is in concordance with mutual respect for the interests of all participants, or with a reciprocal and general justification.; i.e. each member gave his consent to this random division of the fruit of cooperation, no one is excluded, and all have an equal chance of winning. It would have been absolutely different if any of the participants had been excluded from the draw. The advantage of this conception of non-domination is that it does not rely on a specific 'pattern' of relational power and distribution of power resources, but, as a consequence, is exposed to a high level of indeterminateness regarding the size of inequality in this 'distribution'. For example, Forst's account of domination runs this risk of indeterminateness. According to him (Forst 2014, 2017), the most adequate strategy to turn analysis of power into a critique of power is to develop a critical theory of relations of justification. In his view,

> this theory has a material component – namely, a critical understanding of dominant justifications for particular social relations – and critique aims specifically at false, or at least one-sided, justifications for asymmetrical social relations that fall short of the criteria of reciprocity and generality, in short, relations of domination.
>
> (Forst 2017: 51)

Precisely, when political and public domain is at stake, domination should be defined 'as rule without adequate structures of justification being in place' (Forst 2017: 51). Then the normative point is to provide and ensure justificatory or discursive (noumenal) power to all social actors involved in (structural) social relations; in other words, what should be ensured is what Forst calls 'fundamental (minimal) justice' (Forst 2012: 119–120; 196–197; 2014: 36, 115–116).

To be clear, for Forst this 'discursive' or 'noumenal' power is not 'immaterial'. Indeed, the task of fundamental justice is to produce a basic structure of justification which calls for

> certain rights and institutions and a multiplicity of means and specific capabilities and information, up to real possibilities for intervention and control within the basic structure, not a 'minimalist' structure, yet one justified in material terms solely on the basis of the principle of justification. The question of what is included in this minimum must be legitimated and evaluated according to the criteria of reciprocity and generality.
>
> (Forst 2012: 119)

Unfortunately, as we have already seen (see also Chapter 1, Section 1.2), reciprocity and generality (as well as mutual respect) criteria are compatible, in principle, with an unrestricted level of inequality in power resources among social actors.

Of course, Forst (or relational egalitarian scholars) can say that if primary rules would assign and 'distribute' key power resources (or what Forst calls 'noumenal capital') in a way that these criteria are satisfied, social actors involved in the resulting asymmetrical social relations of power are not dominated because these rules are legitimate or better 'adequately' justified. Nonetheless, this is not equivalent to saying that social actors are not dominated because *they have 'adequate' power to be co-author of the primary rules.* This latter form of non-domination has a concrete chance to occur only if primary rules do not allow an unrestricted level of inequality in key power resources among social actors. Or better if social actors are 'relatively' or 'proportionally' empowered by those key power resources in order to establish, shape, and stabilise primary rules.

At the end of this long discussion, I think that we have strong reasons to say that if we want to maintain that domination means obeying the foreign will of others as opposed to 'obeying only oneself' or 'being one's own master', our conception of domination cannot disregard the question of the range of asymmetrical 'distribution' of key power resources between citizens. However, this normative ascertainment does not place us between choosing two opposite undesirable alternatives: unless we want to pursue perfect equality in terms of key individual power resources (non-domination), we are condemned to accept a certain degree of domination. A third alternative normative path is much more viable and feasible. What indeed we should avoid is the *risk of domination*; that is, we should judge as unjust those primary rules that allow, in principle, an unlimited or unrestricted inequality in the 'distribution' of key power resources. This forces us to establish a certain theoretical and empirical 'limit' range (or proportion) for each of these key power resources. Thus, two main tasks need to be accomplished. First of all, the need to set up a list of key power resources. Secondly, the need to judge as unjust those primary rules that allow, *in principle*, an unlimited or unrestricted inequality in the 'distribution' of key power resources.

Regarding the first task, there must be an identification of those categories of power resources that are essential, and for this reason 'key' resources, to establish and shape primary rules of society; such as political power, material power, power of official positions, epistemic power, symbolic power, etc. Of course, a certain degree of contextualisation is necessary. The content of these key power resources depend on the fundamental features of the type of society we take into account; for instance, the case of a modern, industrialised, and liberal society is different from that of ancient societies. However, although I confine the analysis to contemporary liberal democratic societies, in this work I only focus on material power (and I would not have the space to do otherwise) which, in my view, should be understood in terms of the amount of economic resources an individual possesses with respect to others. Here, I can merely mention what the content of other categories of key power resources may be and, briefly, to show why it is fundamental to take into account these key resources as analytically separate, and yet, inevitability related to each other. Let me offer some examples.[41]

As a start, we can observe that the most common, and simplest, way to understand political power is as power resources based on formal political liberties and political rights. Throughout history, political liberties and political rights have been a fundamental and highly contested form of power. For instance, individuals and groups have been deprived of them on the basis of slave or citizen status, race, gender, religion, and so on. The struggle for formal political liberties and rights is still one of the most powerful political claims in many authoritarian countries. Nowadays, it is true that only a few countries officially reject formal political liberties and rights, but many impose serious obstacles to their fulfilment. This latter scenario is much closer than one could imagine, and even a consolidated liberal democracy like the USA has imposed and, surprisingly, continues to impose obstacles to the exercise of political participation and voting. These limitations were, and are, thought to affect specific social actors characterised by their identity and material condition (mainly, poor black people). Unfortunately, not all institutional arrangements and mechanisms that make voting for black people very difficult, or in some cases practically impossible, have been banned by the *voting act*.[42] Nowadays, in particular after the 2013 US Supreme Court's sentence (*Shelby County v. Holder*, 570 US 529), although states cannot impose requirements like a fee for voting, they still maintain or have re-established severe restrictions to access the right to vote. These requirements make both in-person voting and mail ballots more difficult; for example, by imposing new or harsher voter ID requirements, shortening the timeframe for voters to request or automatically receiving a mail ballot, expanding voter purge practises in ways that risk improper removals, and increasing barriers to voter registration.[43] All these restrictions have a very uneven effect on citizens because their impact is vastly increased on those citizens who have fewer material means to circumvent them; for example, losing entire days of work to be able to navigate all these practises and obstacles required to vote. And it is by no means a coincidence that black citizens occupy the most disadvantaged social and employment positions. Now, what kind of power resources do poor, black people lack? And therefore what form of domination is at stake?

We can observe two main aspects of this phenomenon. First, poor black citizens see their formal political rights recognised and yet seriously limited in their exercise, and second, these restrictions on the exercise of political participation and voting achieve the purpose only, and only because, black people statistically occupy the bottom of material distribution much more than other social and cultural groups. Nonetheless, in this case, I think it would be inaccurate to say that poor black citizens are exposed to the risk of political domination or material domination, because these substantive restrictions are designed to their disadvantage only because of their cultural and racial identity – they are black citizens – and they statistically occupy the bottom of material distribution for the same reason. In other words, they lack adequate symbolic power; what in the current debate is understood as a form of injustice as misrecognition. Indeed, although poor black US citizens are sorely restricted in their exercise of political rights, it is different in the case in which citizens, regardless of their cultural and racial identities, are fully deprived of or have their political rights and formal political liberties largely curtailed, as happens in an authoritarian regime. In this latter case, it is more appropriate to argue about political domination, rather than symbolic domination. At the same time, the risk of symbolic domination can occur even in a society that instead is sheltered from the risk of material domination because the level of economic inequality is not so high as to give rise to this risk. Indeed, if the bottom of distribution is occupied by black people, overwhelmingly and disproportionately to the population as a whole, the risk of symbolic domination is at stake. To be clear, the risk of material domination is not able to detect the risk of symbolic domination, but for the simple fact that the latter concerns another key power resource – symbolic power – rather than material power.

A similar discussion can be made for other key power resources such as the power of official positions, whether in government and public organisations or at the helm of a firm large enough to belong to primary rules or the basic structure of society. In this case, it is not only possible that some categories of citizens are excluded from the access to official positions (or they do not enjoy a fair equality of opportunity), but it may occur that those who occupy these official positions have a quite unlimited and unconstrained decision-making power. Again the risk of domination that occurs in the case of disproportionate power of official positions is analytically distinct from the risk of political domination (based on formal political liberties and political rights), material domination, or symbolic domination. The same applies for epistemic power which might include resources such as the access to pluralistic and self-transparent information and adequate access of education.[44] Also in this case, if citizens are disempowered with respect to others in the epistemic power, they are exposed to the risk of epistemic domination. In order to pursue a compelling normative and empirical investigation it is fundamental to take into account these analytically distinct yet closely related key power resources, each of which correspond to a different form of domination.

At this point, the second task should be quite simple to understand. As I have long said, the object of the approach to proportional justice is the question of how primary rules are established and shaped. Thus, once we have identified, at our best, the key power resources, we should judge as unjust those primary rules that allow, *in principle*, an unlimited or unrestricted inequality in the 'distribution' of key power resources. This forces us to establish a certain theoretical and empirical 'limit' range or *proportion* for each of these key power resources.

Again in this book I focus only on the risk of material domination and, hence, what I call the principle of proportionality is a distributive principle that concerns income and wealth ratios (see Chapter 4). Of course, the different nature of each key power resource determines the way in which the approach to proportional justice applies to them. It is very different to establish a permissible range in economic resources than in the official positions. I admit that in some cases the use of the term 'distribution' of key power resources can sound odd. But I think that the normative point is quite clear. For example, although it may seem that there is nothing to be 'distributed' once a social actor held a certain official position, what we need to do is not make disproportional the decision-making power that derives from this position by circumscribing and limiting the scope of the decision-making power, doing it as collegially as possible, and setting up countervailing power mechanisms. To be clear, nothing new. The modern idea of 'checks and balances' based on the division of government between executive, legislative, and judiciary branches of a pluralistic political system, and the presence of a system of basic liberties, political rights and universal suffrage is a complex, and quite effective, manner to allow a certain degree of distribution of (formal) political power (see also Hearn 2012; Pansardi 2016). The point is that the modern democratic constitution-making does not aim to make some key power resources perfectly equally distributed. It simply aims to make the distribution of political power based on formal political liberties, political rights and the power of 'public' official positions not disproportionate; that is, it informs public and political rules in such a way as to prevent an unlimited inequality of these key power resources.

To pursue a perfect equal distribution of key power resources is an implausible and also unrealistic goal. A theory of power and domination should simply include this social fact, and yet it should not neglect the centrality of asymmetrical 'distribution' of key power resources into the concept of domination. In other words, if it is true that social power is a question of *power-ratio*, we have to resist the idea that non-domination can be reached no matter what the range of the asymmetrical 'distribution' of key power resources between individuals would be. Otherwise, we commit the mistake of neglecting how social power works or to draw a notion of potentially paternalistic non-domination. Hence, I believe that the only viable alternative for a conception of social and political justice that also claims to take into account the question of power is to avoid the *risk of domination*; that is, not to allow *in principle* an unlimited and unrestricted inequality in the 'distribution' of key power resources.

I am aware that this strategy may sound to many both frustrating and unsatisfactory because it seems to condemn us to the indeterminateness of the concept of non-domination. However, I am quite convinced that avoiding the *risk of domination* is, first and foremost, all we can realistically and reasonably expect to achieve, and, secondly, is what makes the difference that matters. For example, we can discuss, and certainly disagree too, about the permissible range for income and wealth inequality which protects us from the *risk of material domination*, but we cannot accept that the primary rules are established and shaped in such a way as to allow, *in principle*, an unlimited and unrestricted income and wealth inequality. This is the difference that passes between a society that ignores the normative significance of the size of economic inequality and another one that, instead, establishes a certain limit range or proportion of economic inequality, and consequently arranges political and socioeconomic institutions to ensure that this range is effectively respected. Only the second case, *in principle*, rules out laissez-faire capitalism and a neoliberalist society because their very essence is to reject any a priori limit to economic inequality. Although it is true that our liberal societies are traditionally careful with the 'distribution' of political power based on formal political liberties and rights, and the power of 'public' official positions, much more must to be done, and quite urgently, about other key power resources, such as the power of 'private' official positions (what Anderson (2017) calls 'private government'), symbolic power, epistemic power and, for sure, material power.[45]

Notes

1 Note that here cooperation should be conceived in the wider sense of sharing a socioeconomic and political order.
2 See Allen (1999), Pinzani (2005), Haugaard (2012), and Forst (2015).
3 See Dahl (1957), Lukes (2005, 2018), Pettit (1997), Lovett (2010), and Forst (2015, 2017, 2018).
4 See Bourdieu (1977), Foucault (2020), Hayward (2000), Marx (2013), Thompson (2018), and Azmanova (2020).
5 It is possible to be in a position of absolute disempowerment; however, regarding our most common socioeconomic and political relations what matters is the relative dimension.
6 For an overview of the neo-republicanism debate, see Laborde and Maynor (2008).
7 This means that, for neo-republicanism, 'interference without domination' is possible; that is, not non-arbitrary interference. On this point lies the main difference with the libertarian negative conception of liberty.
8 See Pettit (2008), Casassas (2008), Dagger (2006), and Lovett (2009).
9 The other four features of Dagger's republic civic economy (2006) – workplace republicanism; community interests; progressive consumption tax; social minimum – are not adequate to reduce wealth and income inequality; moreover, a progressive consumption tax might even have the opposite result, no matter how progressive (Atkinson 2015).
10 For the same objection, see Forst (2013).
11 Indeed, I assume that in some cases it is impossible to fully respect persons' moral and political deliberative autonomy, but for the simple fact that some persons might be not able to exercise their autonomy because they are affected by some severe physical and mental disabilities, or because it is not yet fully developed, as in the case of children. Of course, in either of these cases the best that we can do is apply a 'paternalistic' use of power in which the non-arbitrariness consists exactly in trying through our goodwill to track ideas and interests of these persons or in children. However, these are not cases of domination in my view. In Pettit, instead, there seems to be no particular difference in the case of children; he says (1997: 119) 'children should enjoy the standard intensity of non-domination, in the sense of being protected as well as anybody else against arbitrary'. This is further proof that the deliberative autonomy of the power-subject does not play a central role in neo-republicanism.
12 See Marx (2013), Foucault (2020) and Bourdieu (1977, 1990).
13 Structure power is also often used as synonymous with systematic power; although, for some scholars we can speak about systematic power only when structures take literally the form of a system, or sub-system, insofar as they strictly follow a certain, and maybe unique, functionalistic or operational logic (Thompson 2013b; Azmanova 2018, 2020). For the moment, I will take the two as synonymous.
14 According to Hayward (2011: 470),

> inter-agentive nondomination obtains when all participants in power relations are free from rule by other agents who are socially enabled to set the terms of those relations. Impersonal or systemic nondomination obtains when participants in a power relation achieve collective agency vis-a-vis its terms.

15 Italic emphasis is mine.

16 Note that Azmanova (2018: 10, note 3) acknowledges that it would be better to define this form of power as 'relative' rather than 'relational', although for simplicity she retains Strange's formulation.
17 In this sense Azmanova (2018) tries to be faithful to Marx's claim that improving the living standards of the working-class (higher wages or other benefits) would not end exploitation and subjection. However, Azmanova seems to conceive this assumption as a proof that also for Marx it would be possible to make all workers included and perfectly equal in their resources and they will still suffer structure and systematic domination. I seriously doubt that such an inference could be derived from Marx's theory. Indeed, I think that Marx's claim simply means that given that the structure of the private property of the means of production always gives the capitalist class the capacity to extract surplus value from workers, this surplus maintains and increases the differential of the key power-resources (mainly wealth) possessed by capitalists and workers. In other words, capitalistic structures simply represent an insurmountable obstacle to make all members of a society included and perfectly equal.
18 Here Azmanova does not follow structural functionalism in which a society is seen as internally distinct in relatively autonomous economic, administrative, sociocultural, and legitimation systems or subsystems, each of which contributes to social integration. By contrast, she recovers the original Marx's holistic understanding of capitalism as a comprehensive system of social relations enacted through everyday practises. However, she abandons Marx's structure-superstructure dichotomy employed to describe the relation of political rule to socioeconomic processes. In this way, for Azmanova (2020) a democratic capitalism is understood as an institutional order that combines democracy as a political system with capitalism as a social system.
19 The solution is what Azmanova (2012b, 2020) describes as a 'political economy of trust' (or a socioeconomic certainty).
20 There are some accounts that try to solve the dualism between agency and structures, see Dowding (2008b), Gourevitch (2013, 2015) and Cicerchia (2019).
21 Giddens (1979, 1984) also defines structures in terms of *the rules* and resources that enable people to act and interact.
22 I do not exclude that alternative forms to understand social power and domination are valid for different aims (not necessarily normative).
23 For the criterion of publicity, see Freeman (2007).
24 Here I follow the most common terminology, although other scholars chose other terms. For example, Dahl (1957) calls them bases of power, and Forst (2017: 45) distinguishes them between simple resources (like a gun) and 'noumenal capital' for those 'resources' based on social recognition and standing that are enabled by social structures, such as a priest, an officer, or an entrepreneur.
25 I do not deny that for some specific empirical and normative analysis, the measurement of people's outcomes is useful and maybe the best kind of evaluation. For example, when we are interested in assessing people's level of poverty, an approach (like the capability approach) that focuses on the actual ability of someone to achieve outcomes may be the most adequate. For Dowding (2008a) the difference depends on if we want to make a measurement that focuses on 'token' or instead 'types' of individuals.
26 For the same objection, see Pansardi (2012b) and Dowding (2008a).
27 For example, sheer violence is understood as the absence of power for Arendt (1972). Many others follow this intuition, see Forst (2017). Alternatively, for an account of power that also includes violence, see Gilabert (2018).
28 Not surprisingly, for libertarians, there is a crucial distinction between individual liberty understood as the absence of external interference or physical obstacles by others and power as being able to do something or act in some ways. Libertarians claim that justice requires protecting individual negative liberty rather than ensuring some forms of individual power. It is self-evident that if power were to include acts of coercion, this distinction would collapse.

29 However, this social fact tells us that the fear of coercion (and even violence) never disappears from the horizon of social power, even in a democratic society based on the rule of law in which the use of coercive power claims to be justified. And for the same reason, I believe that it may be misleading to define what I call here social power as a form of 'soft power' (Nye 1990). Moreover, although it is true that social power that *prime facie* does not include coercive power is prevailing in modern societies, it also existed in ancient societies; for instance, 'taxation' for Romans citizens of the Roman Empire worked as a form of social power.

30 Here, Forst seems to associate what I call social power with a form of power that he calls 'Rules',

> where the power-holder not only uses his or her capacity to decisively influence the space of justifications for others, but where certain comprehensive (religious, metaphysical, historical, or moral) justifications (and usually a mixture thereof) determine the space of reasons within which social or political relations are being framed— relations which form a structured, durable, and stable social order of action and justification.
>
> (Forst 2017: 49)

31 In his response to Hayward, Forst seems to acknowledge the necessity to investigate the dimension of power that upholds social structures; for example, he argues about a third level of analysis of 'the character and formation of noumenal resources or background conditions that carry and support such structures, especially the justification narratives they rest on' (Forst 2018: 306). However, I believe that his analytic distinction between these three levels, 'the exercise of inter-agentive power, 'structural forms of power', and 'powers and conditions that support structures', reproduce a misleading distinction between interagentive and structural power.

32 For this perspective, we can agree with Young (1990) that power is not a 'good' that can be distributed itself. Nonetheless, power resources can be 'distributed'.

33 Some might object that people value a certain personal quality by following a specific social pattern, and therefore we give worth to a certain type of beauty or intelligence. While this is absolutely true, what matters is how these valuable personal qualities, according to the current social pattern, are rewarded. The case is totally different if an important resource of 'socially generalisable' power, for example official political position, is open only to people with a certain personal quality, the beautiful, the wise, the strong, etc.; in this case the problem is that the excluded (the ugly, the foolish, the weak) are totally deprived of this key power resource.

34 Similarly, Shapiro (2003) points out how asymmetrical relations of material power have significant opposite effects on adaptive preferences and attitudes of both rich and poor. When the gap between the rich and poor is so massive, the former begin to think that they never will share the same destiny of the poor while the latter abandon certain goals from their field of aspirations. The paradoxical result is that 'exceedingly high levels of inequality might actually dampen redistributive demands from the very poor' (Shapiro 2003: 133).

35 Dowding (2016) calls these powerful actors as 'systematic lucky'.

36 Note that a social actor's capacity to establish and shape, by mobilising certain power resources, primary rules, can be effective according to what, in the debate, is identified as different views or dimensions of power (see Section 2.1). For example, a social actor might mobilise his material power (his wealth) to prevail over someone in a political election or referendum consultation (Dahl's first dimension), to control the political agenda (Bachrach and Baratz's second dimension), or to influence and create a political and cultural hegemony in a way that puts some specific topics off the table (Lukes' third dimension).

37 Here, I think that I more or less share Pansardi's (2013, 2016) conclusions that domination ultimately rests on the degree of asymmetry of individual power resources. However, I introduce two fundamental differences. First of all, I emphasise the strict intertwine between individual power resources and social structures that govern social relations in

which individuals are involved. A relation that, instead, is usually missed by the social exchange theory of domination on which Pansardi's account seems to be dependent (see Stoppino 2001). Secondly, I take a step forward from her conclusions and I define non-domination as not being exposed to *the risk of domination* (in its various forms).

38 However, it does not mean that we cannot use the notion of self-authorship in a specific field of our social life.

39 Indeed, this seems to be what Thompson has in mind by offering a criterion to identify when 'surplus benefit' occurs: 'where some group or some individual is worse-off than if they had not been in that relation or of some other scheme is possible wherein a goal could be reached without that kind of dominance' (Thompson 2018: 48). Similarly, Haugaard (2018: 19) explicitly advocates a maximin principle in an asymmetrical 'distribution' of power.

40 As we saw, this is not true for Azmanova (2020), but unfortunately only for what she defines as 'relational domination'.

41 To be clear, I simply offer some examples of the content of key power resources, but certainly other scholars may do far better than me, see Dowding (1991), Stoppino (2001) and Winters (2011). Here, my aim is to defend the theoretical and methodological approach of proportional justice.

42 It was signed into law by President Lyndon B. Johnson on 6 August 1965.

43 For more details, see *Brennan Center for Justice*'s report (2021a; 2021b).

44 In this regard, the risk of epistemic domination is not equivalent to Fricker's epistemic injustice. Fricker (2007: 1) admits that 'the idea of epistemic injustice might first and foremost prompt thoughts about distributive unfairness in respect of epistemic goods such as information or education', but she instead explores a distinctively epistemic kind of injustice which concerns 'testimonial injustice' and 'hermeneutical injustice'. Fricker's epistemic injustice includes an important ethical dimension, but one that my approach of proportional justice cannot take into account.

45 However, in the last decade, we have witnessed an erosion of the classic institutions of 'checks and balances' and political rights. The cases of Hungary and Poland are among the most obvious.

Bibliography

Allen, Amy. 1999. *The Power of Feminist Theory: Domination, Resistance, Solidarity*. Boulder: Westview Press.

Anderson, Elizabeth. 2017. *Private Government how employers rule our lives (and Why We don't Talk about it)*. Princeton: Princeton University Press.

Arendt, Hannah. 1972. *Crises of the Republic: Lying in Politics; Civil Disobedience; on Violence; Thoughts on Politics and Revolution*. London: Mariner Books.

Atkinson, Anthony B. 2015. *Inequality: What Can Be Done?* Cambridge: Harvard University Press.

Azmanova, Albena. 2020. *Capitalism on Edge: How Fighting Precarity Can Achieve Radical Change Without Crisis or Utopia*. New York: Columbia University Press.

Azmanova, Albena. 2018. 'Relational, Structural, and Systemic Forms of Power: The "Right to Justification" Confronting Three Types of Domination', *Journal of Political Power*, 11(1): 68–78.

Azmanova, Albena. 2016a. 'Empowerment as Surrender: How Women Lost the Battle for Emancipation as They Won Equality and Inclusion', *Social Research*, 83(3): 749–776.

Azmanova, Albena. 2016b. 'The Right to Politics and Republican Non-Domination', *Philosophy and Social Criticism*, 42: 465–475.

Azmanova, Albena. 2014. 'Crisis? Capitalism is Doing Very Well. How is Critical Theory?' *Constellations: An International Journal of Critical and Democratic Theory*, 21(3): 351–365.

Azmanova, Albena. 2012a. 'De-Gendering Social Justice in the 21st Century: An Immanent Critique of Neoliberal Capitalism', *European Journal of Social Theory*, 15(2): 143–156.

Azmanova, Albena. 2012b. 'Social Justice and Varieties of Capitalism: An Immanent Critique', *New Political Economy*, 17(4): 445–463.

Bachrach, Peter and Morton Baratz. 1962. 'The Two Faces of Power', *American Political Science Review*, 56: 947–952.

Barry, Brian. 2002. 'Capitalists Rule OK? Some Puzzles about Power', *Politics, Philosophy & Economics'*, 1(2): 155–184.

Boltanski, Luc and Laurent Thévenot. 2006. *On Justification: Economies of Worth*. Princeton: Princeton University Press.

Bourdieu, Pierre. 1990. 'Fieldwork in Philosophy'. Trans. by M. Adamson, in Pierre Bourdieu (ed.), *In other Words: Essays Toward a Reflexive Sociology*, pp. 3–33. Stanford: Stanford University Press.

Bourdieu, Pierre. 1977. *Outline of a Theory of Practice*. Trans. by R. Nice. Cambridge: Cambridge University Press.

Brennan Center for Justice. 2021a. 'Voting Laws Roundup: May 2021', *Brennan Center for Justice*, 28 May 2021, https://www.brennancenter.org/our-work/research-reports/voting-laws-roundup-may-2021a/, (accessed on 3 February 2022).

Brennan Center for Justice. 2021b. 'Voting Laws Roundup: October 2021', *Brennan Center for Justice*, 4 October 2021, https://www.brennancenter.org/our-work/research-reports/voting-laws-roundup-october-2021b, (accessed on 3 February 2022).

Casassas, David. 2008. 'Basic Income and the Republican Ideal: Rethinking Material Independence in Contemporary Societies', *Basic Income Studies*, 2(2): 1–8.

Cicerchia, Lillian. 2019. 'Structural Domination in the Labor Market', *European Journal of Political Theory*, 21(1): 4–24.

Dagger, Richard. 2006. 'Neo-republicanism and the Civic Economy', *Politics, Philosophy and Economics*, 5(2): 151–173.

Dahl, Robert A. 1961. *Who Governs? Democracy and Power in an American City*. New Haven and London: Yale University Press.

Dahl, Robert A. 1958. 'A Critique of the Ruling Elite Model', *American Political Science Review*, 52(2): 463–469.

Dahl, Robert A. 1957. 'The Concept of Power', *Behavioral Science*, 2(3): 201–215.

Dowding, Keith. 2016. *Power, Luck and Freedom. Collected Essays*. Ed. by Keith Dowding. Manchester: Manchester University Press.

Dowding, Keith. 2008a. 'Power, Capability and Ableness: The Fallacy of the Vehicle Fallacy', *Contemporary Political Theory*, 7: 238–258.

Dowding, Keith. 2008b. 'Agency and Structure: Interpreting Power Relationships', *Journal of Power*, 1(1): 21–36.

Dowding, Keith. 1991. *Rational Choice and Political Power*. Aldershot: Edward Elgar Pub.

Forst, Rainer. 2018. 'Noumenal Power Revisited: Reply to Critics', *Journal of Political Power*, 11(3): 294–321.

Forst, Rainer. 2017. *Normativity and Power: Analyzing Social Orders of Justification*. Trans. by Ciaran Cronin. Oxford: Oxford University Press.

Forst, Rainer. 2015. 'Noumenal Power', *The Journal of Political Philosophy*, 23(2): 111–127.

Forst, Rainer. 2014. *Justification and Critique: Towards a Critical Theory of Politics*. Trans. by Ciaran Cronin. Cambridge: Polity Press.

Forst, Rainer. 2013. 'A Kantian Republican Conception of Justice as Non-domination', in Andreas Niederberger and Philipp Schink (eds.), *Republican Democracy*, pp. 154–168. Edinburgh: Edinburgh University Press.

Forst, Rainer. 2012. *The Right to Justification*. Trans. by Jeffrey Flynn. New York: Columbia University Press.

Foucault, Michel. 2020. *Discipline and Punish: The Birth of the Prison*. Harmondsworth: Penguin Press.

Fraser, Nancy. 2009. 'Feminism, Capitalism, and the Cunning of History', *New Left Review*, 56: 97–117.

Freeman, Samuel. 2007. 'Public Reason and Political Justification', in Samuel Freeman (ed.), *Justice and the Social Contract: Essays on Rawlsian Political Philosophy*, pp. 215–256. Oxford: Oxford University Press.

Fricker, Miranda. 2007. *Epistemic Injustice: Power and the Ethics of Knowing*. Oxford: Oxford University Press.

Giddens, Anthony. 1984. *The Constitution of Society: Outline of the Theory of Structuration*. California: University California Press.

Giddens, Anthony. 1979. *The Central Problems of Social Theory: Action, Structure, and Contradiction in Social Analysis*. London: Macmillan.

Gilabert, Pablo. 2018. 'A Broad Definition of Agential Power', *Journal of Political Power*, 11(1): 79–92.

Gourevitch, Alex. 2015. *From Slavery to the Cooperative Commonwealth: Labor and Republican Liberty in the Nineteenth Century*. Cambridge: Cambridge University Press.

Gourevitch, Alex. 2013. 'Labour Republicanism and the Transformation of Work', *Political Theory*, 41(4): 591–617.

Habermas, Jürgen. 1987. *The Theory of Communicative Action. Volume II*. Trans. by Thomas McCarthy. Boston: Bacon Press.

Haugaard, Mark. 2018. 'Justification and the Four Dimensions of Power', *Journal of Political Power*, 11(1): 93–114.

Haugaard, Mark. 2012. 'Rethinking the Four Dimensions of Power', *Journal of Political Power*, 5(1): 35–54.

Hayward, Clarissa R. 2018. 'On Structural Power', *Journal of Political Power*, 11(1): 56–67.

Hayward, Clarissa R. 2013. *How Americans Make Race: Stories, Institutions, Spaces*. New York: Cambridge University Press.

Hayward, Clarissa R. 2011. 'What Can Political Freedom Mean in a Multicultural Democracy? On Deliberation, Difference, and Democratic Governance,' *Political Theory*, 39(4): 468–497.

Hayward, Clarissa R. 2006. 'On Power and Responsibility', *Political Studies Review*, 4: 156–163.

Hayward, Clarissa R. 2000. *De-facing Power*. Cambridge: Cambridge University Press.

Hayward, Clarissa R. 1998. 'De-Facing Power', *Polity*, 31(1): 1–22.

Hayward, Clarissa R. and Steven Lukes. 2008. 'Nobody to Shoot? Power, Structure, and Agency: A Dialogue', *Journal of Power*, 1(1): 5–20.

Hearn, Jonathan. 2012. *Theorizing Power*. Hampshire: Palgrave Macmillan.

Hunter, Floyd. 1953. *Community Power Structure*. Chapel Hill: University of North Carolina Press.

Isaac, Jeffrey C. 1987a. 'Beyond the Three Faces of Power: A Realist Critique', *Polity*, 20(1): 4–31.

Isaac, Jeffrey C. 1987b. *Power and Marxist Theory: A Realist View*. Ithaca: Cornell University Press.

Kant, Immanuel. 1996. *The Metaphysics of Morals*. Trans. by Mary Gregor. Cambridge: Cambridge University Press.

Laborde, Cecile and John W. Maynor. 2008. *Republicanism and Political Theory*. New Jersey: Wiley-Blackwell.

Lovett, Frank. 2012. 'What Counts as Arbitrary Power?' *Journal of Political Power*, 5(1): 137–152.

Lovett, Frank. 2010. *A General Theory of Domination and Justice*. Oxford: Oxford University Press.

Lovett, Frank. 2009. 'Domination and Distributive Justice', *Journal of Politics*, 71(3): 817–830.

Lukes, Steven. 2018. 'Noumenal Power: Concept and Explanation', *Journal of Political Power*, 11(1): 46–55.

Lukes, Steven. 2005. *Power: A Radical View. Second Edition*. Basingstoke: Palgrave Macmillan.

Lukes, Steven. 1974. *Power: A Radical View*. London: MacMillan.

Marx, Karl. 2013. *Capital. Volume One and Two*. Trans. by Edward Aveling and Ernest Untermann. London: Wordsworth Editions.

Maynor, John W. 2006. 'Modern Republican Democratic Contestation: A Model of Deliberative Democracy', in Iseult Honohan and Jeremy Jennings (eds.), *Republicanism in Theory and Practice*, pp. 125–139. London: Routledge.

Mills, Wright C. 1956. *The Power Elite*. Oxford: Oxford University Press.

Morriss, Peter. 2002. *Power: A Philosophical Analysis. Second Edition*. Manchester: Manchester University Press.

Neuhouser, Frederick. 2013. 'Rousseau's Critique of Economic Inequality', *Philosophy & Public Affairs*, 41(3): 193–225.

Nye, Joseph S. 1990. 'Soft Power', *Foreign Policy*, 80: 153–171.

Oppenheim, Felix E. 1981. *Political Concepts: A Reconstruction*. Chicago: University of Chicago Press.

Pansardi, Pamela. 2016. 'Democracy, Domination, and the Distribution of Power: Substantive Political Equality as a Procedural Requirement', *Revue Internationale de Philosophie*, 70(275): 91–108.

Pansardi, Pamela. 2015. 'Republican Democracy and the Priority of Legitimacy Over Justice', *Philosophy and Public Issues*, 5(2): 43–57.

Pansardi, Pamela. 2013. 'A Non-normative Theory of Power and Domination', *Critical Review of International Social and Political Philosophy*, 16(5): 614–633.

Pansardi, Pamela. 2012a. 'Power to and Power Over: Two Distinct Concepts of Power?' *Journal of Political Power*, 5(1): 73–89.

Pansardi, Pamela. 2012b. 'On Abilities and Power Again: A Reply to Peter Morriss', *Journal of Political Power*, 5(3): 495–499.

Pettit, Philip. 2012. *On the People's Terms: A Republican Theory and Model of Democracy*. Cambridge: Cambridge University Press.

Pettit, Philip. 2008. 'A Republican Right to Basic Income?' *Basic Income Studies*, 2(2): 1–8.

Pettit, Philip. 2006. 'Freedom in the Market', *Philosophy, Politics, and Economics*, 5(2): 131–149.

Pettit, Philip. 2004. 'The Common Good', in Keith Dowding, Robert E. Goodin and Carole Pateman (eds.), *Justice and Democracy: Essays for Brian Barry*, pp. 150–169. Cambridge: Cambridge University Press.

Pettit, Philip. 2001. *A Theory of Freedom: From the Psychology to the Politics of Agency*. Oxford: Oxford University Press.

Pettit, Philip. 1999. 'Republican Freedom and Contestatory Democracy', in Ian Shapiro and Casiano Hacker-Cordon (eds.), *Democracy's Value*, pp. 163–190. New York: Cambridge University Press.

Pettit, Philip. 1997. *Republicanism: A Theory of Freedom and Government*. Oxford: Oxford University Press.

Pinzani, Alessandro. 2005. 'It's the Power, Stupid! On the Unmentioned Precondition of Social Justice', in Andreas Føllesdal and Thomas Pogge (eds.), *Real World Justice: Grounds, Principles, Human Rights, and Social Institutions*, pp. 171–197. New York: Springer Publishing.

Pitkin, Hanna. 1972. *Wittgenstein and Justice*. Berkeley: University of California Press.

Rousseau, Jean-Jacques. 1997. 'The Social Contract', in Victor Gourevitch (ed. and trans.), *The Social Contract, and Other Later Political Writings*, pp. 39–152. Cambridge: Cambridge University Press.

Scheffler, Samuel. 2015. 'The Practice of Equality', in Carina Fourie, Fabien Schuppert and Ivo Wallimann-Helmer (eds.), *Social Equality: On What It Means to Be Equals*, pp. 21–44. Oxford: Oxford University Press.

Shapiro, Ian. 2003. *The State of Democratic Theory*. Princeton: Princeton University Press.

Skinner, Quentin. 2012. *Liberty before Liberalism*. Cambridge: Cambridge University Press.

Stoppino, Mario. 2001. *Potere e teoria politica*. Milano: Giuffrè Editore.

Strange, Susan. 1989. 'Toward a Theory of Transnational Empire', in Werner Väth (ed.), *Political Regulation in the "Great Crisis"*, pp. 25–42. Berlin: Edition Sigma.

Strange, Susan. 1988. *States and Markets*. London: Pinter.

Taylor, Charles. 1979. 'What's Wrong with Negative Liberty', in Alan Ryan (ed.), *The Idea of Freedom*, pp. 175–193. Oxford: Oxford University Press.

Thompson, Michael J. 2018. 'The Two Faces of Domination in Republican Political Theory', *European Journal of Political Theory*, 17(1): 44–64.

Thompson, Michael J. 2013a. 'Reconstructing Republican Freedom: A Critique of the Neo-republican Conception of Freedom as Non-domination', *Philosophy and Social Criticism*, 39(3): 277–298.

Thompson, Michael J. 2013b. 'A Functionalist Theory of Social Domination', *The Journal of Political Power*, 6(2): 179–199.

Walzer, Michael. 1983. *Spheres of Justice: A Defense of Pluralism and Equality*. New York: Basic Books.

Wartenberg, Thomas E. 1990. *The Forms of Power: From Domination to Transformation*. Philadelphia: Temple University Press.

Winters, Jeffrey A. 2011. *Oligarchy*. New York: Cambridge University Press.

Young, Iris M. 2011. *Responsibility for Justice*. Oxford: Oxford University Press.

Young, Iris M. 2009. 'Structural Injustice and the Politics of Difference', in Thomas Christiano and John Christman (eds.), *Contemporary Debates in Political Philosophy*, pp. 362–384. New Jersey: Wiley-Blackwell.

Young, Iris M. 1990. *Justice and the Politics of Difference*. Princeton: Princeton University Press.

3

INEQUALITY AND PROPORTIONALITY IN CURRENT DISTRIBUTIVE THEORIES OF JUSTICE

Material inequality is a central issue in the history of political philosophy, and not only since the 19th century, when the idea of social justice emerged; it was already one of the most important topics in the classical idea of distributive justice in Greek philosophy. The ancient principle, to each (or from each) his own, is the most classical manner to assign the way in which the benefits and burdens of society are distributed, and consequently what types of inequality are legitimate or not, and therefore whether they should be eliminated or mitigated. Of course, much depends on our idea of justice and the kind of distributive principles we adopt.

As I said, this normative choice depends on the scope and object of our investigation, and I hope at this point that these aspects of the distributive justice I look for are clear and well defined. To recall, under subjective and objective circumstances of justice (or, in other words, the fact of radical pluralism and the fact of domination), and once *the primary object of distributive justice* inevitably focuses on the primary rules of society, the question of 'authority' is inescapable. Again, given that primary rules determine what people can legitimately claim according to their contribution and participation in social interactions and cooperation, they should not be taken as a natural fact or as a given. On the contrary, the main question becomes: who has the power to establish, shape and stabilise primary rules over the time? This question forces us to clarify the relation between the principles of distributive justice and the subjects of justice, in my case those individual citizens who share a politically unified entity. Thus, I focus exclusively on domestic concerns for distributive justice.

I consider the three following strategies for addressing the problem of 'authority' as unsatisfactory. First of all, our view of distributive justice cannot simply refrain from offering normative guidance to our political action by the mere fact of pluralism, such as the case of the pluralistic view which states that 'we should be pluralists

DOI: 10.4324/9781003189428-4

about morality' (Temkin 2000: 155; 2017). Moral values and ideas, such as equality, justice, utility, and freedom, compete and conflict with each other in many cases, and therefore a pluralistic view does not say much about the ranking of these different values and ideas. This is the problem that Rawls identified with intuitionism. Therefore, we need to provide, albeit limited and partial, a semblance of order or priority between different 'moral' ideas, values, and duties.

Second, our view of distributive justice cannot be fully external or exogenous to the 'authority' of the subjects of justice. In this case, distributive justice is conceived as something that produces results of the right sort, and, from this perspective, even an appointed judge might perfectly implement it. Although we may be well intentioned and convinced that we have found the 'true' or 'correct' conception of distributive justice, in the light of radical pluralism, an external view is not able to respect moral and political deliberative autonomy of those who are the subject of justice. Their 'authority' is downgraded and, as a consequence, individuals are simply conceived as passive, subjective recipients of justice.

Third, our view of distributive justice cannot be fully internal or endogenous to the 'authority' of the subjects of justice. There are two extreme versions of this view. According to a genuine libertarian conception, the social rules that govern individual relations should never be the object of distributive justice. From this point of view, distributive justice is simply the result of voluntary individuals' transactions and interactions free from external interference and threat from others. It is clear that the objective circumstances of justice make this view fully inadequate. People do not have the possibility to live isolated or separated, like in the hypothetical case of the small island. Their lives depend on social rules that govern the social relations in which they are inexorably involved. By insisting on a libertarian view, we would disregard the fact that those who have the power to establish and shape these rules might impose their own will and opinion on others (a result that even libertarians should have to avoid). The opposite version of an internal view, instead, conceives the moral and political autonomy as the subject of authority of a unique collective agent; for example, a political community. The main idea is that the conflicts of distributive justice should be exclusively regulated by political and public confrontation. Given the impossibility to find a unanimous agreement, the best realistic option is to find the largest consensus possible through, for example, a radical democratic process of antagonistic pluralism, which excludes violence and arbitrary coercion and in which decisions can be reversed in the next confrontation. In this sense, once you have participated in the process of political and public confrontation, you would have nothing to complain about regarding the 'distributive' results and decisions, whatever they may be. In this case, the problem is that the idea of collective authority seems to respect pluralism only *ex ante*: once the political confrontation is completed, the decisions that follow do not seem to have particular limits of contents and application. In addition, it is not clear what kinds of prerequisites the public confrontation should satisfy to ensure that all participants have the effective means and power to engage in it.

At this point in the discussion, what can we conclude to come closer to solutions to the problem of 'authority'? In this chapter, I will attempt to indicate a certain path towards finding a solution, one that is also able to give us a compelling answer to the question of permissible economic inequalities. In the first section, I will argue that the path opened by Rawls with the idea of the political conception of justice still gives us, under the subjective and objective circumstances, the most compelling theoretical and methodological account to elaborate normative requirements and principles of justice. Thus, following Rawls, I will draft the main features of what we may call a political conception of distributive justice, one that in my own view takes the form of proportional justice. Of course, we cannot exclude a priori the possibility that, in the current literature, a distributive principle or criterion is already available that adequately takes into account the size of material inequality (wealth and income) between the best-off and the worst-off in such a way that I could be exempted from introducing my specific material distributive principle of justice: the principle of proportionality. Hence, in the further sections, I will show that this is not the case. In the second section, I will argue about Rawls' difference principle and identify the main problem as being that the difference principle itself is insensitive to the width of the gap between the best-off and the worst-off. Although I do not neglect the distributive implications of the fair value of political liberties inscribed in the first principle of justice, I argue that Rawls' two principles of justice fail to offer normative guidance as to what is the *fair* ratio between the income and wealth shares of the worst-off and the best-off. In the third section, I identify three broad families of distributive principles – prioritarianism, moderate egalitarianism, and sufficientarianism – that share the normative requirement with the difference principle to give 'priority' to the worst-off's claims, while avoiding an overly demanding requirement in their favour. Unfortunately, all versions of these three families fare even worse than the difference principle regarding the constraints on the scale of material inequalities. In the fourth section, I will briefly reconstruct Robeyns' limitarianism, arguing that although it takes an important step in the right direction, Robeyns' limitarianism surprisingly misses the target. The main problem is not being above or below a riches line of economic resources that are needed for a fully flourishing life, but rather the distance between the best-off and the worst-off. Thus, limitarianism prescribes a severe limitation of individual wealth that is ineffective to reach the goal of the democratic argument.

3.1 A Political Conception of Distributive Justice

I believe that the path opened by Rawls with the idea of the political conception of justice still offers, under the subjective and objective circumstances, the most compelling theoretical and methodological account to deal with the problem of authority in elaborating normative requirements and principles of justice. First, a political conception of justice clearly defines and circumscribes the 'object' of the distributive justice that Rawls identifies as the background justice or the basic structure of society (or primary rules). Second, it provides us a 'political' constructivist method to advance and elaborate on the 'contents' of the principles of distributive justice. However, I want to clarify that to endorse Rawls' idea of a political conception of justice does not mean to abandon substantive distributive requirements. Thus, following Rawls, in this section I will draft the main features of what we may call a political conception of distributive justice.

I believe that Rawls' political conception of justice can be considered a certain combination of all three views mentioned above. On the one hand, given the fact of the irreconcilable pluralism (Rawls 2005: lviii), Rawls also agrees that political and public deliberation and confrontation can be the only way to lead with the disagreement. Under subjective and objective circumstances of justice, we have seen that people cannot refrain from deciding how to establish and shape social rules. Therefore, it is better to find an agreement between as many people as possible. But, as we have seen, we need to guarantee that the winners of public and political confrontation and deliberation will not impose their will and opinion on others. In other words, we should distinguish between what Rawls (2007: 277) calls principles as a matter of policies and principles as a matter of justice. The former are subordinate to the principles of justice, just as the latter are a priori almost independent from the former. By following Mill, Rawls (2007: 276) says that 'justice cannot be overridden by reasons of policy'. Therefore, on the other hand, the principles of justice have the function to impose *limits* and *background requisites* that the public and political confrontation and deliberation should satisfy. In this respect, the 'object' of Rawls' political conception of justice offers us a sophisticated strategy of how to impose limits on the extent of the policy (broadly understood here) and on the legitimate use of public power and intervention. Given that citizens have to live with an irreconcilable disagreement, the principles of justice cannot extend their scope and validity to all areas of social life. In other words, they must leave room for non-public spheres, or for forms of association and community within a 'political' society (Rawls 2005: 40–43). Therefore, the political conception of distributive justice only applies to the basic structure of society; or in my view, to the primary rules of society.[1]

And what about the contents of the principles of distributive justice? Also in this case, Rawls' political conception offers us a 'political' constructivism method. This method permits us to provide types of moral judgments that are themselves confined to 'the domain of the political' (Rawls 2005: 38). According to Rawls, this specific domain of morality is independent of epistemology, metaphysics and any particular comprehensive doctrine (moral, religious, ethical, etc.). In this sense, although all citizens affirm a comprehensive doctrine, a political conception of justice is presented as *freestanding* and expounded apart from, or without reference to, any such wider background (Rawls 2005: 12). It means that we have a first fundamental criterion to advance the contents of the distributive principles justice; that is, we cannot expect to find an agreement among reasonable citizens if this 'political', but always moral (Rawls 2005: xlvii, 395), content includes principles that are grounded on a particular comprehensive doctrine. In Scanlon's contractualism terms (1982; 1998), we can say that only *freestanding* principles of justice cannot be reasonably rejected by those people affected by them.

Again, here the point is to know what exactly it means to be reasonable. Indeed, to reject a principle we need to prove that it is unreasonable. As Rawls admits (2005: 375, Reply to Habermas), the idea of a political conception of justice presented as *freestanding* can take many forms, not only liberal as in the case of Rawls' *Political Liberalism*, but also conservative, radical and even conceptions of the divine right of kings or dictatorship may also belong to a political conception of justice. Of course, the latter are not compatible with a democratic regime. From this perspective, Rawls seems to conceive of the reasonable as a moral and political attitude of democratic people who consider each other as free and equal citizens. Although this formulation of the idea of reasonableness can be adequate, I think that being a reasonable person means to endorse a 'universal' moral attitude, something that should not necessarily be restricted only to liberal democratic societies. Restricting the idea of reasonableness in this way offers the critics of Rawls the impression that the concept of reasonableness is, at best, a simple virtue of tolerance or a liberal value. The risk is to weaken the idea of a political conception of justice presented as *freestanding*. In other words, a political conception of justice represents a much stronger moral claim than what Rawls seems ready to admit to. Furthermore, our idea of reasonableness cannot also be too indeterminate, otherwise it provides no criteria or requirements to evaluate a reasonable rejection of a principle. I said (Chapter 1) that the idea of reasonableness, understood as to take the effects or consequences of our actions on others very seriously, means that reasonable persons know that their actions can both directly and indirectly cause harm or injury to others; that is, no violence, coercion, or domination which means to impose their will and opinion on others. Moreover, they also know that they are able to eliminate or alleviate the suffering condition of others, even if this condition does not depend on our direct and indirect actions. This implies the common requirements of social virtues such as: sympathy, beneficence, love, care, recognition, solidarity, etc. (O. O'Neill 1996). Hence, keeping in mind these normative clarifications, how can we proceed? The guidelines seem easy enough to follow.

Now, we know that a political conception circumscribes our object of distributive justice to primary rules and that all principles independent of any particular comprehensive doctrine cannot be reasonably rejected. Thus, first of all, we can exclude those principles based on requirements of social virtues because they need to be effective in some particular conceptions of good or some perfectionist views. This means that these principles cannot be a basis for establishing and shaping primary rules, and therefore to provide limits and background requisites for public deliberation and confrontation; or, in other words, for the matter of policies. The point is that it lies outside the scope and object of a political conception of distributive justice to eliminate or alleviate those citizens' sufferings or limitations that are not product or result (directly or indirectly) of the actions of others and, above all, of the primary rules (or basic structure of society in Rawls' language). However, Rawls' idea of a political conception of justice does not deny that the requirements of social virtues cannot be a matter of public policy. Indeed, it is legitimate that citizens can deliberate about the use of economic resources to address what can happen to citizens by reason of their own particular circumstances, or to help others' societies in a natural disaster; or to implement others' public policies to collectively satisfy the requirement of social virtues. Clearly, and again, these kinds of policies are subordinated to background requisites fixed by a political conception of justice.

However, someone can argue that there is a way to provide a freestanding justification for collectively satisfying the requirement of social virtues. Indeed, we can say that to eliminate or alleviate the suffering condition of others we do not need to endorse a comprehensive and perfectionistic conception of good life or well-being; for example, in case we appeal to an 'objective' conception of basic needs of human beings. I think that it is possible, but only in case this 'objective' conception is very minimal; for instance, a conception that protects individuals from absolute deprivation. If we succeed in this task we can include as a principle of a political conception of distributive justice the 'distribution' of certain 'goods' (or to prescribe policies and specific institutions) that allow all citizens to satisfy their very basic needs. This is a way in which Rawls could justify the provision of a social minimum.[2] Moreover, I think that this minimal requirement deploys another important function as a background requisite that allows a procedural political conception of justice to work properly. In the end, if citizens do not see their basic needs met, at least to a minimum level, it is impossible to establish their actual will and their possibility to participate in social cooperation and interaction. Therefore, we cannot be sure if their individual conditions are a result or not by the primary rules.

And, what about the other background requisites? Certainly, as I said, the public power cannot be extended to all spheres of social life, making room for a class of merely 'ethical' duties whose compliance should not be coercively enforced. Most important, the result of public deliberation and confrontation, whatever it is, cannot deprive citizens of certain 'goods' (or to hinder their 'use'). These 'goods' represent the background requisites of a political conception of distributive justice. But, what are those 'goods' that should be 'distributed'? As we know, Rawls calls these goods 'social primary goods': rights, liberties, powers and opportunities, income and wealth, and the social bases of self-respect. His justification is that 'these are things any rational person is presumed to want, irrespective of her particular plan of life' (Rawls 1971: 62; 1982).

There are three plausible, and yet apparently different, interpretations for this statement. According to the first interpretation, these primary goods are so dominant and central to social life that no person is able to pursue her particular plan of life and follow her worldview, whatever they might be, if she is deprived of even just one of them. The second one, instead, is that these primary 'goods' are fundamental and strictly necessary to allow citizens to participate and engage in public confrontation and deliberation. According to the third interpretation, some of these primary goods are addressed to allow the public and political participation, while others are necessary to pursue the individual conception of goods. Those who advocate this last interpretation usually find confirmations in the division of labour between the two principles of justice in Rawls' theory. As explained in Chapter 1, according to this interpretation, justice is divided into enabling and distributive justice. In Rawls' theory, enabling justice is governed by the first principle that establishes the preconditions of social cooperation by enabling and empowering citizens to participate in social and political life as free and equal persons. Meanwhile, the distribution of the benefits and burdens of the social cooperation that take place between citizens thus empowered is the subject of *distributive justice*, which in Rawls' theory are arranged according to the requirements of the second principle of justice (von Platz 2020b: 98).

I believe that these three interpretations are more closely related to each other than it might seem. First of all, given the fact of pluralism, if it is possible to identify those 'goods' that are so dominant and central to social life (at least in a modern and complex society) that no person must be deprived of them to enable the pursuit of her particular plan of life, whatever it might be, it is so only because what make them dominant and central is the very existence of primary rules. I hope that this fundamental aspect has already emerged clearly from the discussion in previous chapters. Indeed, we have seen that an individual's actions, choices and ideas are not only influenced but also *partially* formed by the way primary rules are set. Furthermore, we have already seen that there is a strict interplay between the distribution of individual power resources and primary rules. It is the latter that determines a certain asymmetrical distribution of power resources and, in turn, only through these power resources can individuals establish, shape or stabilise those primary rules. Therefore, the first and the second interpretation are strictly linked. Far from taking a deterministic position, what we need to ensure is that people should reasonably consider themselves co-authors of primary rules. In this way, along with avoiding systematic and arbitrary violence and coercion, the primary rules are able to avoid that individuals do not run the risk of being dominated. From this perspective, as demonstrated in Chapter 1, the third interpretation can be misleading. Under a political conception of distributive justice, the requirements of the second principle of justice should be conceived to enable and empower citizens to participate in social and political life as free and equal persons, just as much as those of requirements of the first principle. In other words, if the second principle of justice, under the special conception, concerns the distribution of primary goods as income and wealth (and powers and opportunity insofar as sufficiently correlated to them, Rawls 1971: 97), it should prescribe a distribution of these primary goods that allows citizens to be co-author of the primary rules.

Here, I will not enter into the debate on whether Rawls' primary goods are all those 'goods' we need to ensure the background requisites of a political conception of distributive justice. We can discover that some of them can be replaced or excluded, or something else should be included. Neither can I provide here a complete list of these 'goods.' However, two fundamental things can be said about the nature of these 'goods.' First of all, once we have realised that, under subjective and objective circumstances, a just distribution should be assessed by taking into account the fundamental question of whether people have the power to be co-authors of the primary rules, the 'goods' should be understood as power resources. Secondly, a political conception of distributive justice does not concern all kinds of individual power resources, but only those resources that are indispensable to establish and shape primary rules. I call them key power resources insofar they are 'socially generalisable' (in a certain type of society) and for which their asymmetrical 'distribution' can be a subject of mutual and public claim. Moreover, I believe that it is possible to identify some categories of power resources that, with a certain degree of generalisability, are essential to establish and shape primary rules of every complex society: political power, epistemic power, symbolic power (or status power), authority power (or power of official positions), and material power. In my view, a political conception of distributive justice is satisfied only if social actors are not 'relatively' disempowered by those key power resources to establish, shape and stabilise primary rules that govern the social relations in which they are involved. Thus, all of the key power resources should be distributed according to what I call the approach of proportional justice. In this sense, in my view, a political conception of distributive justice takes the specific form of proportional justice.

However, unfortunately here I do not have the space and time to focus on each of these key power resources. This book concerns the distribution of material power that (at least, in the contemporary liberal democratic societies) corresponds to economic resources in terms of income and wealth. For the topic of this chapter, it is fundamental to keep in mind that a political conception of distributive justice does not treat income and wealth as resources that citizens simply want to pursue their life plans and their comprehensive doctrines, but rather as a key power resource that allows citizens to be co-authors of primary rules. From this perspective, we can find a strategy to reconcile what Young (1990) and, more recently, Forst (2014) call the two pictures of justice: distributivist and relational conceptions of justice.

I believe that Rawls' theory contains, and seeks to integrate, these two different conceptions. And I think that we must still try to follow and realise his intuition. Unfortunately, the current debate has gone in the opposite direction, making these two conceptions increasingly incompatible and divergent. Moreover, this contraposition has the effect to heighten the division of labour between the two principles of justice in Rawls' theory, in which usually the distributivist accounts are thought to address the requirements of the second principle, while the relational account those of the first principle. On the contrary, I sustain that when the object of justice is the primary rules, both distributivist and relational conceptions of justice taken alone (at least as they are very often presented in the debate) are not able to provide a compelling view. Very briefly, the problems concerning the two conceptions are the following.

On the one hand, the distributivist conception of justice adopts a distribution-centred and a recipient-oriented point of view, and thus the basic question is what 'goods' you have. It means that it identifies distributive justice in terms of subjective or putatively objective states of the provision of goods or well-being (Forst 2014: 20). The main shortcoming is that it tends to overlook the relevance of the question of power, and in this way, it cannot detect the dimension of social injustice as domination. To catch the point, we can see how the distributivist conceptions judge these two different cases: one in which someone suffers deprivations as a result of a natural disaster or a car accident and another in which the same deprivation is a result of an economic and political scheme.[3] For a distributivist conception of justice, individual deprivation in the case of a natural disaster or car accident and in that of economic and political schemes are equivalent.[4] As a result of this moral view, individuals are understood as passive recipients of goods, rather than as active subjects of justice. The distributivist conceptions see justice as redress: individuals are considered as subjects of justice because they lack something and the others (presumed the most affluent and powerful) have the duty to compensate them. But this means that a moral view as such misses the 'political' point of distributive justice (Forst 2014: 20, see also Chapter 1, Section 1.1).

On the other hand, the relational conception of justice focuses on how people are treated in terms of intersubjective relations rather than in terms of what people have. In this case, the moral point of view is not the subjective or putatively objective states of the provision of goods or of well-being, but depends on the nature of our social and political relations of these states of affairs and people's conditions (Forst 2014).[5] Thus, from this perspective, the 'political' point of distributive justice is the central issue. Relational theorists usually focus on the arbitrariness of certain difference in social and political status, 'like those stigmatizing differences in status, whereby the badly-off are caused to experience themselves as inferior, and are treated as inferiors, or when inequalities create objectionable relations of power' (Gosepath 2021: 13). Yet it is not clear what the relational approach itself requires in distributive terms. It is not surprising, given that this view is often presented as a genuine alternative to the distributive justice paradigm (Scheffler 2015). However, this contraposition can be misleading after distributive justice is understood in the broad sense as presented in this chapter. Indeed, the relational conceptions of justice also need to prescribe that a political society should assign or distribute some kinds of 'goods', like political rights, basic liberties, access to public offices, basic needs and so on.

Therefore, the real difference with the distributive camp explicitly concerns a relative disinterest in predetermined and well-defined (re)distributive criteria or principles of justice and, partially as a consequence, a scant attention to the size of economic inequality. Exemplary is the case of Habermas (1990: 94; 1995: 131), who believes that political philosophy should focus exclusively on the procedural aspects of the public use of reason and deriving the system of rights from the idea of its legal institutionalisation, and thus leaving the substantive questions open; for example, what Rawls' two principles of justice are concerned with. In this sense, there is a strong tendency in the field of relational conception of justice to deal only with the requirements of the first principle of justice, or 'political justice'. For this view, it seems that the normative autonomy of political justice and the test of the acceptability of a political conception of justice presented as *freestanding* can be ensured only by watering down the distributive justice that concerns material resources or goods; for instance, the distribution of income and wealth. The argument is grounded on a strong scepticism that there is a uniquely justifiable public criterion or principle of material distribution. In this sense, Rawls' difference principle can be just one among many others, and therefore the choice should be left to public deliberation and confrontation (Salvatore 2004). Curiously, this normative position is also shared by some libertarians (Gaus 2011; Vallier 2014; Shoelandt and Gaus 2018) who sustain that, given the fact of pluralism which includes also those citizens with inegalitarian moral commitments (albeit reasonable), a robust egalitarian distributive principle, like the difference principle, should be abandoned.[6] Even those relational egalitarian scholars (Fraser 2010; Forst 2012, 2014; Scheffler 2015) who are less reluctant about material distribution, provide normative requirements that remain quite indeterminate and they (willingly) do not include any well-defined pattern of distribution.[7] Here, the most serious problem is that innumerable distributive schemes seem to be compatible with the relational conception of justice (in all these different versions), but also including those allowing a potentially unlimited economic inequality.

Now, is this permissive attitude towards the size of inequality justified within relational approaches? No, it cannot be. They can avoid saying a 'definite' word about the normative pattern of material distribution, only if two assumptions are proved. First of all, they should prove that all types of material goods only concern the means of pursuing a particular plan of life from which a political conception of distributive justice should remain silent. But, certainly, it is not true in the case of economic resources in the form of income and wealth, which are also means to allow citizens to influence and control politics, public agendas and cultural hegemony. And this material power, given the competitive and relational nature of economic and political dimensions, depends not so much on what one has, but *on how much more one has compared to others*. Alternatively, they should prove that, although economic resources matter for political and 'enabled' justice, economic inequality is no longer problematic once the insulation strategy is implemented. Also in this case, I have argued enough about the insufficiency of the insulation strategy. Therefore, the worst-off in a society could and should reasonably reject social arrangements that leave them so *distant* from the best-off's shares of economic resources that they risk domination.[8] A relational and political conception of justice cannot disregard this normative requirement. This means that we should reject all those distributive principles of justice that allow, in principle, an unlimited gap in income and wealth between the best-off and worst-off. Hence, if not Rawls' difference principle or other competitive distributive principles, then we have, at least, a well-defined pattern of material distribution that can be justified from a *freestanding* point of view and can be included, along with other things, in a political conception of distributive justice. It is what I call the distributive principle of proportionality, understood as a commitment to set a (relational) limit on economic inequality between the best-off and the worst-off.

To conclude, to say that the distributive principle of proportionality is presented as *freestanding* also means that it is able to offer a reason to reduce economic inequality that avoids the famous levelling-down objection. According to the most famous formulation, 'the objection appeals to cases where, if some inequality were removed, that would be worse for some people and better for no one' (Parfit 2000: 110).

In other words, in order to consider the removal or reduction of some inequality as an improvement, it should be 'better' in some respect, at least, for someone. This objection seems to be particularly challenged for those, like me, who sustain that the size of inequality between people matters. To draw a clear picture of what is at stake here, see three different socioeconomic distributions.

Here for simplicity, and because it is what matters from my point of view, I take into account only the relative inequality between the best-off and the worst-off.[9] Hence, in (A) we have perfect equality, in (B) we have an inequality ratio of 1:2, while in (C) it is double 1:4. If we move from (C) to (B), and even more from (C) to (A) nobody seems to gain an improvement of this reduction of inequality, and the only value at stake is to pursue a less unequal state of affairs. Although I believe that we have compelling reasons to justify 'levelling-down' outcomes, I think that, in a pluralistic society, the levelling-down objection should be taken seriously. Therefore, I sustain that we should offer a normative reason to reduce the size of material inequality that (1) is compatible with the reasonable pluralism, (2) the proposed alternative distribution should improve the condition of some members of the society (a person-affecting conception), (3) the loss of wealth suffered by some should not be more than what is strictly necessary for the desired improvement.

From this perspective, the distributive principle of proportionality satisfies not only the first condition, insofar as it is grounded on a *freestanding* justification, but also the second and third conditions. Let us assume by hypothesis that it is required to move from (C) to (B) in case the ratio 1:2 is considered a reasonable formula to avoid the risk of material domination. First, in (B) the worst-off would see their conditions improved as they enjoy a fairly equal political and economic influence and power with respect to others. Second, if in (B) the worst-off would not incur in the risk of material domination, the principle of proportionality does not require a reduction in economic inequality any more than is strictly necessary to avoid this risk. Therefore, we do not have reasons to pursue (A) or a less unequal material distribution than the permissible ratio in (B).

In the current debate there is an extensive discussion about the nature of the reasons we have to reduce inequality. It is possible to identify three main reasons: intrinsic, instrumental and constitutive (Gosepath 2021: 15). Parfit considers the levelling-down objection devastating for an intrinsic concern for equality, because the objection is the proof that inequality is not always bad. He labels the view that considers equality intrinsic good and inequality intrinsic bad telic egalitarianism. As a result, Parfit infers that the only reason to eliminate or reduce inequality between

TABLE 3.1 Equality and the Levelling Down Objection

Socioeconomic distributions	*Worst-off*	*Lower-middle class*	*Upper-middle class*	*Best-off*	*Ratio*
A			All citizens at 10		1:1
B	15	20	25	30	1:2
C	20	50	60	80	1:4

people, in some respects, is because 'equality has many kinds of good effects, and inequality many kinds of bad effects' (Parfit 2000: 86). In other words, we value equality or disvalue inequality for non-intrinsic or instrumental reasons; namely, the badness or injustice of inequality has to do with its consequences or effects on people. In these terms, according to Parfit's definition, deontological egalitarianism also endorses a non-intrinsic or instrumental view because it aims for equality, not to make the outcome better, but insofar as inequality involves a violation of some deontic constraint (on this point, see Hirose 2015: 64–65). In the last two decades, Parfit's view has greatly influenced the egalitarian debate and the literature on distributive justice in general. Nonetheless, Parfit's view is (albeit involuntary) misleading regarding this distinction. From his view, it seems that we have only two options: one in which we believe that inequality matters, morally speaking, *per se regardless of its* effects on people, and another in which inequality matters only for a non-intrinsic reason as synonymous with instrumental ones. But this distinction is incomplete.

First of all, when we are moved to find reasons to authorise actions to pursue a certain state of affairs or achieve a certain outcome, it is quite trivial to say that these reasons are grounded on a person-affecting conception.[10] Secondly, it is not true that deontological conceptions of justice are inevitably instrumental views. For example, we can be aligned with constitutive egalitarianism (Gosepath 2021: 15). This means that we can attribute 'intrinsic' value to equality in the sense, for example, that equality together with other moral values or ideas (for instance, freedom) is constitutive to the conception of justice. Thus, 'equality stands in relation to justice as does a part to a whole' (Gosepath 2021: 16). In this case, equality is 'intrinsic' as opposed to a simply instrumental notion. This means that certain inequalities can be considered unjust if, and only if, we take into account the difference between what some have and what others have. Moreover, in order to advocate an 'intrinsic' as 'constitutive' concern for inequality, we do not need to be egalitarians in *stricto sensu*. We might be agnostic regarding the place, if any, that the value of equality occupies in our conception of justice that is grounded, alternatively, on autonomy, dignity or respect. Similarly, the principle of proportionality spells out a 'constitutive' (person-affecting) concern for material inequality. Indeed, given that the risk of material domination depends on economic resources that one has with respect to others, the economic inequality is an 'intrinsic' constitutive dimension of this risk. Therefore, the principle of proportionality embodies a constitutive reason to reduce material inequality.[11] In this way, finally, we can further distinguish constitutive reasons from instrumental reasons to object to inequality among people in the sense that the latter are simply 'contingent' reasons to enact it; for example, the negative effects inequality has on the health of those who have less. These instrumental reasons do not take inequality to be a constitutive and inherent dimension of their evaluations.[12]

At this point, in the following sections, I can take into account the most important distributive principles of justice to prove that they do not adequately deal with the size of economic inequality. However, a clarification is needed first. In the current debate, the question about the patterned principle of distribution usually comes at the end of some other fundamental questions. Beyond the fundamental question that is the centre of my discussion up to this point – *why* does inequality matter? – in the current debate, philosophers try to answer other relevant questions:[13] 1) inequality *between whom*? Whether between all human beings, groups, individuals involved in a social relation of a certain kind, politically unified societies, future generations, or even between different species; 2) Inequality of '*what*' (the currency)? Or, in other words, what 'good' or set of 'goods' should be distributed? For example, in Rawls' theory, these goods are those that make up the index of primary goods; 3) How to *measure* (the metric) this 'what'? Or in other words, the question of the metric of distributive justice, whether welfare, resource, primary good, or capability. Indeed, we might agree about the set of 'goods' that justice requires to be distributed and, at the same time, we can disagree about how to measure them. For example, Rawls' metric for social primary goods is an objective and impersonal resource-based account; i.e. primary goods are only considered as objectively indispensable means that allow individuals to pursue (or 'access') their ends, regardless of their individual preferences and tastes, characteristics, or whether they are successful in achieving their ends. Other accounts, alternatively, are sensitive to individuals' preferences and tastes (Classical welfarism) or individuals' characteristics that are beyond the individuals' controls (Dworkin's resourcism) or individuals' achievements of an objective list of valuable and basic 'functionings' (Sen's capability approach);[14] 4) Finally, according to which *patterned principles* should this 'what' be distributed? Whether according to Rawls' difference principle, prioritarian principle, sufficientarian principle, or Robeyns' limitarian principle. Again, we may agree on the answer to all previous questions, and nonetheless disagree about the most appropriate distributive principle of justice, and *vice versa*. Thus, it is possible to argue about the question of distributive principles independent of different accounts of the subjects, the currency, or the metric of justice. For this reason, in the next sections, I will focus on the debate about the choice of material distributive principles (or *patterned principles*), regardless of any eventual disagreements about the other previous three questions.

However, in order to avoid any misleading interpretations and easy objections, it is necessary to very briefly say something about them. I believe that, also in this case, we should be guided by the scope and object of our investigation; in my case, the normative framework of a political conception of distributive justice. Therefore, and 1) regarding inequality *between whom*, given that, as I said, we can identify a politically unified society as a specific context of primary rules (like a state or a federation of states), the ultimate subject of the principle of proportionality are all individuals who live under domestic primary rules. Moreover, a political conception of distributive justice should take into account only those 'goods' (the currency), and opt for a measurement of these goods (the metric), that can be justified from a *freestanding* view; that is, it cannot be grounded on particular comprehensive or perfectionistic doctrine or a particular plan of life. This means that, 2) regarding inequality of '*what*', these 'goods' should be the key power resources that function as objectively indispensable means to allow citizens to establish, shape and stabilise primary rules. Material resources in terms of income and wealth are one of them. In addition, I have already explained why we cannot conceive the notion of power in terms of achievement (Chapter 2, Section 2.3). Hence, and 3) regarding how to measure this 'what', key power resources should be measured, like Rawls' primary goods, by an objective and impersonal resource-based account. Once these clarifications have been made, we can move forward.

3.2 Rawls' Difference Principle

I believe that there are, at least, three main reasons to still consider Rawls' *Justice as fairness* (Rawls 1971, 2001, 2005) the broad paradigm to follow in elaborating the distributive principles of justice. First of all, Rawls introduced the contemporary view that the idea of social justice also consists of some forms of substantive egalitarianism insofar as material inequality between people always requires a 'special' justification to those who might not benefit (or be damaged) by it. Secondly, in Rawls' *Justice as fairness* equal weight is given to both distributive and relational conceptions of justice by combining the two. Indeed, although in his theory social justice is relational in its nature, a certain distribution of resources (material and not) is taken as 'constitutive' to it. Contrary to those philosophers who seem to give priority to one or the other conception, I think that this is the correct way to proceed. Third, Rawls' justice as fairness is conceived by the same scope and object that I have already defined. It applies to what Rawls calls the basic structure (or, in my terms, the primary rules) of a democratic and pluralistic society. In doing so, social justice does not concern all kinds of inequalities between citizens, rather only those that might affect the adequate development and exercise of the two moral powers of democratic citizenship: a capacity for a sense of justice and for a conception of the good.[15] These two powers are associated with the idea of society as a fair system of cooperation. Cooperation is guided by publicly recognised rules and procedures that those who cooperate can reasonably accept; therefore, cooperation involves the idea of fair terms of cooperation which specify an idea of reciprocity (Rawls 2005: 16). Thus, according to the idea of reciprocity, the terms of distribution of the benefits and burdens of social cooperation must allow only reciprocal advantages. But, what would be the distributive principles that apply to the basic structure?

Rawls defines egalitarianism as democratic equality (or democratic citizenship), and it is the result of the two principles of justice (ordered lexicographically) chosen by the parties placed in the original position and behind the veil of ignorance. The two principles of justice establish how the basic structure of society must fairly distribute an index of primary social goods which is composed of rights, liberties, powers and opportunities, income and wealth, and the social bases of self-respect.

More precisely, the first principle concerns the just distribution of basic liberties and rights:

a. Each person has the same indefeasible claim to a fully adequate scheme of equal basic liberties, which scheme is compatible with the same scheme

> of liberties for all; and in this scheme the equal political liberties, and only those liberties, are to be guaranteed their fair value.
>
> (Rawls 2005: 5)

Instead, the second principle establishes the permissible social and economic inequalities.

> b. Social and economic inequalities are to satisfy two conditions: first, they are to be attached to offices and positions open to all under conditions of fair equality of opportunity; and second, they are to be to the greatest benefit of the least-advantaged members of society.
>
> (Rawls 2005: 6)[16]

The second principle of justice is composed of two parts. The first part is what Rawls calls the "fair equality of opportunity" (or FEO), and the second is called "the difference principle". The point is, how exactly can we identify the least favoured, and how can we measure the benefit that socioeconomic inequalities must bring to them. To solve this problem, Rawls introduces the 'special conception', an alternative to the general conception in which the difference principle is applied to all primary goods including liberty and opportunity, with no lexical constraints. According to the special conception, the greatest benefit to the least advantaged is identified in the following manner:

> In a well-ordered society where all citizens' equal basic rights and liberties and fair opportunities are secure, the least advantaged are those belonging to the income class with the lowest expectations. To say that inequalities in income and wealth are to be arranged for the greatest benefit of the least advantaged simply means that we are to compare schemes of cooperation by seeing how well off the least advantaged are under each scheme, and then to select the which the least advantaged are better off than they are under any other scheme.
>
> (Rawls 2001: 59–60)

From this perspective, we are authorised to understand the difference principle as a distributive principle of justice that focuses on income and wealth distribution. However, two premises need to be made. First of all, we do not have to commit the mistake of thinking that the difference principle is the main, or the only, distributive principle in Rawls' theory of justice. I agree with Daniels (2003: 245, 248–249) and von Platz (2020a: 7, note 6) that what Rawls defines as democratic equality requires reference to all parts of the two principles of justice taken as a whole, even if lexicographically ordered. In this sense, for example, the first principle is also a distributive principle of justice, but one that explicitly focuses on the 'distribution' of basic liberties and rights, and also has indirect and derivative implications on socioeconomic distribution. However, in Rawls' theory of justice is the difference principle (under the special conception) that concerns income and wealth distribution. Thus, it is legitimate to evaluate whether the difference principle is itself sensible to the size of economic inequality. Secondly, even if Rawls (2001: 64) uses the idea of maximising the expectations of the least advantaged, the difference principle is essentially a relational principle of justice grounded on the idea of reciprocity. This means that it does not matter how well off the least advantaged are. They might be very affluent but the difference principle still requires them to justify economic inequality between themselves and the others. On the one hand, the difference principle (under the special conception) provides a specific distributive pattern to establish when the absolute share of the worst-off makes wealth and income inequality permissible; that is, when any deviation from the line of perfect equality maximises, under any feasible alternative, their absolute share of income and wealth. According to Rawls, if permissible economic inequality does not realise this 'maximisation', it represents a violation of the idea of reciprocity because it allows the best-off to benefit at the expense of others. From this perspective, the difference principle embodies a strong commitment to equality. On the other hand, the distributive pattern that the difference principle prescribes is insensible to the size of inequality between the least advantaged and the most advantaged. Therefore, the difference principle is a relational criterion based on the idea of reciprocity but it is not a 'comparative' one.[17] Allow me to reveal how it works.

Rawls' default position is perfect equality. It means that the difference principle permits movement from the line of perfect equality in economic resources if, and only if, the consequent inequality maximises the economic condition of the least advantaged (Rawls 1971: 78; 2001: 59–60; 2005: 6). In this sense, the difference principle is guided by the maximin rule (Rawls 1971: 152–153; 2001: 94–97). The main implication is that the difference principle, other things being equal, allows both any reduction of economic inequality (the strong commitment to equality) no matter how large, for the sake of a gain for the worst-off group, no matter how small, and any increase of inequality in return for small gains to the less favoured (Hirose 2015: 26).[18]

Now imagine the previous socioeconomic distributions to which we add (D):

TABLE 3.2 Difference Principle and the Priority Over Efficiency[a]

Socioeconomic distributions	*Worst-off*	*Lower-middle class*	*Upper-middle class*	*Best-off*	*Ratio*
A			All citizens at 10		1:1
B	15	20	25	30	1:2
C	20	50	60	80	1:4
D	18	55	65	144	1:8

[a] Keeping in mind Rawls' figures (1971: 76–77), it means that the distribution in (c) corresponds to the highest point on the curve OP which represents the maximisation of x2's (least advantaged) economic expectations; meanwhile the distribution in (d) is the point on the curve OP in which the expectations of x1 no longer improve x2's expectations, and on the contrary reduces it.

If these are the options, things are quite easy. The worst-off would welcome the move from (A) to (B), and to (C), but they will veto (D), because they know that a more favourable distribution is possible, no matter how large the loss for individuals in the non-worst-off groups is. But let us assume that, given the introduction of an efficient innovation, the following distribution is possible:

In the maximin logic that underpins the difference principle, other things being equal, it would be unreasonable to reject (E). Even when moving from (C) to (E) the gap between the worst-off and best-off has increased from an inequality ratio of 1:4 to 1:10. The same is true in case of a further increase of inequality towards (F) in which the ratio is 1:20.

The moral of the story is that the size of economic inequality between the best-off and worst-off, through the lenses of the difference principle (under the special conception), does not matter. The reason to reject (D) is due to the violation of the idea of reciprocity, rather than the magnitude of the ratio. Rawls himself confirms this normative point,

> the difference principle specifies no definite limits within which the ratio of the shares of the more and less advantaged is to fall. [In addition,] we should leave this ratio to fall where it may, as the outcome of pure background procedural justice. This is perfectly acceptable unless, on due reflection, the actual ratio strikes us as unjust.
>
> (Rawls 2001: 68)

The problem is, as Rawls admits, that within justice as fairness:

TABLE 3.3 Difference Principle and the Maximin Rule[a]

Socioeconomic distributions	*Worst-off*	*Lower-middle class*	*Upper-middle class*	*Best-off*	*Ratio*
E	22	60	70	220	1:10

[a] Now, the curve OP starts growing again until it reaches the highest point that corresponds with the distribution in (E). Here, the difference principle is presented, as Rawls prefers, in the simpler form; that is, it is blind to the gains and losses for the non-worst-off people insofar as none of them becomes the worst-off. This means that it would be judged as the same (E) 22; 60, 70, 220 and an alternative possible distribution (E') 22, 80, 90, 100. However, in order to lead with this case, Rawls (1971: 83) permits a leximin interpretation according to which we should pursue and prefer (E') because by taking the level of the worst-off as equal, it maximises the level of the second worst-off (and so on until the last person or group).

TABLE 3.4 Difference Principle and the Size of Inequality

Socioeconomic distributions	*Worst-off*	*Lower-middle class*	*Upper-middle class*	*Best-off*	*Ratio*
F	24	80	90	480	1:20

> we do not have any further criterion to judge whether the ratio is unjust, for all our principles are met. It is simply that the actual ratio may disturb us and make us wonder. It is as if a state of reflective equilibrium is a bit upset.
>
> (Rawls 2001: 68, note 36)

Obviously, this passing appeal to an unjust ratio that conflicts with our intuitions comes close to a declaration of surrender, given that Rawls is aware (2001: 68) that 'it seems impossible to specify plausible limits on this ratio that can gain wide assent'. Nonetheless, things are more complex if we take into account that under the special conception we can implement the difference principle only after both the first principle and fair equality of opportunity are satisfied. In other words, the background procedural justice might impose limits on the magnitude of economic inequalities. Many commentators of Rawls[19] look mainly at two elements: a) the idea of the fair value of political liberties and b) the constraints to which the institutional background is subject for the sake of compatibility with the two principles of justice.[20] Let me examine each of them briefly.

Rawls introduced the distinction between liberty and the worth (or value) of liberty in *A Theory of Justice* (1971: 201–205), a distinction that gained centrality in his following works. In *A Theory*, Rawls is aware that 'the worth of liberty to persons and groups is *proportional* to their capacity to advance their ends' (Rawls 1971: 204, italic my emphasis). Therefore, he admits that freedom as equal liberty is the same for all while the worth of liberty is not the same for everyone. In *A Theory*, Rawls assumes that the worth of liberty depends on the level of resources available to a person, therefore, given that under the special conception in which income and wealth 'are sufficiently correlated with those of power and authority' (Rawls 1971: 97), the difference principle is considered a normative criterion to also maximise the worth of liberty (Rawls 1971: 204). But this assumption is not pacific at all.

Daniels (1975) was the first author to detail this problematic aspect, convincingly showing that the 'worth of liberty is especially sensitive to relative differences in the index of primary social goods and is not a simple monotonic function of it' (Daniels 1975: 271). He suggests to Rawls to make explicit that 'since liberty has priority over other social goods, no trade-off can be allowed between [the] worth of liberty and the index of primary goods' (Daniels 1975: 279). However, this second alternative seems to propose a radical solution by refusing to allow any inequalities in wealth and power that can cause inequalities to the realm of liberty. In other words, only material equality might ensure equal worth of liberty. Rawls correctly thinks that it is possible and necessary to accommodate Daniels' consideration, but avoids this radical conclusion. Hence, Rawls (1982: 42–45; 2005: 5) reformulates the first principle of justice as prescribing not only a scheme of equal basic rights and liberties, but also a guarantee of the fair value (notice, not the equal value) of political liberties (and only of those liberties). In other words, it is not sufficient that I have the same political rights as every other citizen. It is also required that *the value* of my political liberties be fair. My share of influence cannot be infinitely less than yours, quite independently of whether we have, on paper, the same political rights.

If that is the case, justice as fairness does not allow inequalities in wealth that make the value of some citizens' political liberties significantly lower than that of others.

However, this provision in the first principle alone does not authorise us to say that the fair value of political liberties could only be guaranteed by limiting wealth and income inequalities. Indeed, as we have already seen in Chapter 1, very few philosophers deny that excessive economic inequalities upset political equality, but state that, in theory and in principle, we cannot also deny that the fair value of political liberties can be ensured by the insulation strategy. Hence, if the simple provision of the fair value of political liberties is not sufficient, Rawls needs to prescribe something more solid and specific. Here the constraints of the institutional background seem to play their main normative role.

Although Rawls was not explicit in considering the insulation strategy insufficient to guarantee the fair value of political liberties, he (Rawls 1971: 225–226) seems to rely much more on certain forms of background institutions to avoid excessive economic inequality and, above all, the concentration of wealth in private hands. In *Justice as Fairness: A Restatement* (2001), Rawls expressly specifies the kinds of social systems that are compatible with the two principles of justice. Famously, these are property-owning democracy and liberal (democratic) socialism (Rawls 2001: 136). Only these two institutional settings, we learn, do not permit very large inequalities in the ownership of real property (productive assets and natural resources) and thus avoid the risk that few wealthy people control the economy and, with it, much of political life (Rawls 2001: 137–138).

Unfortunately, the constraints of the institutional background does not also offer us a fully satisfactory solution. What if institutional settings are different (and more unequal) than property-owning democracy or liberal socialism – for example, welfare-state capitalism – guaranteeing higher absolute shares of income and wealth for the worst-off? We should recall that Rawls assesses his five ideal models of social systems by taking the two principles of justice as a benchmark, and not *vice versa*. Rawls is clear about the importance of thinking about justice on the basis of principles. Thus, we need some normative prescriptions on the two principles of justice, and in particular on the difference principle, to expressly sanction the size of economic inequality when it is considered excessive. Otherwise, we have a clear conflict between the two principles of justice and the normative prescriptions about regimes and economic distributions. We should either abandon the difference principle's formulation under the special conception or give up our preference for institutions that limit excessive material inequality.

To conclude, I think that we have two options. First of all, given that for Rawls the only way to ensure the fair value of political liberties is to avoid excessive economic inequalities, we can say that the difference principle's prescription, according to which social and economic inequalities are to be to the greatest benefit of the least advantaged members of society identified by the level of income and wealth (Rawls 1971: 97; Rawls 2001: 59), is valid only if a certain permissible ratio of economic inequality is not overcome. Although this reading is plausible, it comes with some highly theoretical costs. Indeed, it means downgrading the difference principle to a second-order material distributive principle of justice. If the size of economic inequality between the worst-off and the best-off is what primarily matters, we need a *freestanding* distributive principle that explicitly sanctions this normative assumption; that is, to prescribe limits within which the ratio of the shares of the more and less advantaged should fall. If economic inequalities are so important, Rawls' two principles of justice fail to offer normative guidance as to what is the *fair* ratio between these shares of the worst-off and the best-off. By contrast, the second option is, instead, to take the bull by the horns, and reformulate the difference principle in terms of the principle of proportionality which introduces limits to material inequality between best-off and worst-off.[21] I admit that this understanding can represent a radical (re)interpretation of the difference principle, as Rawls presented it and how it is understood by the vast majority of philosophers. Thus, I leave this possibility open and postpone a plausible defense of this reading for another time.[22]

3.3 Prioritarianism, Moderate Egalitarianism, and Sufficientarianism

As I have said, Rawls introduced the contemporary view that the idea of social justice consists of some forms of substantive egalitarianism insofar as material inequality between people always requires a 'special' justification to those who might not benefit (or be damaged) by it. From this perspective, it seems incumbent to deal with the bottom of distribution, and more precisely with the worst-off. Not surprisingly, in the current debate, thanks to the success of Parfit's article entitled 'Equality or Priority?' (1997), this kind of justification is usually understood as a sort of 'priority' attached to the worst-off's claims or interests. In the literature, the effort was to find an alternative to the difference principle, because it imposes egalitarian obligations of reciprocity among citizens that critics judge as too demanding. Given that the background position is the line of perfect equality, the difference principle has the effect of prescribing that any tiny improvement of the worst-off condition (above that line) can justify a loss of gains for the better-off, no matter how large it would be. As we have already seen, although the difference principle itself is insensitive to the size of inequality, and that it allows, in principle, to move from (E) to (F), it also prescribes to move, other things being equal and if it is feasible, toward (G), for the simple matter of the fact that the worst-off's shares are maximised (but again regardless of the inequality ratio, which in G just accidently decreases).[23]

TABLE 3.5 Difference Principle and the Strong Commitment to Equality

Socioeconomic distributions	*Worst-off*	*Lower-middle class*	*Upper-middle class*	*Best-off*	*Ratio*
G	25	40	60	150	1:6

In the current debate, we can identify three broad families of distributive principles – prioritarianism, moderate egalitarianism, and sufficientarianism – that share the normative requirement with the difference principle to give 'priority' to the worst-off's claims, but also offer an alternative by avoiding that even a tiny improvement for the worst-off can justify a huge loss for the better-off. Although these three broad families differ hugely from each other in many respects, here I am interested in their main common element. Scholars who advocate prioritarianism, moderate egalitarianism, and sufficientarianism dispute Rawls in the specific manner in which the difference principle benefits all participants of the social cooperation. Under the difference principle, no one can say they are not benefiting from distribution. It respects the idea of reciprocal advantages, even if those who are better-off would indeed enjoy more advantages under another material distribution that do not maximise the worst-off's position. But this specific feature leads critics to say that the difference principle does not take the non-worst-off seriously, or that it does not give weight to the concerns of all, because it rules out any kind of trade-off between resources of the worse-off and the better-off.

Therefore, on the one hand, prioritarianism, moderate egalitarianism, and sufficientarianism share the same normative requirement of the difference principle according to which material inequality is objectionable when this translates into an unjustifiable shrinking of the shares destined to the worst-off or the badly-off. But, on the other hand, they are distributive principles that, unlike the difference principle, deny that we are obliged to benefit the worst-off *as much as possible.* Furthermore, this normative consideration can be adopted from both distributivist and relational views. Let me begin with prioritarianism.

The priority view, or generally prioritarianism, can be defined in different ways, but all of them share the normative core with Parfit's definition according to which 'benefiting people matters more the worse off these people are' (Parfit 2000: 101) or 'we have stronger reasons to benefit people the worse off these people are' (Parfit 2012: 401).[24] Parfit's starting point is that inequality is not bad or unjust itself, and therefore we should find a reason different from equality to judge the goodness or rightness of a certain distribution or outcome. According to Parfit, this reason is to improve the condition of the worst-off because they are people who are at a lower *absolute* level, regardless of how worse-off than others. This means that prioritarianism is grounded on two strong assumptions. First of all, it assumes that 'the amount of good certain benefits do for a person should be determined only by the absolute level of his or her own well-being, independently of the well-being of other people' (Hirose 2015: 87). In other words, it is a non-relational and non-comparative distributive principle. It means that no reduction of inequality depends on its size or how people fare relative (or compared) to others. Secondly, it assumes 'the law of diminishing moral goodness' according to which 'if benefits go to people who are better-off, these benefits matter less' (Parfit 2000: 105). These two features together allow prioritarianism to be semi- or decent-utilitarianism. Like utilitarianism, they endorse a non-relational view, and they judge the goodness or the rightness of the entire distribution as a whole (see Segall 2015). But, unlike utilitarianism, it avoids the extreme and implausible consequence of maximising the total sum or average of people's well-being or resources regardless of how badly-off they are. For this reason, they can also be considered non-relational egalitarians or 'decent' inegalitarians. Thus, prioritarianism gives us a reason to reduce material inequality, depending on the trade-off between the gains and the losses of the worst-off and the better-off. In other words, 'a small benefit to one worse-off person can be outweighed by a sufficiently large amount of good enjoyed by a sufficiently large number of better-off people' (Hirose 2011: 103). Many are attracted by prioritarianism specifically for this non-absolute or non-exclusive 'priority' attached to the worst-off or worse-off which avoids a potentially huge loss of efficiency for any small gain in favour of them. However, beyond this appeal, prioritarianism is controversial in many respects, and many might find its strong non-relational point of view implausible (see Hirose 2011, 2015).

However, the priority view is not the only manner in which we can take into account, in some manner, the gains and losses of all individuals determined by a certain distribution. Indeed, this normative requirement can also be advocated from a relational point of view, as is the case with the second family I identify: moderate egalitarianism. For example, we can prescribe a distributive principle as such from a contractualism point of view, such as in Nagel's principle of unanimity (1979) and Scanlon's principle which no one can reasonably reject (1982; 2018). For sure Nagel's and Scanlon's accounts are genuine (Rawlsian inspired) egalitarian theories; however, I define them as moderate egalitarianism to emphasise the main point of divergence with the difference principle; i.e. they reject its strong commitment to equality.

Nagel, unlike Rawls, believes that justice should require the choice of principles to be made with information concerning the probability of enjoying different levels of advantage. This means that his principle of unanimity requires that a certain state of affairs (for example, a material distribution) should be 'least unacceptable to the person to whom it is most unacceptable'. Unlike the prioritarian view, what matters is whether a person is worst-off with respect to others, but, like prioritarianism, it requires comparing the possible gains and losses of two individuals. Therefore, unlike Rawls' difference principle, it allows that a small benefit to one worst-off person can be outweighed by a sufficiently large amount of good enjoyed by a better-off person.[25] However, by taking into account all possible social schemes and material distribution, this kind of calculation can be very difficult or nearly impossible to be fully accomplished.

Scanlon's contractualism seems to agree with Nagel's intuition, but without compromising himself with a complicated calculation of losses and gains among individuals (or groups). Recently, Scanlon (2018) provides many relational reasons to explain why economic inequality can be objectionable. For many of these reasons the size of economic inequality is a constitutive dimension of why it is objectionable; in particular, in cases in which inequality might give the rich unacceptable forms of power over those who have less or undermine the fairness of political institutions. However, he does not derive a distributive patterned principle from these reasons. The only pattern of economic distribution is provided when Scanlon investigates reasons we have to reduce income inequalities that arise from economic institutions that are unfair.[26]

Scanlon (2018: 150) tries to show that in order to be disturbed by the unfairness of the actual increase of the ratios 'between incomes of the rich and of the poor, and between the incomes of workers and top managers in large corporations in the U.S', we do not need to assume the strong egalitarian commitment that Rawls' difference principle implies. On the one hand, like Rawls, he assumes that

> the problem does not lie in the ratios themselves, and that the explanation for why they are troubling does not rest on any particular view of what the ratios should be. The problem lies rather with the lack of justification for the factors that give rise to these disparate income levels.
>
> (Scanlon 2018: 150)

In other words, the problem is not the magnitude of the gap, but the unjustifiable manner in which the gap was created (see Scanlon 2018: 138, note 9). On the other hand, unlike Rawls, we do not need to think that any level of economic inequality is unjust unless it results in the maximisation of the economic condition of the worst-off. He also wants to avoid the strong egalitarian commitment of the difference principle. Thus, he provides a weak criterion according to which 'justifiable inequalities must either be unavoidable consequences of the exercise of important personal liberties or result from features of the economic system that are required in order for it to function in a way that benefits all' (Scanlon 2018: 151). This means that in order to condemn inequality, we need to prove that economic institutions are set up in a way to only benefit the rich, or better, that they exclude the worst-off from the benefits. Indeed, in the last three decades, the increasing economic inequality in the USA has followed this line exactly (see Wolff 2017). Therefore, we have strong reasons to change the economic institutions in the USA in order to also benefit other groups at the bottom of distribution, but it is not necessary to benefit them *as much as possible*. Economic institutions that benefit all are fair, but Scanlon does not provide an argument to establish how much the benefit for the worst-off should be. Thus, he does not compromise himself with a calculation of the gains and losses of individuals or social groups in two or more alternative distributions. Of course, Scanlon is aware that this 'standard of justifiability' is rather weak and that virtually any level of inequality may end up being justified. He therefore adds a further argument, according to which inequality must be reduced if 'there are other ways of achieving the same productive advantages while distributing the benefits more equally' (Scanlon 2018: 151), something that aims to resemble the difference principle commitment to inequality.[27]

The third broad family that attaches certain forms of 'priority' consideration to the worst-off is sufficientarianism (broadly understood). But, unlike Rawls' difference principle, prioritarianism and moderate egalitarianism, this view sustains that we should give priority to benefiting those who are badly-off: people whose resources (or well-being) is below a certain threshold level. Therefore, sufficientarian accounts have in common the normative idea that there is a threshold that demarcates a 'shift in our reasons to benefit people once they have secured enough' (Shields 2012: 102). A threshold of the level of 'goods' that everyone should reach. Sufficientarianism is usually taken as an exemplary case of the distributive view that explicitly proposes this threshold.[28] In addition, a sufficientarian account can deploy a single threshold or multiple thresholds, and in the latter case they can be vertical or horizontal.

> Vertical threshold views define three or more ranges on one continuum by positing two or more thresholds. [...] Alternatively, horizontal threshold views specify a threshold for different distributable goods, essentially combining different continua and positing one or more thresholds in two or more of those continua.
>
> (Timmer 2021a: 425–426)

However, it is fundamental for my investigation to keep in mind that what really characterises this family is the normative significance of the threshold (single or multiple). This means that the threshold itself is paramount. Recently, Timmer (2021a) developed an account of the concept of thresholds in distributive justice. In general terms, in a continuum of levels of a distributable 'good' that signals how much someone has of that distributable 'good', a threshold establishes a certain level that everyone should reach (or not overcome, in the case of limitarianism). Therefore, 'this threshold demarcates two ranges of levels. The first range contains the level of the threshold itself and all levels above the threshold. The second range contains all levels below the threshold' (Timmer 2021a: 425). For this reason, all sufficientarian accounts assume some form of 'positive thesis' that bringing people above some threshold is especially important or it has absolute priority over others' distributive claims.[29] However, if sufficientarianism wants to be a candidate, and compete with other distributive principles, for providing the foundation for a full-fledged theory of distributive justice, it must say something regarding the both sides (or ranges) of the threshold: below and above. Not all accounts have this kind of ambition.[30] Hence, I will focus only on those sufficientarian accounts aiming to say something about the entire distribution.

To satisfy this ambition, sufficientarianism usually comes with both the positive thesis and the negative thesis. Harry Frankfurt (1987, 1997, 2015) is considered the first author to explicitly put forward a version of sufficientarianism. He frames the negative thesis in these straightforward terms: 'if everyone had enough, it would be of no moral consequence whether one had more than others' (Frankfurt 1987: 21). It is not surprising that the negative thesis is the main target of the objections moved against sufficientarianism. Indeed, if the positive thesis might be relatively non-controversial, because most philosophers (and most common people) think that all citizens should be above a certain threshold of decency, the negative thesis is less intuitive.

As Casal (2007) resumes the point, why should one start from the default position that the inequality between the super-rich and those just above the threshold is normatively irrelevant? This is known as the indifference objection. Note that, unlike my specific focus here, this objection very rarely regards the size of the inequality, but, rather, the fact that above the threshold no justification for inequality is required. This normative prescription is considered implausible. Sufficientarian accounts should prove that there is something very special in being sufficiently well-off (or very well-off?) that makes people indifferent to the further distribution of goods. A *prime facie* answer would be that inequality between people above the threshold will be only trivial, like in the famous example of a fine bottle of wine provided by Crisp (2003). But this means that the threshold of sufficiency is posed extremely high. Thus, the first dilemma is about where to collocate a single threshold to deploy, at the same time, this twofold normative claim: both positive and negative theses. Indeed, a very high threshold risks underestimating the objective importance to bring as many people as possible above (or as close to) a certain threshold; meanwhile a very low threshold has the opposite effect of being blind to the rest of the distribution, which is almost the totality (Casal 2007; Huseby 2010, 2020). In the current debate, those who advocate sufficientarianism have made a great effort to answer the indifference objection. Three strategies can be identified: a) vertical multiple thresholds; b) positive shift-thesis, c) horizontal multiple thresholds.

a. Sufficientarians who admit that a single threshold is not able to accommodate both the positive and negative theses; they might maintain a single currency of distribution but opt for multiple thresholds in a way that identifies the lowest threshold with the positive thesis and the highest with the negative thesis, with the possibility to introduce middle thresholds too.[31] Then, they might adopt a sort of lexical prioritarianism within each of the ranges between multiple thresholds. The problem with this solution is that multiple, vertical threshold sufficientarianism does not seem to differ, in practice, with weight prioritarianism. In addition, they have the great difficulty to justify the moral relevance of each of these thresholds. Finally, it does not matter the distance between the lowest and the highest thresholds.
b. In an alternative scenario, sufficientarians might endorse Shields' shift-sufficientarianism (2012; 2016). Shields fully rejects the negative thesis, and in exchange he proposes to combine a non-absolute-priority interpretation of positive thesis with his shift thesis. According to him, '*The Positive Thesis:* We have weighty non-instrumental reasons to secure at least enough of some good(s). *The Shift Thesis:* Once people have secured enough there is a discontinuity in the rate of change of the marginal weight of our reasons to benefit them further' (Shields 2016: 34–35).[32] Although Shields' sufficientarianism is able to avoid the indifference objection, this success comes with a high price. Indeed, while Shields' proposal renders the sufficiency view more plausible and compatible with many others distributive views, he simply admits that in order to lead with the distribution above the threshold we must abdicate from

a sufficientarian reasoning and opt for an alternative distributive principle (for instance, some versions of prioritarianism for the negative thesis).

c. Finally, sufficientarians might opt for a multiple, horizontal thresholds approach in which there are multiple currencies that it is important to have enough of, but with only one threshold per currency. Axelsen and Nielsen (2015; 2017; and Nielsen 2018, 2019) propose this account.[33] Distinguishing different currencies allows them to maintain the negative thesis only for those currencies that are non-positional, while they reformulate the negative thesis in relational terms for those currencies that are positional; that is, goods whose value depends precisely on how much of them individuals have compared to others. For example, education, political and social statuses are regarded as the paradigm for positional goods because the competitive value of my education, my political influence, or of my access to social life depends on how well educated or politically and socially influential other people are; while health is usually considered a non-positional good.[34] This sufficientarian account is particularly interesting for my discussion because it admits that the size of inequality between the best-off and the worst-off matters, at least in some cases.

Axelsen and Nielsen (2015) define their sufficientarian account as 'freedom from duress'. According to them, 'freedom from duress entails freeing people from significant pressure in certain central areas of human life, while others are to be considered beyond the scope of justice' (2015: 407).[35] They acknowledge that some of these areas are characterised by positional goods. For example, they note that 'wealth allows one to obtain greater political influence, status, and enormous market advantages with respect to access to good health, education, and security, while poverty creates great obstacles to obtaining these functionings' (2015: 423). However, they maintain that it is not inequality itself that creates the problem, only that inequality might create a specific type of absolute insufficiency or deficiency: social deprivation. In this way they are able to avoid the indifference objection, at least for positional goods.

The normative aim is to take into account the question of inequalities but with the grammar of sufficiency. Hence, they distinguish between absolute non-comparative insufficiencies and absolute social insufficiencies (Axelsen and Nielsen 2015, 2017). More precisely, Nielsen (2018, 2019) defines the latter as social norm-bound deficiencies in which material inequalities give rise to socially harmful treatment of some group or agent (such as discrimination, social exclusion, and oppression). In these cases, individuals might not have 'enough' resources to enjoy a 'sufficient' threshold of social positional goods like political power or influence. Or, to put it another way, material 'inequality places a group of individuals below an absolute threshold in terms of social value' (Nielsen 2018: 14). Given that I am exclusively interested in what they call social insufficiency, could we conclude that this kind of sufficientarianism is the distributive principle I was looking for? Unfortunately, no. Although they reformulate the negative thesis in relational terms for those currencies that are positional, what remains inadequate is the idea that the notion of the threshold of sufficiency can compellingly capture these relational forms of distributive injustice. Let me briefly explain this point.

According to Axelsen and Nielsen (2015: 420), one central area of human life is political dimension or political power and influence as positional social good (they might prefer to say, the *capability* to fairly participate in political life). They recognise that the objective social insufficiency in this dimension also depends on wealth and income inequality between the best-off and the worst-off. Therefore, this kind of absolute insufficiency is determined by the relative size of economic inequality between them.[36] If they want to be sufficientarians, at a certain point, there must be an absolute threshold of economic resources reached, and exceeded, in which individuals do not suffer insufficiencies in terms of political power and influence; or with my words, they do not suffer the risk of material domination. However, a threshold as such does not exist. Recall Timmer's definition of the threshold notion, it demarcates two ranges of levels: below and above. The point in this case is that what signals the risk of domination, or a social norm-bound deficiency, is a unique *range*: the relative size of economic inequality of the economic resources of the best-off and the worst-off. The only way to signal the absence of the social norm-bound deficiency in the political dimension is a certain *range* of economic resources that reflect a continuation of thresholds in which no one suffers this deficiency or insufficiency. In other words, it is the size of inequality that might constitute social harm. Thus, a principle that focuses on a threshold gives us misleading and inadequate normative guidance on how to assess whether a certain material distribution is just or not. It is easy to perceive the deceptive picture:

In distribution (X), we may see that only those who stay at 70 do not suffer a social insufficiency – material domination – because the relative size of inequality between them and the best-off at a ratio 1:10 is not troubling. Therefore, we are led to believe that if no one is below 70, we will eliminate this type of social insufficiency. In other words, at 70 everyone will have enough, as in the case of (X'). But this outcome is a possibility only in the case that economic institutions permit maintaining the same level of efficiency and increase economic resources to those who are at the bottom of the distribution. But, on the contrary, a loss of efficiency in the short or middle run would occur. Thus, we just might reach outcome (X"). Nonetheless, in this material distribution in which some are below 70, no one suffers that type of social insufficiency because the ratio between the worst-off and the best-off is 1:10. Most importantly, we might not be so lucky. In an unfavourable

TABLE 3.6 Sufficiency and the Size of Inequality

Socioeconomic distributions	*Worst-off*	*Lower-middle class*	*Upper-middle class*	*Best-off*	*Threshold of social sufficiency*
X	30	40	70	700	70
X'	70	80	90	700	70
X"	40	50	70	400	70
X'''	25	35	60	250	70

scenario, the only way to avoid the risk of domination may be a more serious loss of efficiency (though possibly only a temporary effect) that will result in (X'''), but in which the ratio remains 1:10 and no one suffers the risk of domination. Note that this scenario can be rejected by sufficientarians only if they can prove that there is a threshold of material sufficiency above 25, for instance 30, below which no one can sink. However, it is true only if 30 represents an absolute level of economic resources to satisfy basic needs; but if it is the case we have no reasons to assume the implausible empirical hypothesis that the reduction of a considerable inequality that embodies the risk of domination cannot be converted into more resources for those who are on the threshold of the minimum satisfaction of basic needs.[37] I think what this unequivocally shows is that the idea of the threshold of sufficiency is not itself able to lead with what Axelsen and Nielsen call social insufficiencies or social norm-bound deficiencies.[38] The normative point is not the sufficiency, but the inequality ratio.

To conclude, we can deduce that the main aim (at least for what matters to my discussion) of these three broad families of distributive principles, alternative to Rawls' difference principle, is to avoid that by giving priority to the worst-off, justice would be required to swing too strongly in their favour, no matter how large the loss for the better-off. In this respect, prioritarianism, moderate egalitarianism, and sufficientarianism might be better than the difference principle. Indeed, we can agree that it is difficult to understand (unless we adopt a particular view of equality or fairness) what is so disturbing about not maximising the benefits for the worst-off at all costs. However, all versions of these three families do even worse than the difference principle regarding the constraints to the size of material inequalities. They are either fully insensitive to or too permissible of the size of inequality, or they take into account the question of the gap but without offering a compelling distributive principle to lead with it. Maybe the solution is to impose limits on the absolute wealth? This is what Robeyns proposes with her limitarianism account.

3.4 Limit the Richness: Robeyns' Limitarianism

In the current debate, Robeyns' limitarianism advances the idea that 'we all have a duty not to be rich' (Robeyns 2017: 2); or, more precisely, 'it is not morally permissible to have more resources than are needed to fully flourishing in life' (Robeyns 2017: 1). Like sufficientarianism, limitarianism entails a threshold, but this time the threshold focuses on the people situated at the top of the distributive ladder.[39] The idea is intriguing for at least three reasons. First, the focus on the top of distribution marks a novelty in the field because theories of distributive justice often deal with the bottom of the distribution.[40] Second, her account provides a principle to limit wealth and a formula to specify quite exactly how much is *too much* in absolute terms, a quantitative commitment quite uncommon in normative thinking. Third, her account aims to eschew the levelling-down objection because having too much is not perceived as intrinsically bad or unjust. Rather, as she puts it, 'limitarianism as a distributive view is justified in the world as it is (the non-ideal world), because it is instrumentally necessary for the protection of two intrinsic values: political equality and the meeting of unmet urgent needs' (Robeyns 2017: 4).[41] However, although Robeyns' limitarianism takes an important step towards an appropriate concern in normative theory about the danger that economic power can pose to political equality, her account is not adequately equipped to avoid this threat. Let me, first, reconstruct Robeyns' limitarianism and then show the limits of her approach.

Robeyns provides two main justifications for limitarianism: the democratic argument and the argument from unmet urgent needs. The argument from unmet urgent needs (Robeyns 2017: 10) rests on three main empirical conditions: (a) the condition of extreme global poverty, (b) the condition of local or global disadvantages, (c) the condition of urgent collective action problems. All three are determined by the poor's lack of adequate economic resources and Robeyns proposes to use the rich's *surplus money*, identified as what remains after they have purchased all they need to have a fully flourishing life, to satisfy the poor's urgent needs: 'the argument for urgent unmet needs is based on the premise that the value of surplus income is morally insignificant *for the holder* of that income, but not for society at large, at least under certain alternative usages' (Robeyns 2017: 13). For *surplus money* she means 'the difference between an individual's financial means and the threshold that distinguishes rich from non-rich people' (Robeyns 2017: 7). In turn, the rich are those people who enjoy 'the state in which one has more resources than are needed for maximally flourishing in life' (Robeyns 2017: 2). The democratic argument rests on the idea that extreme wealth may disrupt political equality, producing large inequalities in political influence. Robeyns also starts from the consideration that the insulation strategy is largely insufficient to defend political equality. According to Robeyns, what undermines political equality is the same factor that impedes meeting urgent needs, that is, *surplus money*; on the contrary, if citizens hold no more than what is necessary to flourish fully in life, then they will have nothing left to buy political influence.

It is evident that the benchmark of limitarianism is to determine accurately the *surplus money*, or, in other words, who counts as rich and who does not. In this respect, it is important to notice that the threshold that distinguishes between rich and non-rich is set in absolute terms, rather than relative ones. In this way Robeyns' purpose is to avoid two problems related to relative measures. The first is the insensitivity to changes in absolute income and wealth level. To use Robeyns' example, if the Swedish government distributes the annual profits of a new oil source and each Swedish citizen (or household) receives EUR 50,000, 'the number of rich, richer, and richest on a relative riches measure will stay exactly the same' (Robeyns 2017: 16). Yet the amount of *surplus money* changed considerably in favour of the top classes. The second concern is the identification of the wealthy with the best-off independently of how rich or poor the best-off are. A relative notion of riches cannot capture the case in which a 'person can have an excellent or even the very best position in comparative terms, but could in absolute terms be in a dire situation' (Robeyns 2017: 17). To use again Robeyns' example, having access to a knife or a torch in an overcrowded refugee camp in Darfur might make a person well-off in comparative terms, possibly even best-off. And yet one could hardly describe that person as rich (Robeyns 2017: 17). However, although Robeyns opts for an absolute measure, she makes it somewhat sensible to the context. For instance, an income of EUR 100,000 a year may not make you *rich* in Western Europe but it certainly does in Sub-Saharan Africa. She calls measures sensitive to context 'contextual measures' to distinguish them from 'distribution-relative measures'. As she puts it:

> [d]istribution-relative measures define riches or poverty as being at a certain distance from the average of the distribution. *Context-relative or contextual measures*, on the other hand, make *some* (generally weaker) reference to the context of the measurement in the definition of the riches or poverty-line, without making that reference a function of the distribution itself.
>
> (Robeyns 2017: 18)

Another important methodological feature of limitarianism is that, although Robeyns opts for money as the currency of her account, she advocates the capability approach as a metric of justice; i.e. given that people are diverse in their ability to convert economic resources into valuable functionings, they need different amounts of resources to meet the same set of capabilities. The reference to the context reappears here. For example, Robeyns plausibly supposes that in contemporary Europe or North America

> one must have access to the goods that enable one to be mobile within a radar of a few hundred miles. Hence people need either to be able to afford a decent car or have access to public transport that enables the same functioning. Certainly, however, one would not need to have access to a private jet.
>
> (Robeyns 2017: 26)

With these methodological considerations in mind, Robeyns proposes a metric of affluence that she calls *the power of material resources* (PMR) which corresponds to economic resources owned by each household unit. She (Robeyns 2017: 20–23) calculates the *PMR* by summing the gross total income of a household deriving from all sources (labour, entitlements, profit, returns on financial capital), the monetary estimate of any transfer in favour of the household other than earnings (e.g. having one's rent paid by a rich uncle) and the life annuity of household assets. From this sum the following is subtracted: a) expenditures from income-generating activities, such as net expenditures on child care and other forms of family care, expenditures for commuting or the improvement of one's human capital within a household; b) taxes paid on income and on the annuity. The result is then corrected through two factors: 1) the Conversion Factor (CF) that accounts for the capabilitarian insight that different people may need different amounts of money for reaching the same level of functionings (CF=1 if the person is perfectly able to translate money into functionings) and 2) the household Equivalence Scale (ES) that allows the rescaling of the household income to what that income means for each person living in that household. Then, once we have chosen the list of basic capabilities for a fully flourishing life in a specific context, we need to calculate how much money is necessary to buy these goods and services. The resulting amount corresponds to the riches line. For example, if this line lies on EUR 200,000 a year (Robeyns 2017: 26), no household unit should own more economic resources than that amount. Any amount above this absolute threshold (i.e. EUR 200,000 a year) can be considered as surplus money.

Unfortunately, things are more complicated than Robeyns supposes, and limitarianism is not able to provide a compelling remedy to satisfy the democratic argument; or, in my view, the risk of material domination. Although Robeyns is not unaware of the difficulties that limitarianism faces, the way she defends herself is not entirely convincing. Prof. Caranti and I (Caranti and Alì 2021) have already provided an extensive critical remark on Robeyns' account; for example, we underlined some criticisms that concern Robeyns' methodological choice of capability approach.[42] Here, my focus will be more restricted; for instance, I will remain faithful to my strategy to bracket off the debate concerning the question of the metrics of justice. Trying to be as straightforward as possible, I argue that the main problems of Robeyns' limitarianism are generated by her choice to target *surplus money* for protecting political equality. Most importantly, the main difficulties could be circumvented if one abandoned the hope to defend political equality by targeting *surplus money* and opted for a focus on limiting *the distance* in material resources between the best-off and the worst-off in society. Let me briefly show how.

Robeyns' democratic argument works only if it is reasonable to think that people on the riches line or close to it will not renounce some of the money needed for their basic capabilities to buy some political influence. Robeyns assumes, or needs to assume, that the cost of this operation would be existentially too high, otherwise it is easy to imagine that people on the line would have money to buy political influence that people who have barely enough to meet their basic urgent needs clearly do not. If this assumption is not made, it becomes natural to think that money becomes a threat to political equality not when some have a *surplus*, but when some have '*much more than others*'. This problem becomes particularly acute because Robeyns herself recognises the possibility that in a world with a top threshold people may still buy luxury items, if they are ready to give up some basic functionings (Robeyns 2017: 27–28). Now, if they can do so for what many would consider a whim (Robeyns' example is *flying* to a party), *a fortiori* they should be considered as capable of giving up their ability to secure basic functionings (or a certain level of them) to buy political influence.[43] Hence people near the threshold will be more influential than average or poor citizens even in the limitarian world. To rephrase this crucial point, even if nobody has surplus money, and even if the best-off are placed quite below the supposed rich-line, they might have significantly more economic resources at their disposal to influence politics than other citizens who, as far as limitarianism is concerned, may have very little. All of this poses a clear and immediate threat to political equality and suggests again that what matters for protecting political equality is the magnitude of the economic gap between the best-off and the middle or lower class, even if the best-off are well within the limit set by Robeyns.

Thus, in order to discourage the exchange between basic functionings and political influence, the riches line needs to be rather low. But this poses a dilemma for Robeyns. The higher the line is, the easier it will be for people close to the line to give up some level of their functionings to acquire political influence. The lower the line, the smaller that risk will be, but the more difficult it will be to leave room for economic efficiency. Indeed, as Robeyns is aware (2017: 34–37), capping wealth through a riches line may damage efficiency up to the point that poor citizens, even with the best redistribution possible, will not have their 'urgent basic needs met'. Robeyns thinks that one is forced to choose between prioritising meeting urgent basic needs at the expense of political equality or prioritising political equality at the expense of meeting urgent basic needs. But this is true only if there is no way to protect political equality without losing systemic efficiency, or without losing less of it than the amount required by limitarianism. But this loss of efficiency is unnecessary to protect political equality.

To better clarify the main shortcoming, we can observe that Robeyns' account is not able to overcome the levelling-down objection, despite Robeyns favours a non-intrinsic conception of limitarianism. To recall: I said that, in a pluralistic society, we should offer a normative reason to reduce the size of material inequality that (1) is compatible with the reasonable pluralism, (2) the proposed alternative distribution should improve the condition of some members of the society (a person-affecting conception), (3) the loss of wealth suffered by some should not be more than what is strictly necessary for the desired improvement. Now, neither the argument from urgent needs nor the democratic argument satisfy the condition of 3.

Regarding the argument from meeting urgent needs, it is dubious that the only way to collect the necessary resources is to cap wealth with a top threshold. It is reasonable to think that allowing people to be rich without imposing a top threshold is compatible with or perhaps even required not by the goal to maximise (in a Rawlsian spirit) the position of the worst-off – a goal Robeyns has no reason to share – but to create the wealth necessary to meet the urgent needs of all citizens (or human beings in general). Robeyns shows herself to be aware of the problem when she admits that protecting political equality through a top threshold may enter into conflict with meeting urgent needs. While most economists think that taxing people more than 70% of their income is detrimental to state revenues, and hence to the possibility of redistributing to meet urgent needs, the democratic argument requires that people are taxed 100% on the income that exceeds the set limit. But if this is what happens to a society ruled by limitarianism, then the loss of wealth some suffer is justified for the pursuing of one moral goal and yet it is not necessary, actually it could be detrimental, to the pursuing of another moral goal. Furthermore, since political equality could be protected also by ensuring that inequality between rich and poor is kept within certain proportions, as already plentifully shown up to this point, Robeyns' democratic argument does not fare much better to satisfy the condition of 3. Limitarianism prescribes a limitation of individual wealth that is unduly severe and, most importantly, *unnecessary* to protect political equality.

To conclude, many difficulties that limitarianism face follow from the idea that what matters to reduce the influence of money in politics is the existence of *surplus money* in the society. First of all, if Robeyns makes room for the possibility that citizens sacrifice some of their functionings to buy luxury items, she should expect *a fortiori* that they make sacrifices to buy political influence. The closer citizens are to the top threshold, the less costly it will be for them to buy political influence. Conversely, the farther they are from it, the costlier this use of their economic resources will be. In short, the best-off will buy political influence at a lower cost than the worst-off. Secondly, and most importantly, since limitarianism has no relative threshold, the distance between the best-off and worst-off can be considerably wide. In particular, the worst-off could be in rather dire conditions and this would evidently put them at the very concrete risk of being 'outweighed' by the best-off in terms of political influence. By contrast, the normative priority should be to make sure that the difference in question never becomes wide enough to be reasonably construed as a form of domination. This entails a change of perspective from a concern with richness measured in absolute terms to a concern with the distance in richness between the best-off and worst-off, that is, with the size of economic inequality. From this perspective, the real enemy of political equality is not richness, as in Robeyns, but unbounded economic inequality.

Recently, the same objection is also proposed, and thus reinforced, by Robert Huseby (2022).[44] Robeyns' reply (2022: 9) seems to accept the core of this objection and open to modifications; for example, she leaves room for a relative threshold but, in any case, to be placed side by side with an absolute one; supposedly, the former to lead with the democratic argument and the second one with the argument from unmet urgent needs. However, she seems to underestimate the breadth and depth of any necessary modifications. For example, as a result, many key concepts of limitarianism would lose their meaning entirely. First of all, as I have already shown about the democratic argument, there would be no riches line or upper threshold, and much less *surplus money*. Second, neither the argument from unmet urgent needs would lead to adopting an absolute riches line. In the case of a society in which the size of economic inequality exposes the less advantaged citizens to the risk of material domination, the economic resources that would derive from a possible redistribution can, and must, go to meet urgent needs, and even in the case in which a society is able to keep economic inequality within a permissible range, those who have the most (and likely not only them) must still contribute to the satisfaction of urgent needs.

Again, what we must be concerned with is that the difference in material resources among citizens does not become so wide that it translates into the risk of material domination. This is the proposal of the principle of proportional justice which, finally, I will present in more detail in the next and last chapter, showing also some comparative advantages over Robeyns' limitarianism.

Notes

1 Here, I will not have the space to identify all varieties of social relations that can be considered as governed by the primary rules within a domestic society. However, compared to Rawls, I think that we should surely include the family and firms (at least those of a certain size).

2 For this point, see Waldron (1993). Rawls (2001: 127–129, note 47) himself agrees with Waldron's interpretation. See also Casal (2007).

3 I take this example from Shklar (1990) and Forst (2014).

4 It is possible to distinguish between teleological and deontological ideas in distributivist conceptions of justice. Teleological conceptions apply simply to what 'goods' people have, no matter how these may have been obtained. For deontological ones, instead, whether that person's deprivation gives rise to moral concern depends on how this deprivation was brought about; for example, if a person's reckless driver caused a car accident. In this case, that person's deprivation does not raise a claim of justice. This view is usually endorsed by luck-egalitarian accounts. The case of the reckless driver is used to advance the abandonment objection (Fleurbaey 1995) or the harshness objection (Anderson 1999) against the luck-egalitarianism view; for a reply see G. A. Cohen (2006) and Segall (2010).

5 In this relational picture of justice we can include many and different accounts and theories; for example, relational and social egalitarianism; Critical Theories account, and theories of recognition and non-domination. Moreover, the relational camp is also characterised by both deontological and teleological conceptions; for example, see the debate between Nancy Fraser and Axel Honneth (2003).

6 These scholars (see Shoelandt and Gaus 2018; von Platz 2020a) usually think to find confirmation of this in Rawls' words (2005: xlvii–l) that *Political Liberalism* identifies a family of 'liberal conceptions of justice', within which *justice as fairness* is just one of the political conceptions of justice among others. From this, they derive that the difference principle is only plausible for those societies with an overlapping consensus able to accept a robust egalitarian distribution. Although it could be true about Rawls' difference principle, I believe that all political conceptions within that family should endorse the principle of proportionality.

7 For sure, there are some important exceptions like Anderson (1999, 2010) and Scanlon (2018) who advocate a specific pattern of distribution; respectively sufficientarianism and moderate egalitarianism.

8 Recently, Schemmel (2021) recognizes this deficit in the relational egalitarians account. His works can be read, among other things, to prove that relational egalitarians 'have an intrinsic reason to limit inequality in the goods produced by such cooperation' (Schemmel 2021: 326). Although his account of relational equality does not prescribe a specific distributive principle to establish this limit, in many passages he argues for reasons to introduce *range constraints* of inequality based on a liberal relational account of non-domination. I think that my view of non-domination overlaps with that of Schemmel in many respects and, above all, in its broad intent to conceive the idea of non-domination on 'grounds of a liberal conception of society and the person' (Schemmel 2021: 12). Albeit I do not have the time and space to elaborate, I think that my principle of proportionality might well accommodate many normative intuitions of his account.

9 Note that if we want to measure the size of inequality, we need to look to relative or comparative inequality rather than to absolute inequality. Otherwise, we might think that between these two distributions (10, 20) and (110, 120) there is the same inequality: 10 units. By contrast, I maintain that the size of inequality in (10, 20) is greater than that in (110, 120); precisely an inequality ratio of 1:2 to 1:1.09. It is particularly true for my argument. Indeed, given that I said that material power depends on *how much one has compared to others*, it is indispensable to take into account the relative inequality. Double the material resource makes the best-off in (10, 20) more powerful than the others in (110, 120).

10 Nonetheless, I agree with Temkin (2000, 2008, 2017) who argues that morality does not preclude us from making 'impersonal' or 'non-person-affecting' judgments. Indeed, it is not true that we have no moral reasons to judge a world as bad where many people live and only some people die because a less unequal distribution of material resources will lead everyone to die or more people to die (for this example, see Temkin 2017). In other words, we might have reasons to judge this unequal state of affairs as bad, even if these reasons do not authorise us to reduce inequality.

11 Elsewhere I define my conception of justice as a non-intrinsic conception, see Alì and Caranti (2021) and Caranti and Alì (2021). Now, I am convinced that it is better to understand my view as a constitutive concern for inequality, in order to emphasise this specific inherent dimension.

12 Scanlon (2018) distinguishes between reasons that are egalitarian in the narrow and in the broad sense. The former are what I call constitutive or inherent reasons to deal with inequality, while the latter are merely instrumental. Similarly, Schemmel (2021) distinguishes between expressive and instrumental reasons. For a set of instrumental reasons against socioeconomic inequality, see Wilkinson and Pickett (2010).

13 See Sen (1980), G. A. Cohen (1989a), Arneson (1989, 2000, 2002), Roemer (1996), Holtug and Lippert-Rasmussen (2007), Brighouse and Robeyns (2010), and Gosepath (2021).

14 See Dworkin (2000) and Sen (2009).

15 See Rawls (2005: 18– 20, 73–75, 81–82, 302; 2001: 18–24).

16 I prefer to quote the two principles of justice as they are formulated in *Political Liberalism*, because this formulation is the most complete that Rawls provided.

17 Thus, from this point of view, although I agree with Freeman (2018) that the difference principle is not a prioritarian principle, I disagree with him that the difference principle (under the special conception) is able to sanction economic inequality according to its size or the distance between the worst-off and the best-off.

18 Rawls (1971: 536) himself admits that the difference principle itself has this feature, although he trusts in other normative elements presented in his theory to avoid, in practice, this result. As Rawls (1971: 536) puts it, 'although in theory the difference principle permits indefinitely large inequalities in return for small gains to the less favoured, the spread of income and wealth should not be excessive in practice, given the requisite background institutions.'

19 See for example J. Cohen (1989b), Daniels (2003), Barry (2005), Freeman (2007), Vita (2007), Forst (2012, 2014), M. O'Neill (2012), and Thomas (2017).

20 Another element that can constrain economic inequalities admitted by the difference principle is the fair equality of opportunity. For a discussion, see Freeman (2013).

21 Freeman (2011) seems to provide an alternative interpretation to solve this puzzle. He sustains that under the difference principle it is not true that the least advantaged are to have more income and wealth than in any alternative economy because it 'is the ultimate standard for distributing not only income and wealth, but also the primary social goods that Rawls calls powers and positions of responsibility' (Freeman 2011: 50). Thus, for example, property-owning democracy does better than welfare-state capitalism in terms of power and authority over productive resources, in such a way as to compensate for a greater absolute share of income and wealth for the worst-off in welfare-state capitalism. However, Freeman's interpretation is plausible only if he maintains Rawls' special conception that aligns the level of income and wealth with power and authority; otherwise, someone may advance the objection that a very high absolute share of income and wealth for the worst-off might be preferable over power and authority. I do not see how this alignment can be maintained unless adopting the principle of proportionality which links economic and political power to the relative size of economic inequality between the worst-off and the best-off.

22 Here I will just note that the principle of proportionality seems to be able to reconcile more adequately (a) the first and second principles of justice and (b) better exemplify the intuitive idea of how procedural justice treats the question of distribution, i.e. 'to design

the social system so that the outcome is just whatever it happens to be, at least so long as it is within a certain range' (Rawls 1971: 85).

23 In leximin, the logic is the same.

24 There are others similar definitions of the priority view, i.e. 'the priority view is the view that the contribution to general good is greater the less well off the person is' (Broome 1991: 199), or 'Priority: A benefit matters more, morally speaking, the worse off the recipient is' (Segall 2015: 344).

25 Nagel's account concerns individuals and not with the representative person of the least advantaged groups. In addition, it does not apply to the basic structure of society. However, nothing forbids us to apply Nagel's principle to the basic structure of society and take into account the representative person of the least advantaged groups rather than individuals themselves.

26 Unfortunately, Scanlon does not offer us any kind of priority among these different reasons.

27 However, Barrett (2019) argues that Scanlon's first clause ('benefits all') is inconsistent with his second clause ('benefits more equally') and that the inconsistency can be solved 'only by allowing sufficiently large gains in the production of total benefits to justify inequality, regardless of how these benefits are distributed' (Barrett 2019: 11). This means that if Scanlon wants to produce the same egalitarian result of the difference principle, he should abandon the first formulation of his criterion to explicitly adopt a maximin (or leximin) rule.

28 However, in the same family should also be included those views that are not sufficientarian themselves. For example, left or real libertarianism usually prescribes a minimal (more or less generous) level of material resources for everyone assigned in the form of a universal and unconditional basic income. This basic income presents a threshold that everyone should reach. However, their moral motivation is to ensure real freedom for all; instead many sufficientarian accounts are grounded on reasons that appeal to human dignity or impartial judgement.

29 About the positive thesis, see Casal (2007), Axelsen and Nielsen (2015) and Shields (2012, 2016, 2020).

30 For example, Shue (1980) provides an account of basic rights that includes a 'positive thesis' but only with regards to the satisfactions of basic needs to respect human rights; similarly, for Nussbaum (2006) who aims to establish a 'minimal' principle for a decent society.

31 See Huseby (2010, 2020), Benbaji (2005) and Spengler (2016).

32 A similar solution had already been sketched by Casal (2007).

33 Nussbaum's sufficientarianism (2006) also contains horizontal multiple thresholds, but she does not have the ambition to propose a sufficientarian account for a full-fledged theory of distributive justice. Her account is a partial conception of justice. On this point, see also Alì and Piroli (2019).

34 For a discussion about the main features of positional goods, see Hirsch (1976), Brighouse and Swift (2006), Axelsen and Nielsen (2015), and Ben-Shahar (2018).

35 The central area of human life is identified by means of the metric of capability and it endorses some pluralist and moderately perfectionist elements.

36 Here I am taking *other things being equal*, such as equal political rights and equal access to public political office.

37 I will go back to this point in Chapter 4, Section 4.1.

38 Most importantly, all that I have said regarding sufficientarianism in general should be much more alarming for those social and relational egalitarian authors who endorse a sufficientarian material distribution. The most exemplary case is Anderson's account (1999, 2007, 2010). Anderson (1999: 326) expressly says that 'once all citizens enjoy a decent set of freedoms, sufficient for functioning as an equal in society, income inequalities beyond that point do not seem so troubling in themselves'. Moreover, Anderson (2008) rarely mentions the necessity to limit economic inequalities; on the contrary she seems to opt, at least as the best option, for some forms of the insulation strategy. For more details on this point, see Schemmel (2021: 233–242).

39 Robeyns has developed her limitarianism in a number of works, see Robeyns (2017, 2019), Kramm and Robeyns (2020), Robeyns et al. (2021), and Robeyns (2022).
40 It is a partial distributive account because it is agnostic regarding what distributive justice requires for those who do not have too much.
41 For an intrinsic conception of limitarianism, see Zwarthoed (2018).
42 These criticisms (Caranti and Alì 2021: 95–99) sustain that it is difficult to identify in a non-arbitrary manner the relevant functionings needed for a 'fully flourishing life'. For a similar criticism to the capability approach, see also Pogge (2010).
43 For a similar objection, see Volacu and Dumitru (2019). Timmer (2019) replies to their objection suggesting that limitarianism is not meant as a sufficient means to promote political equality, but merely as a useful instrument. In this sense, and in more general terms, Timmer (2021b) proposes to downgrade limitarianism from a distributive principle of justice to a principle that can justify specific policies, under certain 'epistemic constraints'. However, the normative force of limitarianism is thereby considerably weakened by Timmer's proposal. Huseby (2022) provides some specific objections to Timmer's defence of limitarianism.
44 Moreover, Huseby (2022) provides a broad investigation aiming to take limitarianism as a contender with familiar distributive principles such as egalitarianism, prioritarianism, sufficientarianism, or utilitarianism; and yet he concludes that 'limitarianism is of very limited value to debates on distributive justice' (Huseby 2022: 2). Here, I do not have the time to discuss the content of his considerations. For a reply, see Robeyns (2022).

Bibliography

Alì, Nunzio and Luigi Caranti. 2021. 'How Much Economic Inequality is Fair in Liberal Democracies? The Approach of Proportional Justice', *Philosophy & Social Criticism*, 47(7): 769–788.

Alì, Nunzio and Diana Piroli. 2019. 'Teoria parcial de justiça e estrutura política democrática na teoria de Nussbaum', *Ethic@: An International Journal for Moral Philosophy*, 18(3): 333–356.

Anderson, Elizabeth. 2010. 'The Fundamental Disagreement between Luck Egalitarians and Relational Egalitarians', *Canadian Journal of Philosophy*, 36: 1–23.

Anderson, Elizabeth. 2008. 'How Should Egalitarians Cope with Market Risks?' *Theoretical Inquiries in Law*, 9: 239– 270.

Anderson, Elizabeth. 2007. 'Fair Opportunity in Education: A Democratic Equality Perspective', *Ethics*, 117: 595–622.

Anderson, Elizabeth. 1999. 'What Is the Point of Equality?' *Ethics*, 109(2): 287–337.

Arneson, Richard J. 2002. 'Why Justice Requires Transfers to Offset Income and Wealth Inequalities', *Social Philosophy and Policy*, 19: 172–200.

Arneson, Richard J. 2000. 'Luck Egalitarianism and Prioritarianism', *Ethics*, 110: 339–349.

Arneson, Richard J. 1989. 'Equality and Equal Opportunity for Welfare', *Philosophical Studies*, 56: 77–93.

Axelsen, David V. and Lasse Nielsen. 2017. 'Essentially Enough Elements of a Plausible Account of Sufficientarianism', in Carina Fourie and Annette Rid (eds.), *What is Enough? Sufficiency, Justice, and Health*, pp. 101–118. Oxford: Oxford University Press.

Axelsen, David V. and Lasse Nielsen. 2015. 'Sufficiency as Freedom from Duress', *The Journal of Political Philosophy*, 23(4): 406–426.

Barrett, Jacob. 2019. 'Efficient Inequalities', *The Journal of Political Philosophy*, 28(2): 181–198.

Barry, Brain. 2005. *Why Social Justice Matters*. Cambridge: Polity Press.

Benbaji, Yitzhak. 2005. 'The Doctrine of Sufficiency: A Defence', *Utilitas*, 17(3): 310–332.

Ben-Shahar, Tammy H. 2018. 'Positional Goods and the Size of Inequality', *The Journal of Political Philosophy*, 26(1): 103–120.
Brighouse, Harry and Ingrid Robeyns (eds.). 2010. *Measuring Justice: Primary Goods and Capabilities*. Cambridge: Cambridge University Press.
Brighouse, Harry and Adam Swift. 2006. 'Equality, Priority, and Positional Goods', *Ethics*, 116(3): 471–497.
Broome, John. 1991. *Weighing Goods: Equality, Uncertainty and Time*. Oxford: Wiley-Blackwell.
Caranti, Luigi and Nunzio Alì. 2021. 'The Limits of Limitarianism: Why Political Equality is Not Protected by Robeyns' Democratic Argument', *Politica & Società*, 1: 89–116.
Casal, Paula. 2007. 'Why Sufficiency is Not Enough', *Ethics*, 117(2): 296–326.
Cohen, Gerald A. 2006. 'Luck and Equality: A Reply to Hurley', *Philosophy and Phenomenological Research*, 72(2): 439–446.
Cohen, Gerald A. 1989a. 'On the Currency of Egalitarian Justice', *Ethics*, 99(4): 906–944.
Cohen, Joshua. 1989b. 'Democratic Equality', *Ethics*, 99(4): 727–751.
Crisp, Roger. 2003. 'Equality Priority, and Compassion', *Ethics*, 113(4): 745–763.
Daniels, Norman. 2003. 'Democratic Equality: Rawls's Complex Egalitarianism', in Samuel Freeman (ed.), *The Cambridge Companion to Rawls*, pp. 241–276. Cambridge: Cambridge University Press.
Daniels, Norman. 1975. 'Equal Liberty and Unequal Worth of Liberty', in Norman Daniels (ed.), *Reading Rawls*, pp. 253–281. New York: Basic Books.
Dworkin, Ronald. 2000. *Sovereign Virtue: The Theory and Practice of Equality*. Cambridge: Harvard University Press.
Fleurbaey, Marc. 1995. 'Equal Opportunity or Equal Social Outcome?' *Economics and Philosophy*, 11(1): 25–55.
Forst, Rainer. 2014. *Justification and Critique: Towards a Critical Theory of Politics*. Trans. by Ciaran Cronin. Cambridge: Polity Press.
Forst, Rainer. 2012. *The Right to Justification*. Trans. by Jeffrey Flynn. New York: Columbia University Press.
Frankfurt, Harry. 2015. *On Inequality*. Princeton: Princeton University Press.
Frankfurt, Harry. 1997. 'Equality and Respect', *Social Research*, 64: 3–15.
Frankfurt, Harry. 1987. 'Equality as a Moral Ideal', *Ethics*, 98(1): 21–43.
Fraser, Nancy. 2010. *Scales of Justice: Reimagining Political Space in a Globalizing World*. New York: Columbia University Press.
Fraser, Nancy and Axel Honneth. 2003. *Redistribution or Recognition? A Political-Philosophical Exchange*. London: Verso.
Freeman, Samuel. 2018. 'Rawls on Distributive Justice and the Difference Principle', in Serena Olsaretti (ed.), *The Oxford Handbook of Distributive Justice*, pp. 1–33. Oxford: Oxford University Press.
Freeman, Samuel. 2013. 'Property-Owning Democracy and the Difference Principle', *Analyse & Kritik*, 35(1): 9–36.
Freeman, Samuel. 2011. 'Capitalism in the Classical and High Liberal Traditions', *Social Philosophy and Policy*, 28: 19–55.
Freeman, Samuel. 2007. *Rawls*. New York: Routledge.
Gaus, Gerald. 2011. *The Order of Public Reason: A Theory of Freedom and Morality in a Diverse and Bounded World*. Cambridge: Cambridge University Press.
Gosepath, Stefan. 2021. 'Equality', in Edward N. Zalta (ed.), *The Stanford Encyclopedia of Philosophy*, https://plato.stanford.edu/archives/sum2021/entries/equality/ (accessed on 25 January 2022).
Habermas, Jürgen. 1995. 'Reconciliation Through the Public use of Reason: Remarks on John Rawls's Political Liberalism', *The Journal of Philosophy*, 92(3): 109–131.

Habermas, Jürgen. 1990. *Moral Consciousness and Communicative Action*. Trans. by Christian Lenhardt. Cambridge: MIT Press.

Hirose, Iwao. 2015. *Egalitarianism*. London: Routledge.

Hirose, Iwao. 2011. 'Prioritarianism and Egalitarianism', in Thom Brooks (ed.), *New Waves in Ethics*, pp. 88–107. London: Palgrave Macmillan.

Hirsch, Fred. 1976. *Social Limits to Growth*. Cambridge: Harvard University Press.

Holtug, Nils and Kasper Lippert-Rasmussen. 2007. *Egalitarianism: New Essays on the Nature and Value of Equality*. Oxford: Clarendon Press.

Huseby, Robert. 2022. 'The Limits of Limitarianism', *The Journal of Political Philosophy*, 30(2): 230–248.

Huseby, Robert. 2020. 'Sufficiency and the Threshold Question', *The Journal of Ethics*, 24(2): 207–223.

Huseby, Robert. 2010. 'Sufficiency: Restated and Defended', *Journal of Political Philosophy*, 18(2): 178–197.

Kramm, Matthias and Ingrid Robeyns. 2020. 'Limits to Wealth in the History of Western Philosophy', *European Journal of Philosophy*, 28(4): 954–969.

Nagel, Thomas. 1979. 'Equality', in Thomas Nagel (ed.), *Mortal Questions*, pp. 106–127. Cambridge: Cambridge University Press.

Nielsen, Lasse. 2019. 'What is Wrong with Sufficiency?' *Res Publica*, 25(3): 21–38.

Nielsen, Lasse. 2018. 'What Is Our Real Concern with Real Inequality?' *Policy Studies Journal*, 46(3): 553–572.

Nussbaum, Martha. 2006. *Frontiers of Justice: Disability, Nationality, Species Membership*. Cambridge: Belknap.

O'Neill, Martin. 2012. 'Free (and fair) Markets Without Capitalism: Political Values, Principles of Justice, and Property-owning Democracy', in Martin O'Neill and Thad Williamson (eds.), *Property-Owning Democracy: Rawls and Beyond*, pp. 75–100. Oxford: Blackwell.

O'Neill, Onora. 1996. *Towards Justice and Virtue: A constructive Account of Practical Reasoning*. Cambridge: Cambridge University Press.

Parfit, Derek. 2012. 'Another Defence of the Priority View', *Utilitas*, 24: 399–440.

Parfit, Derek. 2000. 'Equality or Priority?' in Matthew Clayton and Andrew Williams (eds.), *The Ideal of Equality*, pp. 81–125. New York: St. Martin's Press.

Parfit, Derek. 1997. 'Equality and Priority', *Ratio*, 10(3): 202–221.

Pogge, Thomas W. 2010. 'A Critique of the Capability Approach', in Harry Brighouse and Ingrid Robeyns (eds.), *Measuring Justice: Primary Goods and Capabilities*, pp. 131–149. Cambridge: Cambridge University Press.

Rawls, John. 2007. *Lectures on the History of Political Philosophy*. Ed. by Samuel Freeman. Cambridge: Belknap Press.

Rawls, John. 2005. *Political Liberalism. Expanded Edition*. New York: Columbia University Press.

Rawls, John. 2001. *Justice as Fairness: A Restatement*. Cambridge: Harvard University Press.

Rawls, John. 1982. *The Basic Liberties and Their Priority. The Tanner Lectures on Human Values, Volume III*. Salt Lake City: University of Utah Press.

Rawls, John. 1971. *A Theory of Justice. Original Edition*. Cambridge: Harvard University Press.

Robeyns, Ingrid. 2022. 'Why Limitarianism?' *The Journal of Political Philosophy*, 30(2): 249–270.

Robeyns, Ingrid. 2019. 'What, if Anything, is Wrong with Extreme Wealth?' *Journal of Human Development and Capabilities*, 20(3): 251–266.

Robeyns, Ingrid. 2017. 'Having too Much', in Jack Knight and Melissa Schwartzberg (eds.), *NOMOS LVI: Wealth. Yearbook of the American Society for Political and Legal Philosophy*, pp. 1–44. New York: New York University Press.

Robeyns, Ingrid, Vincent Buskens, Arnout van de Rijt, Nina Vergeldt, and Tanja van der Lippe. 2021. 'How Rich is too Rich? Measuring the Riches Line', *Social Indicators Research*, 154: 115–143.

Roemer, John E. 1996. *Theories of Distributive Justice*. Cambridge: Harvard University Press.

Salvatore, Ingrid. 2004. 'Liberalism, Pluralism, Justice: An Unresolved Strain in the Thought of John Rawls', *Philosophy & Social Criticism*, 30(5–6): 623–641.

Scanlon, Thomas M. 2018. *Why Does Inequality Matter?* Oxford: Oxford University Press

Scanlon, Thomas M. 1998. *What We Owe to Each Other*. Cambridge: Harvard University Press.

Scanlon, Thomas M. 1982. 'Contractualism and Utilitarianism', in Amartya Sen and Bernard Williams (eds.), *Utilitarianism and Beyond*, pp. 103–128. Cambridge: Cambridge University Press.

Scheffler, Samuel. 2015. 'The Practice of Equality', in Carina Fourie, Fabien Schuppert and Ivo Wallimann-Helmer (eds.), *Social Equality: On What It Means to Be Equals*, pp. 21–44. Oxford: Oxford University Press.

Schemmel, Christian. 2021. *Justice and Egalitarian Relations*. Oxford: Oxford University Press.

Segall, Shlomi. 2015. 'In Defence of Priority (and Equality)', *Politics, Philosophy, & Economics*, 14(4): 343–364.

Segall, Shlomi. 2010. *Health, Luck, and Justice*. Princeton: Princeton University Press.

Sen, Amartya. 2009. *The Idea of Justice*. Cambridge: Harvard University Press.

Sen, Amartya. 1980. *Equality of What? The Tanner Lectures on Human Values*. Ed. by S. McMurrin. Cambridge: Cambridge University Press.

Shields, Liam. 2020. 'Sufficientarianism', *Philosophy Compass*, 15(11): 1–10.

Shields, Liam. 2016. *Just Enough: Sufficiency as a Demand of Justice*. Edinburgh: Edinburgh University Press.

Shields, Liam. 2012. 'The Prospects for Sufficientarianism', *Utilitas*, 24(1): 101–117.

Shklar, Judith N. 1990. *The Faces of Injustice*. New Haven: Yale University Press.

Shoelandt, Chad Van and Gerald Gaus. 2018. 'Political and Distributive Justice', in Serena Olsaretti (ed.), *The Oxford Handbook of Distributive Justice*, pp. 283–305. Oxford: Oxford University Press.

Shue, Henry. 1980. *Basic Rights*. Princeton: Princeton University Press.

Spengler, Laura. 2016. '"Two Types of 'Enough'": Sufficiency as Minimum and Maximum', *Environmental Politics*, 25(5): 921–940.

Temkin, Larry. 2017. 'Equality as Comparative Fairness', *Journal of Applied Philosophy*, 34(1): 43–60.

Temkin, Larry. 2008. 'Illuminating Egalitarianism', in Thomas Christiano and John Christman (eds.), *Contemporary Debates in Political Philosophy*, pp. 155–178. Oxford: Wiley-Blackwell.

Temkin, Larry. 2000. 'Equality, Priority, and the Levelling Down Objection', in Matthew Clayton and Andrew Williams (eds.), *The Ideal of Equality*, pp. 126–161. New York: St. Martin's Press.

Thomas, Alan. 2017. *Republic of Equals: Predistribution and Property-Owning Democracy*. Oxford: Oxford University Press.

Timmer, Dick. 2021a. 'Thresholds in Distributive Justice', *Utilitas*, 33: 422–441.

Timmer, Dick. 2021b. 'Limitarianism: Pattern, Principle, or Presumption?' *Journal of Applied Philosophy*, 38(5): 760–773.

Timmer, Dick. 2019. 'Defending the Democratic Argument for Limitarianism: A Reply to Volacu and Dumitru', *Philosophia*, 47(4): 1331–1339.

Vallier, Kevin. 2014. *Liberal Politics and Public Faith: Beyond Separation*. New York: Routledge.

Vita, Álvaro de. 2007. *A justiça igualitária e seus críticos*. São Paulo: Martins Fontes.

Volacu, Alexandru and Adelin C. Dumitru. 2019. 'Assessing Non-intrinsic Limitarianism', *Philosophia*, 47: 249–264.

von Platz, Jeppe. 2020a. 'Democratic Equality and the Justification of Welfare-State Capitalism', *Ethics*, 131: 4–33.

von Platz, Jeppe. 2020b. 'Rawls's Underestimation of the Importance of Economic Agency and Economic Rights', in John Mandle and Sarah Roberts-Cady (eds.), *John Rawls: Debating the Major Questions*, pp. 95–108. Oxford: Oxford University Press.

Waldron, Jeremy 1993. 'John Rawls and the Social Minimum', in Jeremy Waldron, *Liberal Rights: Collected Papers 1981–1991*, pp. 250–270. Cambridge: Cambridge University Press.

Wilkinson, Richard and Kate Pickett. 2010. *The Spirit Level: Why Equality is Better for Everyone*. London: Penguin Press.

Wolff, Edward N. 2017. *A Century of Wealth in America*. Cambridge: Harvard University Press.

Young, Iris M. 1990. *Justice and the Politics of Difference*. Princeton: Princeton University Press.

Zwarthoed, Danielle. 2018. 'Autonomy-based Reasons for Limitarianism', *Ethical Theory and Moral Practice*, 21(5): 1181–1204.

4

THE PRINCIPLE OF PROPORTIONALITY

So far I have defended the idea that economic inequality must be contained within a certain range, if the risk of material domination is to be avoided, and that normative theory should make an effort to define it. Can it be done? Yes, if, in an Aristotelian mood, one is ready to accept the degree of precision allowed by the nature of the problem. Let me start off by spelling out the constraints that the range should respect.[1] They also serve as indications of how the range ought to be sought:

1. The limits of permissible inequality are to be expressed through two ratios: one between the wealth of the best-off segment of the population and the wealth of the worst-off segment; the other between the incomes of the same segments (post-tax and transfer benefits). One should distinguish between wealth and income, not only out of conformity with current scientific standards, but also because wealth inequality is more pronounced, produces more economic inefficiency, and more effectively impacts economic and political power than inequality of labour income.
2. Ratios come with a technical problem, similar to the well-known one about the threshold. Imagine we say that the richest segment's income cannot be 29 times higher than that of the worst-off segment. We would be saying that those who make 29.0001 more times than what the poor make will risk to dominate, while those who make 28.9999 will not. In any event, the general normative point – the necessity to establish some proportion in the resources of the best-off and worst-off – does not change. Notice that even if a satisfactory solution to the 'threshold' problem or other technical problems is not available, one should be ready to sacrifice elegance for the sake of protecting the fairness of political equality through an unambiguous measure of the limit. After all, not only is the threshold problem widespread in any legislative body

DOI: 10.4324/9781003189428-5

(think of tax brackets), but it is certainly not a problem peculiar to proportional justice given that many distributive accounts (think of limitarianism and sufficientarianism) suffer the same difficulty.

3. The permissible ratios should reflect what the best empirical science available at any time indicates as necessary to avoid the risk of material domination. In particular, any account of the limit will have to justify how the best-off and the worst-off segments of the population are identified. To compare the resources of the top 10% with those of the bottom 50% is one thing; to compare the resources of the top 1% and those of the bottom 20% is quite another. The justification must rest on empirical findings on the relation between money and political influence and other relevant facts such as the availability of welfare services. To have a certain income in a society that offers free access to healthcare, schools and college is quite different than having the same amount in a society without those services.
4. A specific justification will have to be provided if the account, as it is reasonable to assume, will focus on the average income and wealth of the worst-off segment. For example, since the poorest individuals in the society earn and own less than the average of the bottom segment, they seem to remain at risk of domination even if the ratio is respected. This suggests the opportunity to make the bottom segment narrow enough to limit this risk. More importantly, the bottom segment should be defined in such a way that there are strong reasons to believe that the poorest in it are poorest not because of some modifiable societal arrangement but because of subjective factors unrelated to the shaping of primary rules. Once this is done, the criterion will take the following form: *no one should have an income (post-tax and transfer benefits) that exceeds the limit of being No. times higher than the average income of the bottom X% of the national population, and no one should possess a wealth (post-tax and transfer benefits) that is No. times higher than the average wealth of the bottom X% of the national population.*
5. The ratios should be prudent in the sense that we are authorised to adopt one only if there are strong reasons to believe that a more permissive limit would entail the risk of domination. In other words, the limit should be permissive enough to allow as much exercise of economic liberties and socioeconomic efficiency as possible. The only acceptable reason to limit one of these values is the risk of material domination.
6. The ratios should be realistic in the sense that they should not aim to make each citizen perfectly equal in terms of political influence. Differences in political influence, even considering only economic factors, will likely remain in any just society.
7. In principle, the ratios should be the same for all liberal democratic societies. However, the specificities of income and wealth distribution in each liberal democracy may suggest the opportunity to cut different segments at the top and at the bottom, something which would obviously impact the final ratios. It follows that we may keep the general validity of the ratios as a regulative ideal (a sort of general formula of democratic distribution), while proceeding at this

initial stage by focusing on one country at a time, privileging those countries in which data on wealth and income distribution are available and research on the relation between money and influence has produced some reliable results.

8. The ratios only apply to the domestic level. I am far from denying that we have obligations of justice to reduce material inequalities at the global level. I simply do not deal with the problem in this book.

Now, and finally, I have what it takes to present and defend the distributive principle of proportionality in even more detail. In doing so, I will show how the principle of proportionality is able to deal with those normative issues concerning the wealth and income distribution that are fundamental to a liberal democracy. By aiming to avoid the risk of domination, we must take into account and lead with multiple lines of enquiry on aspects such as efficiency, absolute poverty, basic liberties, pluralism, and the set of distributive public policies and social reforms that are needed to avoid this risk. The purpose is also to show that the principle of proportionality is better equipped to face all these main issues than other competitive distributive principles; in particular with respect to Rawls' difference principle and Robeyns' limitarianism with which it shares some normative assumptions. Last, but not least, in this way I take the opportunity to rebut some predictable objections to the principle of proportionality.

Hence, the first section take into account the manner in which the principle of proportionality handles the questions of economic efficiency and absolute material conditions of the least advantaged members of the society. In the second section, I argue that the principle of proportionality leaves room for the exercise of economic liberties. Most importantly, even if we have some compelling reasons to consider a wide range of economic liberties as basic liberties as well as freedom of speech and political liberties, this requirement is compatible with the distributive prescription of capping economic inequality. In the third section, I stress that the principle of proportionality, as Rawls' justice as fairness, endorses a noncommittal view about the ideal social systems that are compatible and satisfy the principles of justice. Nonetheless, I argue that in this respect, the principle of proportionality may fare better than Rawls' two principles of justice. Moreover, I sustain that a noncommittal view about the choice of ideal social system has the advantage of leaving the path open for what I call a 'pluralistic distributive approach'. In the fourth section, I define the permissible ratios of income and wealth inequality for one liberal democracy, the United States, for which the preliminary empirical studies are available. The main point is not to provide a final answer, but rather to initiate a debate about the acceptable limit ratios of economic inequality within liberal democratic societies.

4.1 Justice, Efficiency and Poverty

In this section, I take into account the manner in which the principle of proportionality handles the questions of economic efficiency and absolute material conditions of the least advantaged members of the society. In this regard, two possible critiques may be advanced on the principle of proportionality. First of all, some might object that the principle of proportionality requires a huge loss of economic efficiency. Thus, the objection sustains that it is not able to satisfy two main dominating assumptions concerning a just (or fair) economic distribution in our liberal democracies: first, it should be able to raise enough resources to provide an adequate level of public goods, such as defence, law enforcement, and education; and second, it should result in a decent standard of living for the least advantaged members of the society (Murphy and Nagel 2002). Secondly, even in the case that we are able to reject the first objection regarding the incompatibility with efficiency, a second critique concerns the insensitivity of the principle of proportionality towards the absolute material conditions of the worst-off. This critique comes from two opposing perspectives: one in which the worst-off are so affluent (in absolute terms) that they would not run the risk of material domination even if the permissible ratio is not respected; and the other in which the poorest individuals in the society earn and own less than the average of the bottom segment, so that even if the ratio is respected, they might see their urgent needs unsatisfied and, therefore, they may be dominated. Let me begin with the question of efficiency.

Some might think that defending a ratio modelled after strongly egalitarian societies may harm efficiency, and more so than what alternative egalitarian accounts of justice do. Indeed, many scholars, even egalitarians, believe that 'bringing down the top, unless it is a means of bringing up the rest, is not a policy that can be easily defended by politically attractive arguments' (Murphy and Nagel 2002: 187). From this perspective, it seems that the only way to justify a curtailment of economic efficiency is to prove that as a result the worst-off will increase their share of economic resources. This reading would exclude, in principle, any 'levelling-down' outcomes. In other words, and in a Rawlsian mood, some may object that the efficiency costs brought about by the implementation of permissible ratios may leave the worst-off (and possibly other segments of the populations) below the level they would reach without any proportional limit. However, it is possible to rebut this objection. Although the principle of proportionality holds, like Robeyns' limitarianism and Rawls' justice as fairness, the normative priority of justice over efficiency, it performs better than both of them in two fundamental aspects.

Take, for example, justice as fairness. Rawls is ready to sacrifice some efficiency for the sake of justice. And yet, as we saw in Chapter 3 (Section 3.2), the difference principle (under the special conception) would not rule out a change in the existing distribution if this produced (a) a better condition for the worst-off (and therefore an increase of efficiency of the whole system) even if this caused an increase in inequality. Let me return now to the set of socioeconomic distributions already presented in Chapter 3.

As we saw, we can move from (A) a stage of perfect equality not only to (B), but also to (C), and even to (E); regardless of the increase in the ratio of inequality (only D is precluded). By the same logic, also a move to (F), would be permitted, *other things being equal*; that is, provided that the worst-off are not penalised in their

TABLE 4.1 Principle of Proportionality, the Size of Inequality, and Efficiency

Socioeconomic distributions	*Worst-off*	*Lower-middle class*	*Upper-middle class*	*Best-off*	*Ratio*
A			All citizens at 10		1:1
B	15	20	25	30	1:2
C	20	50	60	80	1:4
D	18	55	65	144	1:8
E	22	60	70	220	1:10
F	24	80	90	480	1:20

share of other primary goods. By contrast, the principle of proportionality prevents the move to any system in which the ratio is violated, no matter what the loss of efficiency would be. From this perspective, the principle of proportionality may thus cause a more significant reduction of efficiency than that allowed by Rawls' difference principle. However, in doing so, it should be noticed that it endorses the same priority of justice over efficiency dear to Rawls. It simply better qualifies the nature of this priority.

Indeed, in (F), the least advantaged are better-off in terms of income and wealth than in other socioeconomic distributions, but they are worse-off in terms of the value of their political liberties, because the latter depend on the gap with the most advantaged. The key point is the way we conceive of the *other things equal* proviso. In (F) *other things* are not equal at all, and *if* in (F) the ratio of inequality exposes the worst-off to the risk of material domination, they are severely damaged by that condition. In this sense, the principle of proportionality is able to better sanction the normative priority of justice over efficiency than Rawls' difference principle. Thus, we have reasons to prefer a society that avoids the risk of material domination, even if this is less efficient than a society (F) in which there this risk. And this is true both if it is less efficient than (F) in the aggregate and – here is the difference with Rawls' difference principle – even if in society (F) the worst-off would be better-off in absolute terms. Proportional justice holds that loss of efficiency (in both senses) is a price liberal democracy should pay to avoid the risk of material domination. A requirement that, ultimately, is implicit in the lexical priority of Rawls' two principles of justice that should exclude higher material gains if they are at the expense of the fairness of political influence.

However, an extreme version of the objection would argue that the permissible ratios may take the worst-off not merely below where they could reach without proportional justice, but below a decent level of resources, decency be defined as it may. Aside from the fact that the scenario is quite abstract because qualitative and quantitative research has abundantly shown how too much inequality does not boost but in fact damages growth.[2] In any case, since the principle of proportionality does not aim to eradicate inequality, and is allowing its reduction only for the sake of avoiding domination (*constraint 5*), the objection needs to assume that a society in which the group at the top of the distribution dominates (not merely x times more affluent than the bottom group) is more efficient in keeping the poor above the threshold than one in which inequality stops at the doors of domination. But, as I have said in Chapter 3 (Section 3.3), this scenario needs to assume the implausible empirical hypothesis that the reduction of a considerable inequality that embodies the risk of material domination cannot be converted into more resources for the poorest. Even the rare empirical studies that challenge the idea, supported by numerous, convergent and solid studies, that democracies do a better job than non-democracies to improve the welfare of the poor while producing more public goods and more income redistribution than non-democracies, do not dare claim that non-democracies fare better. Instead, they claim that non-democracies do not do worse than democracies (Ross 2006). Thus, even if one sides with this 'minority report', the choice would be between a world in which the poor are below the threshold of decency and dominated, and one in which they are equally positioned but non-dominated.

In any case, the crucial point is obviously that the principle of proportionality does not rest on some version of limitarianism and, therefore, efficiency is not so severely curtailed as it is with Robeyns' account. Recall that limitarianism, at least in the version that gives priority to the value of political equality over that of meeting urgent needs, is bound to inefficiently tax 100% of the extra income earned by those who are already at the top threshold. However, there is no reason to assume this. From this perspective, the principle of proportional justice has a comparative advantage over Robeyns' limitarianism. Although the principle of proportionality starts, somewhat similarly to limitarianism, from the fact of the risk of political domination in liberal democracies, unlike limitarianism, it holds that the best way to counter material domination is not the imposition of a top threshold meant to eliminate surplus money, but through the introduction of limits on material inequality between the best-off and worst-off. In other words, it makes sure that some are never so much richer than others that their wealth gives them the opportunity to buy a quota of political influence significantly bigger than the one the worst-off can afford. On the contrary, targeting inequality as opposed to absolute measures of wealth is both more efficient as a way of protecting political equality, and costs less in terms of erosion of the values that liberal democracies are committed to, such as personal liberty, general efficiency (hence resources to redistribute in favour of poor citizens), and pluralism.

The most fundamental and obvious difference with limitarianism is that the principle of proportional justice assumes that unbounded inequality is more dangerous than surplus money if one is worried about money-driven political influence. In other words, the principle of proportionality is not about taking away the superfluous from the rich. It is about watching the distance they have with the worst-off, regardless of how many superfluous resources the best-off and, for what it is worth, the worst-off enjoy. If we start from a distribution that violates the ratio, the required change could be brought about by raising the resources of the worst-off as well as by capping the resources of the best-off. In any case, the decisive theoretical feature is that citizens may become increasingly richer provided that taxation or alternative forms of distribution ensure that the distance from the worst-off does not violate the limit ratio. This would leave open the possibility that people work more to buy as many luxury items as they wish on the condition that the worst-off are 'lifted up' so that the permissible ratio is still respected. This allows the principle of proportionality to avoid the incentive objection, which plagues limitarianism, as Robeyns knows (Robeyns 2017: 34–37). Limitarianism demands to cut all economic resources above the riches line. In this way the almost rich are evidently discouraged from producing more. This loss of efficiency is unnecessary to protect political equality and it is bad because it might subtract resources that, for example, could be used to meet basic needs. Robeyns (2017: 34–35; 2019: 261–262) seems to suggest an inevitable trade-off between the two main values she defends. This contrast is significantly eased, if not removed altogether, by the principle of proportionality: the best-off have incentives to contribute to the creation of wealth because they do not have to give up the hope of having surplus money. They are merely asked not to 'fly' too distant from the worst-off.

However, even if we can be confident about the question of efficiency, another objection can be advanced against the principle of proportionality, in particular regarding the *constraint 4*. The core of this critique concerns the insensitivity of the principle of proportionality towards the absolute material conditions of the worst-off. As I anticipated, this critique comes from two opposing perspectives. According to the first perspective of this critique, material domination is unlikely to occur in an affluent society in which inequality is unlimited but the worst-off are rich. Even if the gap between the super-rich and rich is large, the autonomy of the latter would be safe, given their considerable resources. Then, contrary to all I have been arguing, the factor generating domination would not be inequality but the poor's absolute levels of material resources. But this criticism misses the variety of ways in which money can influence politics and, more generally, primary rules. First of all, while it is probably true that in this society nobody – to paraphrase Rousseau – would be so poor as to be forced to 'sell themselves', this is clearly insufficient to conclude that material domination could not occur. Indeed, the best-off would still have a significantly bigger share of material resources to steer the political process in the desired direction. Notice that our Western societies can be considered as quite similar to this hypothetical affluent society, at least if the comparison is with ancient societies. The fact that in absolute terms Westerners today have more resources than mediaeval kings is no guarantee that they are not dominated. Indeed, even in this hypothetical very affluent society, perhaps the worst-off would not 'sell' their votes, but all mechanisms previously described through which money is translated into political and cultural hegemonic influence would still remain in force, because they depend on the competitive nature of the political and economic spheres. Hence they are sensitive to inequality of resources, not how much citizens have in absolute terms.

In addition, following my argument, some could assert that the amount of wealth that the best-off citizens may use to influence politics could be compensated and even outspent by the sum of small contributions coming from the many worst-off.

It could be further suggested that one should worry about how money disrupts the political process only when the total wealth of the best-off segment is bigger than the wealth of the worst-off segment (for example, respectively the top 1% and the bottom 20%, as indicated in the case study, see Section 4). This is evidently compatible with the possibility that the gap between the best-off and worst-off individuals is larger than what the limit allows. There are many problems with this line of thought. First, it is hardly disputable that poor people can devote only a lower percentage of their budget than the one rich people can offer. So the total wealth of the two segments can be the same but the percentage of resources each can allocate to political activities is not. The idea is meant to ensure that each citizen has roughly the same political influence, not that classes or segments of the population collectively do. Guaranteeing equal rights to members of the society as long as they align their political preferences with members of the same class would be a strange notion of political equality in a liberal democracy indeed. Finally, ratios calculated in this way would allow enormous wealth concentration in the hands of a single individual (think of Jeff Bezos) if the sum total of the top segment's wealth respected the ratio.

The opposite perspective of the same critique regarding the insensitivity of the principle of proportionality towards the absolute material conditions of the worst-off, instead, might be worried about the possibility that since the 'poorest' individuals in the society earn and own less than the average of the bottom segment, even if the ratio is respected, they might see their urgent needs unsatisfied and they may be dominated. This scenario could occur because the principle of proportionality focuses on average income and wealth of the worst-off segment (*constraint* 4), rather than on the least advantaged individuals. Here it is necessary to distinguish two scenarios, and to deal normatively with them.

The first scenario is that of a very poor society in which, even if the ratio is respected, the worst-off are so poor that they are materially dominated because they are at the mercy of the more affluent citizens' charity to survive. Note that this form of material domination is not related to Christiano's four mechanisms, but rather concerns some pervasive interactional forms of control and subordination of the poorest. In other words, the most affluent citizens might not have the amount of economic resources necessary to shape the primary rules significantly more than the worst-off do, but nonetheless they might have enough material resources with respect to the poorest to put the lives of the latter under their control and subordination. I admit that in this extreme case the principle of proportionality should give way to a principle of sufficiency or social minimum as the main distributive principle of justice that guides political and social actions. However, we need to make this normative shift for the simple, and unique, fact that what exposes the poorest to the risk of control and subordination (or we could say, interactional forms of domination, see Chapter 2) is not an excessive material inequality but their unmet basic needs.[3] In any case, in a liberal democracy, given its comparatively high capacity to produce wealth and to redistribute, this extreme scenario is a remote possibility.

In the second scenario, the ratio is also respected, and the society is, instead, rich enough that the average income and wealth of the worst-off does not expose them to the form of material domination of the preceding case. Still, some members of society might continue to suffer a condition of poverty due to their subjective factors. In this case, the principle of proportionality does not require any additional redistribution, because, again, the bottom segment should be defined in such a way that there are strong reasons to believe that the poorest in it are poorest not because of some modifiable societal arrangement, but because of subjective factors unrelated to the shaping of primary rules. This theoretical feature is also shared by Rawls' difference principle which states that social and economic inequalities should 'be to the greatest benefit of the least-advantaged members of society' (Rawls 2005: 6), and for the 'least advantaged', Rawls means the least advantaged social group – unskilled workers (Rawls 1971: 78) – rather than single individuals. Not surprisingly, my reply follows the same normative intuition underlying Rawls' theory of justice. Rawls (1971: 54) distinguishes what can happen to a citizen by reason of their own particular circumstances – such as suffering psychological or physical deficiencies or other personal attitudes that do not allow them to fully participate in the social cooperation – and what by reason of the imposition of the basic structure of society. From this perspective, it is not a case of the least advantaged always being identified as representative of social groups, and not as a single individual. Otherwise, it would be impossible to prove the political and social dimension of a certain claim of (social) justice that satisfies the criteria of reciprocity and publicity. As I said in Chapter 3 (Section 3.1), proportional justice assumes that any compelling political conception of distributive justice needs such a fundamental distinction.

However, it is important to recall that two features of what I call a political conception of distributive justice, in this respect, can mark a decisive point to make the choice of focusing on average income and wealth of the worst-off segment less problematic. I said (Section 3.1) that, first of all, a political conception of justice does not deny that the requirements of social virtues cannot be matter of public policies as long as the limits and background requisites fixed by a political conception of justice are respected; and secondly, it is also possible to appeal to an 'objective' and minimal conception of basic needs of human beings to provide a *freestanding* justification for a material distribution that protects citizens from absolute deprivations. Hence, as a result, some individuals might be considered 'relatively' poor, but certainly would not see their basic needs unmet, and in addition nothing prevents us from pursuing a political agenda (in the hope of being convincing in the acts of public deliberation) aimed at improving the condition of the poorest citizens.

Finally, a last objection to be asserted against another theoretical feature of the principle of proportionality: the fact that it remains silent about the fairness of the intermediate social positions between the best-off and the worst-off. The point is that if the most affluent individuals do not have enough to dominate the worst-off, *a fortiori* they will not have enough to dominate the middle class. This allows for a disregard of the normative relevance of intermediate positions. However, in this way, some might argue that there is no guarantee that the permissible ratio is reached or maintained by 'transferring' economic resources to the worst-off from the intermediate segments rather than from the best-off. I admit that, in theory, the principle of proportionality does not forbid this possibility. Similarly, other distributive principles of justice, like Rawls' difference principle, sufficientarianism or limitarianism, exclusively focus on a certain baseline for their normative prescriptions, disregarding the losses and gains of other social groups or individuals. It is a price to pay for providing a principle with a good chance of being practically executed.

In any case, the risk that the permissible ratio would be reached at the cost of intermediate positions by avoiding a sacrifice of the resources of the wealthiest in a way that might sound severely unfair is quite remote. Indeed, a just liberal society should pay attention not only to avoid the risk of material domination, but also to guarantee that positions and offices are open to all under condition of fair equality of opportunity (Rawls 1971, 2005) and to also ensure the fair value of the exercise of economic liberties. In this respect, it is very unlikely that a society that also satisfies these normative requirements will result in a disharmonious economic 'hierarchy' of the income and wealth shares of the different social groups. As a counter-proof of this, in fact, the astronomic concentration of wealth in the hands of the top end of the distribution in our current liberal societies, in some cases almost close to the Belle Époque levels (see Piketty 2014: 248), is an evident sign that the risk of material domination is already with us. In a society with these very high wealth and income inequalities (as in the case of the USA), the 'contribution' of the best-off individuals in reaching the permissible ratio is empirically inevitable. Think again Jeff Bezos with a personal wealth of USD171 Billion (year 2022) (Peterson-Withorn 2022): any reasonable permissible ratio for wealth cannot be reached without considerably curtailing his economic resources, as well as raising the resources of the worst-off.

4.2 Economic Liberties as Basic Rights in a Liberal Democracy

The *constraint 5* establishes that the ratios should be permissive enough to allow not only socioeconomic efficiency, but also the exercise of economic liberties. Thus, we might ask ourselves how much weight should economic liberties have in a liberal democracy. Answering this question is significant in order to know if the principle of proportionality leaves enough room for economic liberties, and if in doing so this space is compatible with the prescription of capping economic inequality. Indeed, some might argue that the kind of protection that we should ensure to economic liberties in a liberal democracy is incompatible with strong distributive requirements, like Rawls' difference principle or the idea of imposing a limit on economic inequality. In this section, I will answer this fundamental question.

Recently, the debate on the idea of economic liberty has gained a new vigour. To have a clearer picture of the content of economic liberties, we can take into account the basic list that James Nickel provided. According to Nickel (2000: 156–157), we can distinguish four main categories of economic liberties: 1) *Working: Freedom to labour and use labour in production.* This concerns the liberty to employ one's body and time in productive activities that one has chosen or accepted; i.e. liberty to sell, buy, trade, and donate labour; 2) *Transacting: Free economic activity.*

This category concerns the liberty to manage one's own affairs, to sell and buy, to make things, to invest and save, hire workers, buy and use land, and to engage in business activities such as to start, run, and close a farm or other commercial enterprises; 3) *Holding: Freedom in the realm of property*. This is the liberty to acquire, hold and transfer property, and to develop property for commercial and productive purposes; 4) *Using: Freedom to buy, use, and consume resources, goods, and services*. This last category corresponds to the liberty to make use of legitimately acquired resources for consumption and production; i.e. liberty to eat, drink, wear, inhabit, and read, or to consume the goods necessary for productive activities.

Traditionally, the liberal thought debate has been animated by a sharp controversy about the kind of protection that we should assign to economic liberties. The assumption that a robust protection of economic liberties and property rights is incompatible with a strong commitment to distributive justice was taken as a given. In a nutshell, if economic liberties are conceived as basic rights, or much more as absolute natural rights, political authority cannot restrict or limit them to pursue redistributive requirements of social justice or other social values. For example, the government cannot impose a minimum wage, a mandatory saving for retirement, taxation on inheritance and bequest for the sake of securing substantive equality of opportunity or pursuing other (re)distributive goals. For this reason, it is not surprising that liberals who usually believe that a society should also pursue the distributive requirements of social justice tend to give the economic liberties a lower level of protection. This usually takes them apart from those liberals who belong to classical liberalism and libertarianism schools who assign a high or absolute level of protection to the full range of economic liberties and property rights, and in so doing, they usually deny the idea of distributive justice. The main difference lies in the different conceptions of economic liberty.

Brennan and Tomasi (2012) distinguish between a thick and a thin conception of economic liberty, according to which one can classify the different kinds of liberalism. According to Brennan and Tomasi (2012), classical liberalism (e.g. Smith, Hume, but also Hayek and Friedman) and libertarianism (Nozick) defend a thick conception of economic liberty, while what is usually called high liberalism (Mill, Rawls, Dworkin, Freeman) endorses a thin conception.[4] In the thick conception, economic liberty is understood as having the same status as civil liberties (for libertarianism, economic liberties have absolute moral status); in contrast, high liberalism reduces the weight accorded to economic liberty when compared with other basic liberties (Brennan and Tomasi 2012: 117). However, in the contemporary debate, this theoretical distinction has been questioned, and there are some attempts to combine a robust protection of economic liberties without thereby denying commitments to distributive justice. The most significant example is neoclassical liberalism (see Brennan and Tomasi 2012; von Platz and Tomasi 2015).

To say something on the controversy about the kind of protection that economic liberties should enjoy in a liberal democracy, we need to provide a compelling argument about the normative status that justifies this kind of protection, whether absolute, high or low; and it is evident that this normative status depends on the idea of justice we advocate. For this reason, the discussion must be split into two aspects. First of all, we need to know if we have a compelling argument – that is, a justification that nobody can reasonably reject – to consider the full or a wide range of economic liberties as basic rights as well as other basic liberties such as freedom of speech and political liberties. In my view, this means to know whether economic liberties should be included on the list of key power resources that make up the background requisites of a political conception of distributive justice. Secondly, once, and if, we have found this argument, we need to assess if a robust protection for economic liberties really implies, as many believe, a downsizing in terms of material distributive commitments so much as to rule out Rawls' difference principle or my principle of proportionality. Beginning with the first step, we can identify four main different conceptions of justice that assign a specific normative standard to economic liberties: libertarianism, classical liberalism, high liberalism, and neoclassical liberalism.

Libertarianism assigns the highest protection to economic liberties which are understood as absolute. This means that 'libertarians tend to think that distributive justice is fully realised by the protection of economic liberties and that any state redistribution of resources impermissibly violates economic liberties' (von Platz and Tomasi 2015: 266). This view depends on the fact that for libertarianism, at least Nozickean ones, economic liberties are natural rights that are constitutive of self-ownership or are based on a principle of natural liberty. As a consequence,

> the economic rights, including property rights that persons can acquire by dealing with each other, are thus theoretically and normatively prior to the authority of the state — to secure these rights is the source, end, and limit of state authority.
>
> (von Platz 2020b: 98)

From this libertarian perspective, economic agency is central for justice. Indeed, only if individuals are fully free to engage themselves in 'voluntary' acquisitions and exchanges is their self-ownership protected from external and coercive interferences. This means that economic liberties pre-exist the political authority and any legal system. It is evident that, according to a libertarian account, a full protection of economic liberties is incompatible with distributive justice other than that which arises from two historical conditions: the first acquisition should not be marked by violence and fraud, and all subsequent transactions ought to be free and non-coercive.

Classical liberalism does not follow libertarianism in conceiving economic liberties, as well as other basic liberties, as absolute. By contrast, not only do classical liberals take property rights to be determined by convention and law and not attribute them pre-legal validity, but they also assign a greater role to the state than libertarians (see on this point Freeman 2011). Indeed, the state's function is to make the free market work properly, for example by avoiding monopolies or correcting externalities (for this end Pigovian taxes and subsidies are acceptable). The state can also provide essential public services and goods, which should be paid for according to the benefit principle requiring that 'taxpayers contribute in proportion to the benefit they derive from government' (Murphy and Nagel 2002: 16). However, on the one side, this means that for classical liberalism economic liberties can be regulated by political authority, on the other side, they attribute to them the same high level of protection of other basic liberties, like freedom of speech and religion or political liberty. For classical liberalism, the reason according to which economic liberties have this high level of protection is usually indirect utilitarian (von Platz and Tomasi 2015; von Platz 2020b). In other words, they are essential tools for promoting individual and also collective well-being, insofar as 'free exercise of economic agency tends to minimise waste, maximise the productive output of society, secure an optimal distribution of goods and resources, and avoid the dangers of concentrated governmental power' (von Platz and Tomasi 2015: 269). From this perspective, distributive justice that arises from government interference with economic liberty is seen as intrinsically inefficient, and therefore as unjust. It is not surprising that, for classical liberalism, the laissez-faire economic system is taken as a requirement of justice. Material distribution should result from individual participation in a free market whose fair functioning is guaranteed by the state, and ultimately should not depend on undue privileges, but on differences in individual talents and abilities. Besides the provision of public goods to secure an educated workforce, although the idea of distributive justice is not entirely absent, it is confined to micro interventions and interferences on individual economic choices. For example, an exception is permitted in a situation in which individuals cannot ensure their self-subsistence, in this case the state should intervene by distributing benefits in order to allow these individuals, as potential consumers, to participate in the free market and therefore increase general well-being. However, under this indirect utilitarian point of view, the protection of economic liberties has the consequence of sharply limiting the scope and the significance of distributive requirements.

On the opposite side of liberal thought, high liberalism instead does not assign a prominent role to economic liberties, and therefore they receive a lower protection than other basic liberties. Certainly Rawls' theory of justice represents the most influential account of this school which, unlike libertarianism and classical liberalism, works within the contractualist framework; that is, the principles of justice are those on which all citizens conceived as free and equal could agree, or on which they cannot reasonably reject. Rawls' theory of social justice is the most exemplary case. Indeed, he (Rawls 2005: 298) thinks that thick economic liberties are not necessary to develop citizens' moral powers. This means that only a few economic liberties qualify as basic rights. Here the basic rights are equivalent to what I called the background requisites of political justice. There is a significant difference between liberties conceived as absolutes and those conceived as basic rights; that is, the latter are not absolute in the sense that they cannot be regulated by political authority under any circumstance. However, basic rights hold a high normative standard with respect to non-basic rights, because a basic right can only be regulated or even 'restricted' in order to secure an equal system of basic rights for all. Again, the consequence is that they cannot be limited or restricted to pursue equality of opportunity, distributive justice, or efficiency. In Rawls' theory, basic rights are included on the first principle of justice and therefore their protection has priority over the achievement of the requirements of the second principle. To recall, for Rawls the requirements of the first principle are conceived to allow citizens to develop and exercise the two moral powers of democratic citizenship: the capacity for a conception of the good and the capacity for a sense of justice. According to Rawls (1971: 42–43; 2005: 228, 232, 298; 2001a: 114), only two categories of economic liberties – the right to hold and have exclusive use of personal property, and freedom of occupation – are necessary for the adequate development and exercise of the two moral powers (in particular the capacity for a conception of the good), and therefore they satisfy the conditions for being considered basic rights.[5] As a consequence, as von Platz (2013: 5) observes,

> apart from these two, Rawls thinks that the scheme of economic rights that a society should provide should be determined by reference to realising the fair value of political liberties, equality of opportunity, and a fair distribution of income and wealth.

In other words, a wide list of economic liberties (think of that provided by Nickel) does not enjoy the same lexicographical priority as basic rights, and it means that there is nothing wrong in regulating and limiting them to pursue, for instance, a material distribution that accomplishes the difference principle.

Finally, neoclassical liberalism assumes a normative position that represents an alternative to classical liberalism and libertarianism, as well as to high liberalism. Precisely, neoclassical liberals, unlike high liberals, endorse a thick conception of economic liberty, but they ground it on an argument that distinguishes them from classical liberals and libertarians. Neoclassical liberals sustain that a thick conception of economic liberty is a necessary condition for citizens to develop and pursue an autonomous life plan (Brennan and Tomasi 2012: 118). In this sense, they 'focus on the moral ideal of citizens living together as responsible self-authors', not as self-owners like in libertarianism (Brennan and Tomasi 2012: 120). Furthermore, they disagree with classical liberalism and libertarianism on the idea that only negative liberties matter. In contrast, they claim that citizens should have the concrete means to pursue their own conceptions of the good life. From this point of view, they share high liberalism's commitment to the material well-being of citizens, accepting some distributive criteria such as those endorsed by sufficientarianism or prioritarianism, but less demanding than Rawls' difference principle or other egalitarian principles.

Although neoclassical liberalism shares the same contractualist framework with high liberalism, it maintains that a full range of economic liberties are basic rights insofar as they are necessary for the proper development and exercise of the powers of moral personality. In this sense, the charge of neoclassical liberalism is that Rawls (and generally high liberals) does not provide convincing and coherent reasons for excluding economic liberties from protection by the first principle of justice. In other words, it represents a sort of unjustified 'exceptionalism' because 'economic liberties are no less important for the development and exercise of the moral powers than the liberties Rawls includes in the list' (von Platz 2020b: 101). For example, Tomasi (2012; and with Brennan 2012) argues that there is no reason to consider economic identity less essential than religious or political identities, and therefore the economic agency should enjoy the same protection as other basic liberties. Again, the consequence of considering the full list of economic liberties as basic rights is that these liberties, as much as political and civil, can be regulated and restricted only for the sake of securing an adequate scheme of equal basic rights for all, rather than to pursue distributive goals. According to Tomasi, and other neoclassical liberals, a revision of this sort would lead Rawls' justice as fairness to be committed to an ideal institutional social scheme that is closed to a sort of laissez-faire capitalism that Tomasi calls 'market democracy' rather than property-owning democracy and liberal socialism, which Rawls instead believes are the only ones that satisfy the two principles of justice.

Some Rawlsians (Freeman 2011, 2012; Thomas 2017) have rejected this criticism, proving that it is not incoherent to exclude a full range of economic liberties from the first principle in order to ensure an adequate development of the two moral powers of democratic citizenship. I do not have the time here to enter into this exegetic debate, and it would not be decisive for my argument. Indeed, as observed by von Platz (2013, 2016, 2020b), although it is not true that, by Rawls' own criterion, the full range of economic liberties should be basic rights, Tomasi's charge of unjustified exceptionalism can remain valid. In other words, 'economic agency is no less central to social cooperation than the ethical and political forms of agency that the first principle protects and enables' (von Platz 2020b: 103), and therefore Rawls' own conception of the moral powers of the democratic citizenship is not adequate.

According to von Platz, given that social cooperation presupposes the capacity for working, Rawls missed taking into account, along with the capacity for a conception of the good and for the sense of justice, the capacity to work productively with others which explains how we engage *in* cooperation. For this reason, he suggests including a third moral power in order to complete the idea of democratic citizenship; that is, the capacity to *work*, to be a productive participant in social cooperation (von Platz 2016: 292; 2020a: 23; 2020b: 104). What is important in von Platz's argument is that the capacity for working empowers citizens and enables them to 'share in the burden of producing all the good things' (von Platz 2020b: 105). In this way, he can avoid embracing a liberal perfectionism view that sees, instead, a valuable 'good' or 'purpose' to be followed in work. Von Platz's emphasis on this sort of productive justice[6] implies normative requirements that distance his proposal from that of Tomasi. For instance, although von Platz, like Tomasi, considers economic liberties as basic rights, his view does not place justice as fairness along the lines of laissez-faire capitalism. By contrast, it makes certain types of capitalism, but not capitalism itself, impermissible in the case that access to productive work for some members of society is a matter left to the discretion of others. In other words, in the case that development and exercise of the productive powers for all citizens is not ensured. From this perspective, von Platz (2020a) argues that his proposal has the result to rescue welfare-state capitalism from Rawls' charge of being incompatible with the two principles of justice.[7]

In any case, beyond the substantive differences between von Platz's and Tomasi's proposals (or more generally between a liberal-social democratic conception of justice and neoclassical liberalism), by assigning a higher normative standard to economic liberties than Rawls did, for both of them the result is that a (liberal) political conception of justice becomes incompatible with the strong egalitarian requirements of Rawls' difference principle.

At the end of this brief overview of the current debate about the normative standard of economic liberties, I believe that we have some compelling arguments to consider a wide range of economic liberties as basic rights as well as other basic liberties, such as freedom of speech and political liberties.[8] At this point in my argument we can quite easily find both libertarianism and classical liberalism's conception of economic liberties - based respectively on natural rights and on utilitarian grounds - inadequate. While, by contrast, the argument provided by neoclassical liberalism grounded on the idea of self-authorship (Kantian in spirit) or von Platz's third moral power to be a productive participant in social cooperation has doubtless a lot in common with my idea of non-domination as co-authorship. Indeed, I share with Tomasi and von Platz the assumption that economic liberties have a fundamental role to protect citizens against domination. As we have already seen, given the fact of pluralism and rejecting a command economy (see Chapter 1, Section 1.3), individuals should be co-authors of the primary rules also in the economic domain itself. In this respect, I am sympathetic with neoclassical liberal scholars who see economic liberties as a necessary condition for which citizens develop and pursue a life plan for themselves, or, as von Platz puts in different terms, a necessary condition for which they engage themselves in productive activities. In other words, economic liberties should be considered as key power resources that enable citizens to be co-authors of the primary rules, insofar as they allow 'adequate access to the development and exercise of the productive powers of all' (von Platz 2020b: 107). In this sense, I believe that my idea of non-domination based on citizens' '*relative*' or '*proportional*' capacity to establish, shape, and stabilise primary rules, already includes von Platz's third moral power.

However, the dilemma is to know whether by sharing the idea of economic liberties as basic rights, my view is inevitably exposed to a contradiction with the limits of economic inequality prescribed by the principle of proportionality. At the first insight, by looking up the current debate, the answer seems to be yes. Indeed, as we have already seen, when economic liberties are conceived as basic rights, even if this does not exclude the idea of distributive justice (like with libertarianism and classical liberalism), in the best scenario, it seems to have the unequivocal effect of weakening the prescriptions of distributive justice. If this is true, the only solution would be the one endorsed by Rawls and high liberals: to downgrade the normative standard of economic liberties. Nonetheless, I think it is short-sighted to derive this conclusion.

For the sake of argument, let us suppose it is true that a provision for a wide range of economic liberties included in the first principle of justice would make it very difficult, if not impossible, to pursue Rawls' difference principle by reason of the fact that Rawls' theory of justice seems to be grounded on a division of labour between the two principles of justice (see Chapter 1, Section 1.3 and Chapter 3, Section 3.1) which distinguishes those principles conceived to assign basic liberties and rights and those principles that define the terms of material distribution. But it is not the case with the principle of proportionality which prescribes a reduction of economic inequality within a certain permissible ratio only for the sake of protection and ensuring the development and exercise of the two (or three) moral powers for all citizens, including the basic rights of economic liberties. The principle of proportionality is not based on a division of labour between political justice and distributive justice; by contrast, it prescribes a certain material distribution in order to ensure and guarantee both the *value* of political liberties and economic liberties. In other words, to pursue the distributive prescriptions of the principle of proportionality, we should regulate and in some cases restrict economic liberties to ensure the exercise of other basic liberties, such as political liberties, or to enable the 'fair' exercise of economic liberties themselves for all. In this respect, what I consider unsatisfactory in Tomasi's and von Platz's accounts is the way they claim to guarantee citizens' effective means (i.e. the value or the worth of liberty) to exercise both political and economic liberties.

First of all, although neither Tomasi (2012) nor von Platz (2020a) neglect the threat that economic inequality poses to political equality, they rely on the insulation strategy to protect the value of political liberties. Although von Platz does not deny that it might be necessary to impose a 'limitarian ceiling on economic inequality alongside the sufficientarian floor' (von Platz 2020a: 27), he sustains that it is impossible in theory to affirm the insufficiency of the insulation strategy (von Platz 2020a: 24–25). I said a lot about why and how the insulation strategy is in *theory* insufficient, and I do not need to dwell on the point any longer. Tomasi instead opts for an unconventional insulation strategy by which inequality and the concentration of wealth and property are no longer problematic because political equality and autonomy can be protected by removing 'divisive economic issues from the legislative agenda and thus [by limiting] the attractiveness of buying power' (Brennan and Tomasi 2012: 123). To achieve this goal, Tomasi (2012) proposes an ideal regime that he calls 'market democracy'. In it, the market guarantees that all citizens have sufficient economic resources to live autonomously without state intervention. In market democracy the role of government is quite limited and economic conflicts about state legislation are therefore avoided *ex ante*. For this reason, the rich ought to have no incentive to translate their superior economic power into political power. This solution is also not convincing. If one is really worried about the material means that should guarantee to all citizens the material means to exercise their economic liberties, one needs to establish a set of socioeconomic rules to ensure this result. This leads once again to the question of *who* should decide on these rules. There are only two realistic hypotheses: the government or the market. In the first scenario, Tomasi (and generally neoclassical liberalism) disregards the problem of economic power interfering in the political system. In the second scenario, one simply shifts the place where economic decisions are taken from the state to the market. In the market, however, unequal economic power allows the richest citizens to control economic relations among agents; for example, the terms of the contracts and agreements between employers and employees, or sellers and consumers (see Thomas 2017, 2020). For this reason, the market will be truly democratic only if it does not permit great inequality and the concentration of wealth and property – a concern that neoclassical liberalism does not seem to have. Thus, Tomasi's proposal commits the same mistake of those who, like von Platz, rely on the classical insulation strategy: they overlook the effect of the primary rules (or the basic structure) of society.

Secondly, I also consider it unsatisfactory the way they claim to guarantee citizens' effective means to exercise their economic liberties; i.e. in terms of absolute material resources in the hands of citizens. In this way, they commit, *mutatis mutandis*, the same mistake as Rawls does of neglecting the value of economic liberties and, therefore, the fact that they are competitive in their use.[9] Someone could affirm that not all liberties are innately competitive. For example, based on this consideration, Joshua Cohen (1989: 738–739, note 32) defends Rawls' choice to take only the case of political liberties into account. Of course, not all kinds of liberties are competitive in their use, for instance civil liberties, but it is sharply counterintuitive to affirm that economic liberties are not, especially in a society that makes use of the free market. Indeed, as I have repeatedly said, what gives citizens the effective means to exercise their economic liberties is not simply, as instead Brennan and Tomasi affirm (2012: 122), that a typical citizen of a Western nation today has more material resources and conditions than a mediaeval king, but that their material resources would be converted into economic power having more or less the same competitive value of the economic power of the most affluent citizen in our contemporary society. For example, think about what it really means to have the chance of winning a legal battle to guarantee the success of an economic activity; what increases my chances is not simply the amount of economic resources that I can afford for my legal representation, but also, and above all, the amount of these resources with respect to those of my opponent, and whether they permit him/her to hire a more expensive and superior lawyer or to afford a longer juridical process than I can. Taking another concrete example, the phenomenon of centrifugation in some famous metropolitan areas such as the San Francisco Bay Area. The cost of living in that region has grown to a point that forces people who have a high level of education and a qualified job to become homeless (see Har 2017). The point is that the 'absolute' condition of those people who live in this uncomfortable situation strictly depends on relative conditions of the new millionaires of the tech boom who are able to afford an astronomical price to rent a house.

To conclude, all those liberals who really care about economic liberty, and want to avoid advocating a simple formal conception of liberty, should endorse a serious concern with the proportionality in citizens' wealth and income. In light of all this, I find the distributive commitments of the principle of proportionality to also be compatible with an effective protection of a wide set of economic liberties for all citizens.

4.3 Ideal Types of Social Systems and a Pluralistic Distributive Approach

No principle of justice that can be considered as such can avoid the difficult question of its implementation in more or less generic social forms. In other words, principles of justice (whether pure procedural or consequentialist) pose two inescapable questions separately: *what is justice?* Or, better, *what is injustice?* And *how should we achieve justice or remove injustice?* For example, a principle of justice might prescribe a certain procedure to assign the fruit of social cooperation, while leaving the question open as to what kinds of social and political policies, technical devices, or political actions we should adopt in order to correctly realise the procedure or to achieve a certain outcome. Of course, it is possible that some principles of justice prescribe something that is unfeasible or very difficult to accomplish under any or certain empirical circumstances. This corresponds to the problem of knowing if a certain theory of justice and its principles can be considered what Rawls (2001a, 2001b) calls a 'realistic utopia', both with respect to the material conditions and the 'nature' of human beings.

The difficulty of implementation and the potential conflicts that may arise between what the principles of justice prescribe and the concrete circumstances in which those principles should apply are the topics of the debate about ideal and non-ideal theory. This debate finds its origins in John Rawls' methodological paradigm.[10] In *A Theory of Justice*, Rawls describes his theory as an ideal theory which is defined by two main assumptions: agents' strict compliance with the demands of justice and favourable natural and historical conditions (Rawls 1971: 8, 215, 245; 2001b: 4–6). Ideal theory tells us what justice is; that is, 'it presents a conception of a just society that we are to achieve if we can. [and therefore] Existing institutions are to be judged in the light of this conception' (Rawls 1971: 246). In opposition, 'nonideal theory asks how this long-term goal might be achieved, or worked toward, usually in gradual steps. It looks for courses of action that are morally permissible and politically possible as well as likely to be effective' (Rawls 2001b: 89). This means that the non-ideal theory is characterised by partial compliance and unfavourable conditions, and therefore it 'studies the principles that govern how we are to deal with injustice' (Rawls 1971: 8). Although Rawls himself admits that the problems that concern non-ideal theory (or partial compliance theory) 'are the pressing and urgent matters, [...] the reason for beginning with ideal theory is that it provides, I believe, the only basis for the systematic grasp of these more pressing problems' (Rawls 1971: 9).

This distinction has generated the suspicion that the ideal approach leaves us without a method for bringing the gap between a set of political principles of justice appropriate to ideal conditions and those appropriate to the non-ideal circumstances in our real world. In other words, if ideal principles are valid in the ideal circumstances, but irrelevant to non-ideal circumstances, they are unable to guide action in the real world. If this critique were well founded, it would inflict a fatal blow to all those principles of justice which are the result of an ideal theory or an ideal methodology. For this reason, it is not surprising that Rawls (1971: 303) explicitly says that ideal theory guides the application of the principles of justice to non-ideal situations. The point is that 'for until the ideal is identified, at least in outline – and that is all we should expect – nonideal theory lacks an objective, an aim, by reference to which its queries can be answered' (Rawls 2001b: 90).

Given that I said that the principle of proportionality shares the same intuition as Rawls about the transitional justice between the principles of justice and its concrete implementation in some specific institutional settings or social systems (Chapter 1, Section 1.3), it is important to elucidate this controversy and to clarify in which sense we could define the principle of proportionality as an 'ideal' principle of justice.

I believe the debate on ideal and non-ideal theory is somewhat misconstrued. Honestly, the origin of these difficulties is also due to Rawls' vocabulary, and his choice of terms like 'perfect justice' or 'ideal theory' itself. In any case, if we investigate the content of the main objections that Rawls' methodology has received, we discover that the disagreement seems to regard how to answer different questions, rather than the same one. Here, I will only focus on one of the main controversies of the contemporary debate about ideal vs non-ideal theory; precisely the controversy about the necessity of the ideal theory to determine justice-improvements; i.e. make the world more just.[11]

Sen (2009) affirms that the ideal theory, or the 'transcendental institutionalism' in his words, is both insufficient and unnecessary. According to him, for instance, to know which one of two mountains is the tallest, one need not know the height of the tallest mountain on Earth. For an historical example, he mentions the movements for the abolition of slavery in the 18th and 19th centuries: 'they were not labouring under the illusion that the abolition of slavery would make the world perfectly just. It was their claim, rather, that a society with slavery was totally unjust' (Sen 2009: 21). Or for an actual case, Sen says (2009: 245) that 'instituting a system of health insurance in the United States that does not leave tens of millions of Americans without any guarantee of medical attention at all', would be widely accepted as a manifest advancement of justice without taking into account the transcendental requirements. From this perspective, he opts for a non-ideal theory that proceeds by means of a comparative approach which focuses 'on actual realizations and accomplishments, rather than only on the establishment of what are identified as the right institutions and rules' (Sen 2009: 10). But contrary to what Sen and others' criticisms of Rawls sustain, an ideal theory is instead truly necessary.

What they miss is that ideal principles of justice aim to answer some priority questions that are essential to guide our actions to, first, specify and identify the kind of injustice we ought to eliminate or compensate, and second, to roughly indicate the path and the permissible actions to do it. The point is not to measure the height of the tallest mountain on Earth, but to understand why we have to climb a mountain at all. Some of the injustices that Sen (2009) or Jonathan Wolff (2015) might call manifest, like slavery, racial segregation, severe gender discrimination, or absolute poverty, in the past, and in some cases unfortunately even nowadays, were not considered injustices at all. These severe forms of injustice were not, and are not, hidden or masked situations, and therefore, unlike what Wolff (2015: 218) sustains, it is not true that 'when exposed and brought to full attention, will immediately elicit a judgment of clear injustice'.

With this I do not deny that there are 'manifest' injustices in the sense of Sen and Wolff, but that their existence does not prove anything against the necessity of 'ideal' or 'transcendental' theories and principles of justice. On the contrary, if some injustices are 'manifest' in the sense of being immediately considered as such by people, it is true because those people engage themselves in some 'ideal' or 'transcendental institutional' judgments. The fact that these judgments can simply be unconscious, as Jonathan Wolff suggests, is quite trivial. Political philosophy and theories of justice are useful simply to make these judgments self-reflected and conscious (no theory of justice 'creates' moral judgments) and then help assess their coherence and validity.

For this reason, first of all, we need a fundamental principle of justice or morality to say that slavery is one of the most severe forms of injustice; remember that many US citizens in the 18th and 19th centuries sincerely believe that it was not. Similarly, nowadays, millions of Americans believe that a universal system of health insurance is not a requirement of (political) justice because health insurance should reflect the moral individual responsibility. In supporting such public policy as a requirement of social justice, Sen needs to engage his argument with reasons that he actually believes are not necessary to grapple with: 'the establishment of what are identified as the right institutions and rules' (Sen 2009: 10). Secondly, we need to have some ideals about what means to live in a non-slave or non-racist society; that is, what basic rights and liberties, what material conditions, or what correct treatments that political and social institutions should ensure for all citizens regardless of their cultural and racial identities. Only in this way, for example, Mills' (2020: 49) three non-ideal principles of corrective racial justice – end racially unequal citizenship, end racial exploitation, and end racial disrespect – make sense, and they can be useful to US society in guiding the transition towards an accomplished non-racial democracy.

Instead, what ideal principles of justice are not able to do is to identify and specify the means and concrete actions to eliminate or compensate injustice; in other words, they cannot answer the question of how to eliminate or compensate injustice. They cannot tell us if we should engage in a political movement to reform an unjust society or instead in some forms of disobedience, or if the disobedience should include even the use of force. They cannot say which policies and tools we should adopt to eradicate present injustices or rectify past ones. In other words, the application and implementation of the principles of justice cannot be but largely empirical and strategic (Freeman 2018: 23). However, even in transitional justice, ideal principles roughly constrain our actions. For example, even in some extreme cases, like Shelby's 'dark ghetto' (2007; 2016), where citizens are treated in a way to legitimise the disrespect of their civil obligations as a form of reasonable and legitimate disobedience under circumstances of severe socioeconomic injustices,[12] the ghetto poor should respect what Shelby (2007: 151–152) calls natural duties which constrain the conduct aimed at causing reckless and gratuitous violence.

To sum up, we can agree that Rawls' ideal methodology is not sufficient to deal with injustices, but is inevitably necessary for this purpose. In this sense, Rawls is right to say that ideal theory is the necessary precursor of non-ideal theory. In other words, as I said at the beginning, a principle of justice should treat as separate the questions: *What* justice or injustice is? and *How* should we achieve justice or remove injustice?

Once this fundamental point is clarified, we should not be afraid to admit a certain gap between the principles of justice and its application and implementation. Much more, I believe that this gap is healthy because it shows how normative political philosophy leaves enough room for political imagination and democratic implementation, and how it also allows better dialogue and symbiosis with other social science disciplines. For this reason, a certain level of abstraction is inevitable and necessary; and this is particularly true for those principles of justice that are thought to be applied primary rules.[13] However, from this level of abstraction, Rawls suggests proceeding step by step via what he calls 'four-stage sequence' which is composed by the choice of the principles of justice and then by their gradual application at the constitutional stage, legislative stage, and the administrative-cum-judicial stage. More recently, Rawls (2001a) introduced a sort of additional stage of application – 'the choice of social system' – which is immediately located after the choice of the principles of justice and before the remaining stages. This choice concerns comparing a set of ideal types of social systems and to decide which of these satisfy the requirements of the two principles of justice.

As we saw, Rawls takes into account a closed list of options composed by laissez-faire capitalism, welfare-state capitalism, liberal market socialism, command socialism, and a property-owning democracy, and his choice falls only on two of these – liberal market socialism and a property-owning democracy; meanwhile he excludes the other three. As Thomas (2020) rightly observes, Rawls' methodology of the choice of a social system has two fundamental features: 'first, he vindicates no single option, rather the disjunctive choice between liberal market socialism and a property-owning democracy. Second, while nearly all the options on Rawls' closed list can claim to have some basis in historical fact, one of his chosen options [a property-owning democracy] does not' (Thomas 2020: 109). Thus, Rawls endorses a noncommittal view and he leaves room for political imagination about the choice of social system. The principle of proportionality shares the same Rawls intuition. Similarly, as I said (Chapter 1, Section 1.3), the principle of proportional justice clearly rules out a libertarian system or a commanded economy because they are respectively incompatible by the fact of domination and the fact of reasonable pluralism; in other words, the very essence of a libertarian system or of laissez-faire capitalism is to reject any a priori limit to economic inequality, and a commanded economy disregards even a very narrow conception of basic economic liberties. At the same time, the principle of proportionality does not force us to choose a specific social system because it is compatible with many of them, provided that they incorporate the requirement to contain economic inequality in well-specified limits (and the other correlated constraints). However, I believe that with respect to the choice of social system, the principle of proportionality may fare better than Rawls' two principles of justice.

In the contemporary debate there is increasing attention placed on the choice of a social system. In particular, the debate has been focused on the compatibility between Rawls' two principles of justice and a variety of ideal type institutional settings. This compatibility depends on the way we understand the content of the two principles, and from this, the lists of ideal types of social systems can expressively increase in number, more than Rawls' closed list of options. Some might favour a property-owning democracy (Mead 1964, 1989; O'Neill and Williamson 2012; Thomas 2017), others a liberal market socialism (Schweickart 1993; Mill 2008; Ellerman 2016), the pluralist commonwealth (Alperovitz 2005, 2012), participatory economy (Hahnel 2005), liberal democratic socialism (Edmundson 2017), market democracy (Tomasi 2012), social democracy (von Platz 2020a), participatory socialism (Piketty 2020), or workplace democracy (Neuhäuser 2021). However, in the debate, there is a dominant trend to critique Rawls' answer to the question of the choice of a social system. Precisely, some influential scholars on the debate, despite their disagreement about the choice of social system (see Tomasi 2012; Edmundson 2017, 2021; Thomas 2017, 2020), have considered Rawls' noncommittal view to be unsatisfactory.

They detect an important ambiguity about the threat that, according to Rawls, excessive economic inequalities poses to the protection of the value of political liberties and the ultimate manner in which this threat should be defused. As summarised by Thomas (2020: 114–115),

> while Rawls is explicit about the threat, he is less explicit about whether he has retained his confidence in an insulation strategy to contain it. Nor, if he takes the very choice of a social system to be the ultimate, successful, pre-emptive strategy of capital dispersal offering the strongest protection against the fact of domination, did he revise the architectonic of his system to reflect that fact.

As we have already seen (Chapter 3, Section 3.2), this ambiguity leaves the possibility open that Rawls' two principles of justice are satisfied by very different social systems, even those types that allow *in principle* unrestricted economic inequality and only rely on some forms of insulation strategy (see for instance Tomasi

2012 and von Platz 2020a). For this reason, and in order to exclude this result, some influential egalitarians scholars (O'Neill 2012, 2017; Edmundson 2017, 2021; Thomas 2017) revise Rawls' methodology to assume a committal view about the ideal (predistributive) social system which is the most effective to prevent wealth and property concentration.

By contrast, I believe that this evident shortfall in Rawls' theory of justice should be resolved at the level of the principles of justice; precisely, by reformulating the difference principle and making it sensitive to the gap in economic inequality (Chapter 3, Section 3.2). Indeed, if we believe that, no matter of how well accomplished an insulation strategy can be, excessive economic inequalities are incompatible with the fair value of political liberties or, in other words, they expose citizens to the risk of material domination, we should set up a principle of justice that unequivocally disallows excessive economic inequalities. And this is the exact prescription of the principle of proportionality. In this way, we can maintain a noncommittal view without troubles.

Indeed, I believe that there are some fundamental reasons and advantages to avoid a committed view that tightens our options and political imagination about the choice of social system.[14] First of all, it does not seem to be plausible and reasonable that all liberal democratic societies should pursue the same ideal type of social system. Democratic autonomy of political societies should be ensured as much as possible. Second, assuming that there is only one social system at our disposal involves the risk of endorsing the idea that we should realise the ideal social system exactly the way it was ideally conceived. By contrast, depending on the non-ideal society that we hope to transform toward a certain ideal social system, the actual non-ideal institutional structures and socioeconomic, cultural and political circumstances of that society might make it more feasible and affordable to opt for one ideal system rather than another, and much more likely for a combination of several different ideal systems.

Thus, the principle of proportionality endorses, like Rawls, a noncommittal view about the choice of social system but, unlike Rawls' two principles of justice, it leaves no doubts about imposing limited ratios in wealth and income inequality to avoid material domination. Once this first and priority 'ideal' stage (following Rawls' vocabulary) is definite, the further fundamental question is how to reshape political and socioeconomic structures of our liberal democracies in a way that reverses the trend of increasing economic inequality, and in doing so, preventing dominant control of the economy and political life from being consolidated in few hands.

In the debate, this question is usually faced from two different strategies: a long-run strategy and a short-to-medium-run strategy (O'Neill 2017; Freeman 2018). The first strategy, as we saw, specifically concerns an ideal social scheme understood as a predistributive system in which we have political and socioeconomic institutions that systematically prevent political and economic domination. Instead, a short-to-medium-run strategy is a less ideal approach which requires a discussion of a set of distributive proposals seeking to contain and reduce, at present, economic inequality of income and wealth. For example, the redistributive strategy (or *ex post* distribution) that accepts the given distribution of wealth and seeks to override unequal market outcomes through transfer policies and social protection is usually considered a short-to-medium-run strategy.

I believe that the best way to proceed is to follow what I call a 'pluralistic distributive approach' which tries to combine the two strategies, in order to, *first of all*, pursue a more productive step-by-step strategy to better understand how to achieve a certain ideal system or, more realistically, some version of it; *second*, to avoid reproducing a very common misleading opposition between predistribution and redistribution strategies (on this point see more in O'Neill 2020). For example, the main reason to raise the upper tax rate (for those belonging to the top 1%) is not primarily to collect revenue (a redistributive policy), but to regulate the labour market, reducing the bargaining power and incentives of the top executives in negotiating higher pay (with a clearly predistributive effect, see Piketty 2014: 510; 2016: 104); *third*, to focus on a plurality of distributive proposals combining: redistribution with predistribution of both public and private forms of capital (e.g. sovereign wealth funds and the universal capital endowment), forms of workplace democracy (including stake-holding mechanisms, control ownership, and access to the dividends of social ownership), progressive tax schemes, and new forms of welfare-state and social security (based on novelty instruments such as the universal basic income[15]).

Here, I do not have the space to provide more details about a 'pluralistic distributive approach'. However, to give but a brief sketch, the main idea is to focus on a set of distributive proposals concerning five broad areas: 1) wealth distribution and capital shared; 2) social security; 3) progressive taxation; 4) countervailing power of economic decision-making; and 5) transnational financial regulations. These can be considered the most crucial areas of contemporary capitalistic socioeconomic structures.

However, from a more empirical point of view, some attempts in this direction have been made (see Wright 2010, 2019; Atkinson 2015; Stiglitz 2015, 2019). For sure, Piketty's participatory socialism (2020) is the most recent proposal to be characterised by a similar pluralistic approach. In his recent *Capital and Ideology* (2020), Piketty seems to complete his previous work – *Capital in the Twenty-First Century* (2014) – in two directions.[16] Firstly, he provides an historical (synchronic and diachronic) investigation of the ideological justifications of economic inequality, that is, of how economic inequality was accepted and legitimised, even when it reached stratospheric dimensions. In contemporary capitalist societies, this ideological function is played by the sanctity of private property understood as permanent individual property. Secondly, he draws a socioeconomic system alternative to capitalism that he calls participatory socialism, which combines a plurality of distributive policies, tools and mechanisms.[17] Let me briefly describe his 'pluralistic' proposal.

Piketty's proposal on workplace democracy starts from historical experience in Germany and Scandinavia and it tries to reinforce the weight of workers' decision-making within larger companies (Piketty 2020: 974). Concerning the structural dispersion of capital, Piketty suggests that an annual progressive property tax could represent the main tool for ensuring the real circulation of capital. The advantage of an annual property tax over more conventional forms of property taxes – for example, inheritance taxes – is that

> it can adapt much more quickly to changes in wealth and in the ability of each taxpayer to pay. There is no need to wait for Mark Zuckerberg or Jeff Bezos to turn 90 years old and pass their wealth to their heirs in order to collect taxes.
>
> (Piketty 2020: 978)

In addition to these measures, Piketty sketches two other forms of progressive taxation: an inheritance tax and an income tax. This triptych of progressive taxation – on property, inheritance and income – mainly aims to finance and put in place a system of capital endowments (see Ackerman and Alstott 1999) that should be paid to each young adult (say, at the age of 25) with the result of disseminating ownership at the bottom while limiting its concentration at the top (Piketty 2020: 983). The idea is to design a progressive tax structure that does not disincentivise work, innovation and productivity while, at the same time, avoiding wealth and income accumulation on the top levels; a sort of step-by-step progressive taxation system that reaches the marginal tax rates of 80% or 90% only for the positions at the very top (Piketty 2020: 985). Finally, Piketty's participatory socialism encompasses other important elements; for instance, a progressive tax on carbon emissions as a partial response to global warming, a fairer educational system, and a form of social federalism on a global level that should allow for a rewriting of the treaties that regulate financial and commercial exchanges in a way that helps nation states to recover their power to collect taxes and impose distributive policies.[18]

Of course, advantages, limits, and functions of each distribution proposal (taken alone and in relation to the others) strongly depend on their effects on social cooperation, job participation, individual responsibility, political liberties, freedom of private initiative, and property rights. Therefore, a pluralistic distributive approach should require a specific normative task that concerns the question of distributive implementations. A further investigation that goes beyond (albeit it should follow a path of coherence and theoretical continuity) the question of which normative reasons and distributive principles can, and ought to, justify the reduction of inequality, which is the core of this present work.

4.4 How to Determine the Permissible Ratios for Income and Wealth Inequalities: The Case Study on the United States

At this point, and finally, I will try to indicate a first attempt of how income and wealth limit ratios could be determined. There is no ambition to provide a final answer. The main point of what follows is rather to start an informed discussion, suggest paths for future research not only in political philosophy, and prove that defining the limits beyond which economic inequality is too much is possible.[19] A good starting point to define the ratios for income and wealth inequalities is to focus on a domestic case in which empirical studies that measure rich citizens' influence on politics and data about the income and wealth distribution are available.[20] Given these conditions, it seems advisable to take the USA as the case study.[21]

Going back to the studies by Gilens and Page (2014) on the relation between affluence and influence in the United States, the authors show that economic elites (identified with the top 10%) have a predominant impact on the public policies of the United States. In the 2017 book *Democracy in America?*, Gilens and Page (2017) offered a more articulated and detailed version of the argument. Other studies have confirmed their empirical analysis, while refining and expanding the conclusions to be drawn from it (Grossmann and Issac 2017; Rhodes and Schaffner 2017). However, while the gist of Gilens and Page's argument seems to hold up, the authors confess ignorance as to exactly which sub-segment of the top 10% has most influence: the top 10% itself, the top 1% or the top one-tenth of 1%? (Gilens and Page 2014: 576). Bartels (2016) individuates the well-off only with those who earn income over USD60,000 (roughly the top 10% in the USA in 2006). Instead, Winters and Page argue that a very conservative assessment lets oligarchy in the USA start with the top 0.1% (Winters and Page 2009: 738), but they recognise that there is no mechanical, infallible way of determining the boundaries of the oligarchic class.

In any event, it should be noted that their notion of oligarchy is much stronger than my notion of domination (Chapter 1, Section 1.2). You are an oligarch not merely if you have a significantly higher share of political power than other citizens, but if *no policy can pass unless the group you belong to agrees with it*; at least no policy that interests the oligarchs, such as those related to protection of wealth concentration (Winters and Page 2009: 733). On the contrary, given my definition, it follows that there are 'dominators' who are not oligarchs. This suggests that broadening the top segment from the 0.1% to the 1% to capture the risk of domination seems to be consistent with the commitment to epistemic prudence (see *constraint 5*). Furthermore, and in support of this assumption, most empirical studies converge on the fact that the risk of domination becomes evident at the very top of distribution, within the top 1%.[22] Of course, if future research were to discover that not the top 1% but the larger top 10% dominates the bottom segment, the ratio would have to be modified, but the logic on which it rests would remain valid.

For similar considerations of epistemic prudence, we should identify the group at risk of being dominated not with the large 'middle class' but with a rather low end, which again as default position we may take to be the bottom 20%. If the middle class is at risk of being dominated by the top earners, *a fortiori* the bottom 20% is. If a focus on the top 1% vs the bottom 20% is reasonable, the upper and lower limits of the ratios are easy to determine (*constraint 4*). If the 1% dominates, then we should not allow inequality to reach the current ratio between the top 1% vs the bottom 20%.

Let me start with income inequality.[23] Given the recent income distribution in the USA, if you make more than USD383,000 (post-tax and benefits) you are part of the top 1%, while the average income of the bottom 20% is USD13,100 (post-tax and benefits).[24] In this case, the ratio would be roughly 1 to 29. This means that to avoid the risk of domination no one should have an income (post-tax and benefits) that exceeds USD13,100*29.

Now, we can observe that this income ratio allows a citizen at the top to earn almost as much annually as someone at the bottom 20% earns (on average) throughout an entire working life of 35 years. Thus, on the one hand, the ratio can hardly be considered as too egalitarian. Moreover, those who are situated at the very top of the distribution are fully able to develop their life plan and are generously rewarded for their potential extra productivity (*constraint 5*). On the other hand, if this range strikes as being not egalitarian enough, one should consider the significant extent to which economic inequality would be reduced if these limits were upheld. An income ratio of 1 to 29 is more egalitarian than the ratio between the annual pay of chief executives of large and medium-sized USA companies and that of all workers in 1960, which was 1 to 42. By contrast, in 2007 this ratio rose to 1 to 344, and it reached an extreme level in the case of America's largest companies. The chief executive of Walmart, for example, earns 900 times the pay of his/her average employee (Lansley 2012: 23–24). Note that it does not mean that the ratio should be exactly 1 to 29. The aim is merely to demonstrate that it is possible to define it in a largely approximate, yet non-arbitrary manner. One should be able to live with the degree of imprecision and approximation that seems to be inherent in this matter. The important point to keep in mind is that there is a huge difference existing between approximation and arbitrariness. Moreover, the ratio 1 to 29 would not ensure that every citizen has exactly the same degree of influence, but this feature is in conformity with *constraint 6*. It means that respecting this ratio would significantly avoid the risk of domination generated by material factors. Finally, the ratio is valid only for the domestic case study on the USA, for which there is enough refined empirical science to generate a reasonable ratio (*constraints 7 and 8*).

Mutatis mutandis, an analogous reasoning could be done for wealth inequality. Data concerning wealth distribution are fewer and less organised than those related to income, because economic studies have mainly focused on the latter (see Piketty 2014). Recently, the scenario has marginally improved and we have (at least for some countries, including the USA) an accurate estimate of how wealth is concentrated at the top 1% (see Alvaredo et al. 2018), while there is a still rather non-articulated estimate for the bottom. Perhaps as a consequence of the fact that wealth concentrates at the top 1%, scholars tend to identify the bottom with the lowest 50% (Piketty 2014) or give agglomerate data for the wealth concentration of the entire bottom 90% (Saez and Zucman 2016). Maintaining the focus on the USA, the top 1% owns 37% of the net worth wealth of the country and 46% of the financial wealth, which is wealth that can be easily used to exercise political influence (E. Wolff 2017). Meanwhile, according to some studies (E. Wolff 2014: 14), the average of the bottom 40% is –USD10,800 (data 2013), or a little more than zero; 25% of all families have less than USD10,000 in wealth (data 2017; Leiserson,

McGrew and Kopparam 2019: 13). Perhaps the figures that are most relevant for the purpose are those that indicate the percentage of wealth owned by the bottom 20%. According to Norton and Ariely, the lowest quintile owns 0.1% of the wealth in the United States (Norton and Ariely 2011) and this is the most conservative figure because all other studies attribute a negative figure.[25] Wealth data are so appalling that they motivated the above-mentioned studies that denounce political domination and 'civil' oligarchy in the USA. Again, assuming that the 1% might dominate, we should set the limit at the entry point of that segment. We can observe that the wealth threshold for accessing the top 1% (for family, data 2012) is USD3,960,000 (Saez and Zucman 2016: 552).[26] Even taking into account a *very* optimistic wealth average of USD10,000 at the bottom 20%, the ratio with wealth of the top 1% would be roughly 1 to 400.

This ratio may strike some as not egalitarian enough. But one should consider that implementing this ratio would already cause a huge wealth redistribution from the top 1% to those who are situated at the bottom. Remember that in the USA in 2014 (Saez and Zucman 2016: 552) the average wealth of the top 1% and top 0.1% was respectively USD13,840,000 and USD371,000,000 (41.8% and 11.2% of national wealth), with ratios 1/1384 and 1/37100 respectively. The case of wealth vividly illustrates that to determine a fair and effective ratio with precision is extremely difficult. And yet even using the most prudent, that is, most favourable to the rich, estimate, the implications of the principle of proportionality are enormous.[27] The fact that there is no rock-solid, mechanical way of hitting on the limit ratio is no excuse for failing to define and defend one.

Notes

1 These constraints have already been presented in a similar shape in Alì and Caranti (2021) and Caranti and Alì (2021).

2 Bowles (2012) and Atkinson (2015), for example, show how wealth inequality is detrimental to the economy. McAdams (2007) argues that at a certain degree inequality incentivizes crime and corruption while hindering growth through direct and indirect effects.

3 Note that this extreme case does not include those that are more common in our social and political reality, a reality in which an extreme level of economic inequality coexists with the absolute poverty of a large part of the population. Brazil is an exemplary case of this scenario. It is one of the most unequal countries in the world in which the top 1% own 27.8% of Brazil's total wealth (see Medeiros, Souza and Castro 2015; Alvaredo et al. 2018; Souza 2018), and if we consider only labour income, the top 1% earns on average BRL 27,744 per month, while the bottom 50% earns just BRL 820 per month. The first group (1%) is composed of 889,000 individuals and the bottom 50% of almost 45 million. But if we take into account all kinds of economic sources, half of the Brazilian population, around 104,000,000 individuals, lives on BRL 413 a month (data from Instituto Brasileiro de Geografia e Estatística 2019). So, while the richest in Brazil have a similar income to the rich in developed countries (Morgan 2017), the rest are disproportionately poorer by comparison. This means there are millions of citizens at the bottom 30% who earn considerably less than the minimum wage established by law (in 2018, BRL 954, data Instituto Brasileiro de Geografia e Estatística 2019). The principle of proportionality fits perfectly in a case such as this.

4 Both Freeman (2011) and Brennan and Tomasi (2012) make a similar distinction among classical liberals, libertarians, and high liberals.
5 For an extensive and accurate discussion on Rawls' conception of economic liberties, see von Platz (2013; 2016; 2020b).
6 About the idea of productive justice, see also Hsieh (2009), Stanczyk (2012) and Edmundson (2021).
7 Note that von Platz (2020a: 21) defends welfare-state capitalism not from a utilitarian perspective, but as a form of social democracy in which citizens are conceived 'as free and equal cooperators working together in the production and distribution of the goods of society'.
8 Here, I leave open the question of how wide the range of economic liberties should be; whether it should include Nickel's entire list, or a less extensive version.
9 Freeman (2013) also detects this deficit in Rawls' theory and he suggests remedying it by including economic agency as part of the fair equal opportunity principle. To be honest, also in this case von Platz (2020a) leaves open the empirical possibility of it being necessary to impose limits on economic inequalities in order to guarantee the fair values of economic liberties, but again he does not derive any distributive principle from this.
10 For a general overview of the debate, see Stemplowska (2008), Stemplowska and Swift (2012) and Valentini (2012).
11 For different versions of this objection, see Phillips (1985), Murphy (2003), Mills (2005, 2020), Sen (2009), and Wiens (2012). I will focus mainly on this controversy because it concerns the object of this section. However, as observed by Valentini (2012) the contemporary debate has also focused on two other related controversies: 'full compliance vs. partial compliance' and 'utopian vs. realistic theory'. Here I do not have the time to address all these topics; however for a discussion, see Simmons (2010), Valentini (2012), Robeyns (2008), Thomas (2013), and Freeman (2018).
12 Rawls (1971: 52) himself seems to admit this possibility.
13 Clearly, a difficult question is to decide the correct level of abstraction and idealisation in order to draw a successful theory able to provide reasonable and feasible normative orientations. For this reason, Rawls believes that certain facts and circumstances – such as the facts of domination and pluralism or the subjective and objective circumstances of justice – are crucial to the design of plausible normative political principles.
14 Gilabert (2015) also advocates the same logical priority but applied it to socialism theories; a very interesting proposal that subverts the tradition of socialist thought.
15 I leave open the question of whether the basic income should be 'universal and unconditional' as suggested by Van Parijs (1995), Van Parijs and Vanderborght (2017) or should include some kinds of conditionality as proposed by Atkinson (2015).
16 This last work can also be read as Piketty's attempt to answer and remediate some objections and criticisms that he received. For the more relevant critical remarks, see Murphy (2015), O'Neill (2017), Farrell (2016), and Boushey, Delong and Steinbaum (2017).
17 O'Neill (2021) also seems to understand Piketty's participatory socialism as a pluralistic distributive approach.
18 However, the kinds of constraints imposed by globalisation should not be overestimated. Indeed, governments (in liberal democracies and elsewhere) still have enough room to implement distributive policies at the domestic level, as Piketty himself confirms: 'they can make progress toward reducing inequality and establishing more just forms of ownership without waiting for international cooperation to be achieved. This is obvious for very large states such as the United States and China (and soon for India). [...] It is also important to note that while smaller states, such as France, obviously have more to gain from international cooperation, they, too, have a great deal of room to manoeuvre if they wish to pursue new policies at the national level' (Piketty 2020: 1107–1108).
19 In Switzerland (5 December 2013), a public referendum took place on a similar proposal trying to establish a ratio of 1 to 12 between the executive's pay and the lowest pay in the company. The proposal was defeated with 65% of the vote (the vote participation

was 53%). It is likely that a ratio of 1 to 12 was perceived as too narrow, which contributed to the rejection of the proposal. Another similar attempt, but successful, was a new legislation approved by Israel's Knesset (parliament) in 2016, according to which total compensation will be capped at 2.5 million shekels (USD652,605) a year, or no more than 44 times the salary (net income, or 35 times the gross income) of the lowest worker at the company; anything above the ceiling will be subject to higher taxes (see Scheer 2016). Although it is the first, and unique, mandatory ratio of top pay to bottom ranking pay applied to a free market economy, this law only establishes a soft cap of salary which means that earnings can surpass the cap, but the excess cannot be deducted from corporate taxes. Moreover, another fundamental limit of this legislation (but like the Switzerland referendum proposal) is that it only applies to wages, and not to individual wealth accumulation.

20 This case study, but only about income inequality, was presented in Alì and Caranti (2021). I need to expressly thank Professor Luigi Caranti to let me, here, include our attempt to extend the case study to wealth inequality.

21 Empirical studies about economic elites' influence on politics are still quite rare for national contexts other than the USA. For an explanation of why this is the case, see Hopkin (2014). For a few exceptions, see Cagé (2020), and for case studies on Brazil, see Avis et al. (2017) and Silveira and Mello (2011).

22 See Alvaredo et al. (2018), American Political Science Association Task Force (2004), Dorling (2014), Piketty (2014, 2020), Milanovic (2019), Reich (2016), Saez and Zucman (2019), Stiglitz (2012), Winters and Page (2009), and Edward Wolff (2017).

23 It should be recognized that the distinction between income and wealth could be overcome by adopting the interesting methodology Robeyns (2017) follows to define her index of Power of Material Resources. In particular, recall that she calculates it by summing the gross total income of a household deriving from all sources, the monetary estimate of any transfer in favour of the household other than earnings and the life annuity of household assets. By doing so, returns from wealth are incorporated into the household income (broadly considered). Moreover, she applies the household Equivalence Scale (ES) to take into account the number of members within a household. While PMR is used by Robeyns to calculate how much is needed to buy the functionings necessary for a fully flourishing life, it could also be used as a precise enough measure of the economic resources of each citizen, disregarding the capabilitarian insight of the Conversion Factor (CF) which brings with it inherent difficulties as a political standard of interpersonal comparison. Also, the measurements will be different whether we take into account the income and wealth of individuals or that of households, and something should be said to justify whether we focus on one or the other. The economic inequality statistics usually use the household rather than individual as the unit of observation; however, 'the choice is dictated primarily by the source of data rather than by an opinion about the most appropriate economic unit' (Davies and Shorrocks 2000: 624). I believe that there are many reasons why one may think that the individual, and not the household, is the appropriate economic unit. First of all, how do you define the household unit? Is it composed of a person living alone, or a group of two or more persons occupying the whole or part of a housing unit, while providing themselves with food and possibly other essentials for living (as suggested by the United Nations' Canberra Group 2011: 25)? Or should it be some legal bond among them, such as marriage, family or fiscal unit. It is very difficult to find a non-arbitrary reason to opt for one or another criterion of household composition. The second, normatively more significant problem concerns the risk of being blind to inequality within the household, above all to gender inequality, see Ponthieux and Meurs (2014) and Bennett (2013). Taking the household as an economic unit means to assume that economic resources are equally shared within the household. By contrast, we want to know who are the very rich who can influence politics and the economy, whether Jeff Bezos or his wife. Fortunately, there are some relevant exceptions regarding income inequality measurements; such as

Piketty et al. (2018). These data allow me to take into account, at least for income ratio, individuals as the unit of the measurement.

24 Data 2014: Piketty et al. (2018: 575). Of course the 'post-tax and benefits' close is crucial.

25 Kuhn, Schularick and Steins (2020), instead, confirm a negative measurement even taking into account the wealth average of the bottom 25%, which is -0.5% of the wealth in the United States (year 2016).

26 Wealth inequality statistics use the household rather than the individual as a unit of observation, and here I can only follow this trend, despite my normative preference for a unit of measurement built on individuals.

27 Interestingly, Piketty's latest book *Capital and Ideology* (2020) contains an element that is rather in line with the approach of proportional justice. He suggests structuring what he calls 'the progressive tax triptych: property, inheritance, income' (Piketty 2020: 1101) for multiples of average wealth and income, assigning to each multiple a progressive tax rate (different for property, inheritance and income). For example, property tax should be organised so that 'the tax rate is 0.1 percent for wealth below the national average, rising gradually to 1 percent at twice the national average, 10 percent at one hundred times the national average, 60 percent at 1,000 times the national average (or EUR 200 million if the average wealth per adult is EUR 200,000), and 90 percent at 10,000 times the national average (which would be EUR 2 billion)' (Piketty 2020: 1104).

Bibliography

Ackerman, Bruce and Anne Alstott. 1999. *The Stakeholder Society*. New Haven: Yale University Press.

Alì, Nunzio and Luigi Caranti. 2021. 'How Much Economic Inequality is Fair in Liberal Democracies? The Approach of Proportional Justice', *Philosophy & Social Criticism*, 47(7): 769–788.

Alperovitz, Gar. 2012. 'The Pluralist Commonwealth and Property-Owning Democracy', in Martin O'Neill and Thad Williamson (eds.), *Property-Owning Democracy: Rawls and Beyond*, pp. 266–286. Oxford: Wiley-Blackwell.

Alperovitz, Gar. 2005. *America Beyond Capitalism: Reclaiming Our Wealth, Our Liberty and Our Democracy*. New York: John Wiley & Sons.

Alvaredo, Facundo, Lucas Chancel, Thomas Piketty, Emmanuel Saez, and Gabriel Zucman (eds.). 2018. *World Inequality Report 2018*. Cambridge: Belknap Press.

American Political Science Association Task Force. 2004. 'American Democracy in an Age of Rising Inequality', *Perspectives on Politics*, 2(4): 651–666.

Atkinson, Anthony B. 2015. *Inequality: What Can Be Done?* Cambridge: Harvard University Press.

Avis, Eric, Claudio Ferraz, Frederico Finan, and Carlos Varjão. 2017. 'Money and Politics: The Effects of Campaign Spending Limits on Political Competition and Incumbency Advantage', *NBER Working Paper*, no. w23508, 13 June 2017, https://ssrn.com/abstract=2984684 (accessed on 25 January 2022)

Bartels, Larry M. 2016. *Unequal Democracy: The Political Economy of a New Gilded Age. Second Edition*. Princeton: Princeton University Press.

Bennett, Fran. 2013. 'Researching Within-Household Distribution: Overview, Developments, Debates, and Methodological Challenges', *Journal of Marriage and Family*, 75(3): 582–597.

Boushey, Heather, Bradford Delong and Marshall Steinbaum (eds.). 2017. *After Piketty: The Agenda for Economics and Inequality*. Cambridge: Harvard University Press.

Bowles, Samuel. 2012. *The New Economics of Inequality and Redistribution*. Cambridge: Cambridge University Press.

Brennan, Jason and John Tomasi. 2012. 'Classical Liberalism', in David Estlund (ed.), *The Oxford Handbook of Political Philosophy*, pp. 115–132. Oxford: Oxford University Press.

Cagé, Julia. 2020. *The Price of Democracy: How Money Shapes Politics and What to Do About It*. Trans. Patrick Camiller. Cambridge: Harvard University Press.

Canberra Group. 2011. *Handbook on Household Income Statistics. Second Edition*. Geneva: United Nations Economic Commission for Europe.

Caranti, Luigi and Nunzio Alì. 2021. 'The Limits of Limitarianism: Why Political Equality is Not Protected by Robeyns' Democratic Argument', *Politica & Società*, 1: 89–116.

Cohen, Joshua. 1989. 'Democratic Equality', *Ethics*, 99(4): 727–751.

Davies, James and Anthony Shorrocks. 2000. 'The Distribution of Wealth', in B. Atkinson and F. Bourguignon, *Handbook of Income Distribution. Volume 1*, pp. 605–675. Amsterdam: North Holland.

Dorling, Danny. 2014. *Inequality and the 1%*. London: Verso.

Edmundson, William A. 2021. *Socialism for Soloists: Spelling Out the Social Contract*. Cambridge: Polity Press.

Edmundson, William A. 2017. *John Rawls: Reticent Socialist*. Cambridge: Cambridge University Press.

Ellerman, David. 2016. *The Democratic Worker-Owned Firm: A New Model for the East and West*. New York: Routledge.

Farrell, Henry (ed.). 2016. 'Crooked Timber Seminar on Thomas Piketty's Capital in the Twenty-First Century', *Crooked Timber*, http://crookedtimber.org/wp-content/uploads/2016/01/piketty-final.pdf (accessed on 2 February 2022).

Freeman, Samuel. 2018. 'Rawls on Distributive Justice and the Difference Principle', in Serena Olsaretti (ed.), *The Oxford Handbook of Distributive Justice*, pp. 1–33. Oxford: Oxford University Press.

Freeman, Samuel. 2013. 'Property-Owning Democracy and the Difference Principle', *Analyse & Kritik*, 35(1): 9–36.

Freeman, Samuel. 2012. 'Can Economic Liberties Be Basic Liberties?' *Bleeding Heart Libertarians*, Symposium on John Tomasi's Free Market Fairness, 13 June, https://bleedingheartlibertarians.com/2012/06/can-economic-liberties-be-basic-liberties/ (accessed on 2 February 2022).

Freeman, Samuel. 2011. 'Capitalism in the Classical and High Liberal Traditions', *Social Philosophy and Policy*, 28: 19–55.

Gilabert, Pablo. 2015. 'The Socialist Principle "From Each According to Their Abilities, to Each According to their Needs"', *Journal of Social Philosophy*, 46(2): 197–225.

Gilens, Martin and Benjamin I. Page. 2017. *Democracy in America? What Has Gone Wrong and What We Can Do About It*. Chicago: University of Chicago Press.

Gilens, Martin and Benjamin I. Page 2014. 'Testing Theories of American Politics: Elites, Interest Groups, and Average Citizens', *Perspectives on Politics*, 12(3): 564–581.

Grossmann, Matt and William Isaac. 2017. 'Oligarchy or Class War? Political Parties and Interest Groups in Unequal Public Influence on Policy Adoption', *Matt Grossmann Tumblr*, http://matthewg.org/Gilens-Parties4.pdf (accessed on 25 January 2022).

Hahnel, Robin. 2005. *Economic Justice and Democracy: From Competition to Cooperation*. London: Routledge.

Har, Janie. 2017. '"We Still Need to Eat": Tech Boom Creates Working Homeless', *AP News*, 8 November 2017. https://apnews.com/article/technology-business-small-business-9309128222ab4c4f92b0d0022e1ec133 (accessed on 23 February 2022).

Hopkin, Jonathan. 2014. 'The Politics of Piketty: What Political Science Can Learn from, and Contribute to, the Debate on Capital in the Twenty-First Century.' *The British Journal of Sociology*, 65(4): 678–695.

Hsieh, Nien-hê. 2009. 'Justice at Work: Arguing for Property-Owning Democracy.' *Journal of Social Philosophy*, 40(3): 397–411.

Instituto Brasileiro de Geografia e Estatística (IBGE). 2019. 'PNAD Contínua 2018: 10% da população concentram 43,1% da massa de rendimentos do país', *Agência IBGE Notícias*, 16 October 2019, https://censoagro2017.ibge.gov.br/agencia-sala-de-imprensa/2013-agencia-de-noticias/releases/25700-pnad-continua-2018-10-da-populacao-concentram-43-1-da-massa-de-rendimentos-do-pais (accessed on 23 February 2022).

Kuhn, Moritz, Moritz Schularick, and Ulrike Steins. 2020. 'Income and Wealth Inequality in America, 1949–2016', *Journal of Political Economy*, 128(9): 3469–3519.

Lansley, Stewart. 2012. *The Cost of Inequality: Why Economic Equality is Essential for Recovery*. London: Gibson Square Books.

Leiserson, Greg, Will McGrew and Raksha Kopparam. 2019. 'Net Worth Taxes. What They Are and How They Work', *Washington Center for Equitable Growth*, 21 March, https://equitablegrowth.org/research-paper/net-worth-taxes-what-they-are-and-how-they-work/ (accessed on 2 February 2022).

McAdams, Richard H. 2007. 'The Economic Costs of Inequality', *John M. Olin Program in Law and Economics*, Working Paper no. 370: 1–28.

Mead, James E. 1989. *Agathotopia: The Economics of Partnership*. Aberdeen: Aberdeen University Press.

Mead, James E. 1964. *Efficiency, Equality and the Ownership of Property*. New York: Routledge.

Medeiros, Marcelo, Pedro H. G. F. de Souza and Fábio Ávila Castro. 2015. 'A estabilidade da desigualdade de renda no Brasil, de 2006 a 2012: estimativa com dados do imposto de renda e pesquisas domiciliares', *Ciência & Saúde Coletiva*, 20(4): 971–986.

Milanovic, Branko. 2019. *Capitalism, Alone: The Future of the System That Rules the World*. Cambridge: Harvard University Press.

Mill, John S. 2008. *Principles of Political Economy and Chapters on Socialism*. Ed. by Jonathan Riley. Oxford: Oxford University Press.

Mills, Charles W. 2020. 'Theorizing Racial Justice', The Tanner Lectures on Human Values, Delivered at Michigan University, 12 February, https://tannerlectures.utah.edu/_resources/documents/a-toz/m/MILLSTANNERLECTURE.pdf (accessed on 2 February 2022).

Mills, Charles W. 2005 '"Ideal theory" as Ideology', *Hypatia*, 20(3): 165–184.

Morgan, Marc. 2017. 'Extreme and Persistent Inequality: New Evidence for Brazil Combining National Accounts, Surveys and Fiscal Data, 2001–2015', *World Inequality Database*, December, https://wid.world/document/extreme-persistent-inequality-new-evidence-brazil-combining-national-accounts-surveys-fiscal-data-2001-2015-wid-world-working-paper-201712/ (accessed on 2 February 2022).

Murphy, Liam B. 2015. 'Why Does Inequality Matter? Reflections on the Political Morality of Piketty's Capital in the Twenty-First Century', *Tax Law Review*, 68(3): 613–630.

Murphy, Liam B. 2003. *Moral Demands in Nonideal Theory*. Oxford: Oxford University Press.

Murphy, Liam B. and Thomas Nagel. 2002. *The Myth of Ownership: Taxes and Justice*. Oxford: Oxford University Press.

Neuhäuser, Christian. 2021. 'Property-owning Democracy, Market Socialism and Workplace Democracy', *Review of Social Economy*, 79:3: 554–580.

Nickel, James. 2000. 'Economic Liberties', in Victoria Davion and Clark Wolf (eds.), *The Idea of Political Liberalism: Essays on Rawls*, pp. 155–176. New York: Rowman & Littlefield.

Norton, Michael I. and Ariely, Dan. 2011. 'Building a Better America–One Wealth Quintile at a Time.' *Perspectives on Psychological Science*, 6(1): 9–12.

O'Neill, Martin. 2021. 'Justice, Power, and Participatory Socialism: on Piketty's Capital and Ideology', *Analyse & Kritik*, 43(1): 89–124.

O'Neill, Martin. 2020. 'Power, Predistribution, and Social Justice', *Philosophy*, 95(1): 63–91.

O'Neill, Martin. 2017. 'Survey Article: Philosophy and Public Policy after Piketty', *The Journal of Political Philosophy*, 25(3): 343–375.

O'Neill, Martin. 2012. 'Free (and fair) Markets Without Capitalism: Political Values, Principles of Justice, and Property-owning Democracy', in Martin O'Neill and Thad Williamson (eds.), *Property-Owning Democracy: Rawls and Beyond*, pp. 75–100. Oxford: Wiley-Blackwell.

O'Neill, Martin and Thad Williamson (eds.). 2012. *Property-Owning Democracy: Rawls and Beyond*. Oxford: Wiley-Blackwell.

Peterson-Withorn, Chase. 2022. 'Forbes' 36th Annual World's Billionaires List: Facts and Figures 2022.' *Forbes*, 05 April 2022. https://www.forbes.com/sites/chasewithorn/2022/04/05/forbes-36th-annual-worlds-billionaires-list-facts-and-figures-2022/?sh=56919ec57e30 (accessed on 10 July 2022).

Phillips, Michael. 1985. 'Reflections on the Transition from Ideal to Non-Ideal Theory', *Noûs*, 19(4): 551–570.

Piketty, Thomas. 2020. *Capital and Ideology*. Trans. by Arthur Goldhammer. Cambridge: Harvard University Press.

Piketty, Thomas. 2016. 'Capital, Predistribution and Redistribution', *Crooked Timber*, Crooked Timber Seminar on Thomas Piketty's Capital in the Twenty-First Century, http://crookedtimber.org/wp-content/uploads/2016/01/piketty-final.pdf (accessed on 2 February 2022).

Piketty, Thomas. 2014. *Capital in The Twenty-First Century*. Trans. by Arthur Goldhammer. Cambridge: Harvard University Press.

Piketty, Thomas, Emmanuel Saez and Gabriel Zucman. 2018. 'Distributional National Accounts: Methods and Estimates for the United States', *The Quarterly Journal of Economics*, 133(2): 553–609.

Ponthieux, Sophie and Dominique Meurs. 2014. 'Gender Inequality', in Anthony Atkinson and Francois Bourguignon (eds.), *Handbook of Income Distribution. Volume 2A-2B*, pp. 981–1146. Amsterdam: North Holland.

Rawls, John. 2005. *Political Liberalism. Expanded Edition*. New York: Columbia University Press.

Rawls, John. 2001a. *Justice as Fairness: A Restatement*. Cambridge: Harvard University Press.

Rawls, John. 2001b. *The Law of Peoples. With "The Idea of Public Reason Revisited*". Cambridge: Harvard University Press.

Rawls, John. 1971. *A Theory of Justice. Original Edition*. Cambridge: Harvard University Press.

Reich, Robert B. 2016. *Saving Capitalism, for the Many, Not the Few*. New York: Icon Books.

Rhodes, Jesse H. and Brian F. Schaffner. 2017. 'Testing Models of Unequal Representation: Democratic Populists and Republican Oligarchs?' *Quarterly Journal of Political Science*, 12(2): 185–204.

Robeyns, Ingrid. 2019. 'What, if Anything, is Wrong with Extreme Wealth?', *Journal of Human Development and Capabilities*, 20(3): 251–266.

Robeyns, Ingrid. 2017. 'Having too Much', in Jack Knight and Melissa Schwartzberg (eds.), *NOMOS LVI: Wealth. Yearbook of the American Society for Political and Legal Philosophy*, pp. 1–44. New York: New York University Press.

Robeyns, Ingrid. 2008. 'Ideal Theory in Theory and Practice', *Social Theory and Practice*, 34(3): 341–362.

Ross, Michael. 2006. 'Is Democracy Good for the Poor?' *American Journal of Political Science*, 50(4): 860–874.

Saez, Emmanuel and Gabriel Zucman. 2019. *The Triumph of Injustice: How the Rich Dodge Taxes and How to Make Them Pay*. New York: W. W. Norton & Company.

Saez, Emmanuel and Gabriel Zucman. 2016. 'Wealth Inequality in the United States since 1913: Evidence from Capitalized Income Tax Data', *The Quarterly Journal of Economics*, 131(2): 519–578.

Scheer, Steven. 2016. 'Israel Passes Law to Cap Bankers' Salaries', *Reuters*, 29 March, https://www.reuters.com/article/israel-banks-wages-idUSL5N1713AP (accessed on 23 February 2022).

Schweickart, David. 1993. *Against Capitalism*. Cambridge: Cambridge University Press.

Sen, Amartya. 2009. *The Idea of Justice*. Cambridge: Harvard University Press.

Shelby, Tommie. 2016. *Dark Ghettos: Injustice, Dissent, and Reform*. Cambridge: Harvard University.

Shelby, Tommie. 2007. 'Deviance, and the Dark Ghetto', *Philosophy & Public Affairs*, 35(2): 126–160.

Silveira, Bernardo and João M. P. de Mello. 2011. 'Campaign Advertising and Election Outcomes: Quasi-natural Experiment from Gubernatorial Elections in Brazil', *Review of Economic Studies*, 78(2): 590–612.

Simmons, A. John. 2010. 'Ideal and Nonideal Theory', *Philosophy & Public Affairs*, 38(1): 5–36.

Souza, Pedro H. G. Ferreira. 2018. 'A History of Inequality: Top Incomes in Brazil, 1926–2015', *International Policy Centre for Inclusive Growth*, Working Papers 167, https://ipcig.org/publication/28529?language_content_entity=en (accessed on 02 February 2022).

Stanczyk, Lucas. 2012. 'Productive Justice', *Philosophy and Public Affairs*, 40(2): 144–164.

Stemplowska, Zofia. 2008. 'What's Ideal about Ideal Theory?' *Social Theory and Practice*, 34(3): 319–340.

Stemplowska, Zofia and Adam Swift 2012. 'Ideal and Nonideal Theory', in David Estlund (ed.), *The Oxford Handbook of Political Philosophy*, pp. 373–390. Oxford: Oxford University Press.

Stiglitz, Joseph E. 2019. *People, Power and Profits: Progressive Capitalism for an Age of Discontent*. London: Allen Lane.

Stiglitz, Joseph E. 2015. *Rewriting the Rules of the American Economy: An Agenda for Growth and Shared Prosperity*. New York & London: W. W. Norton & Company.

Stiglitz, Joseph. 2012. *The Price of Inequality: How Today's Divided Society Endangers Our Future*. New York & London: W. W. Norton & Company.

Thomas, Alan. 2020. 'Rawls on Economic Liberty and the Choice of Systems of Social Cooperation', in John Mandle and Sarah Roberts-Cady (eds.), *John Rawls: Debating the Major Questions*, pp. 109–121. Oxford: Oxford University Press.

Thomas, Alan. 2017. *Republic of Equals: Predistribution and Property-Owning Democracy*. Oxford: Oxford University Press.

Thomas, Alan. 2013. 'Sen on Rawls's "Transcendental Institutionalism": An Analysis and Critique', *European Journal of Political Theory*, 13(3): 241–263.

Tomasi, John. 2012. *Free Market Fairness*. Princeton: Princeton University Press.

Valentini, Laura. 2012. 'Ideal vs. Non-ideal Theory: A Conceptual Map', *Philosophy Compass*, 7(9): 654–664.

Van Parijs, Philippe. 1995. *Real Freedom for All: What (If Anything) Can Justify Capitalism?* Oxford: Oxford University Press.

Van Parijs, Philippe and Yannick Vanderborght. 2017. *Basic Income: A Radical Proposal for a Free Society and a Sane Economy*. Cambridge: Harvard University Press.

von Platz, Jeppe. 2020a. 'Democratic Equality and the Justification of Welfare-State Capitalism', *Ethics*, 131: 4–33.

von Platz, Jeppe. 2020b. 'Rawls's Underestimation of the Importance of Economic Agency and Economic Rights', in John Mandle and Sarah Roberts-Cady (eds.), *John Rawls: Debating the Major Questions*, pp. 95–108. Oxford: Oxford University Press.

von Platz, Jeppe. 2016. 'Social Cooperation and Basic Economic Rights: A Rawlsian Route to Social Democracy', *Journal of Social Philosophy*, 47(3): 288–308.

von Platz, Jeppe. 2013. 'Are Economic Liberties Basic Rights?' *Politics, Philosophy & Economics*, 13(1): 23–44.

von Platz, Jeppe and John Tomasi. 2015. 'Liberalism and Economic Liberty', in Steven Wall (ed.), *The Cambridge Companion to Liberalism*, pp. 261–281. Cambridge: Cambridge University Press.

Wiens, David. 2012. 'Prescribing Institutions without Ideal Theory', *Journal of Political Philosophy*, 20(1): 45–70.

Winters, Jeffrey A. and Benjamin I. Page. 2009. 'Oligarchy in the United States?' *Perspectives on Politics*, 7(4): 731–751.

Wolff, Edward N. 2017. *A Century of Wealth in America*. Cambridge: Harvard University Press.

Wolff, Edward N. 2014. 'Household Wealth Trends in the United States, 1962 to 2013: What Happened over the Great Recession?' *National Bureau of Economic Research (NBER)*, Working Paper No. 20733, December 2014, https://www.nber.org/papers/w20733 (accessed on 7 February 2022).

Wolff, Jonathan. 2015. 'Social Equality and Social Inequality', in Carina Fourie, Fabien Schuppert and Ivo Wallimann-Helmer (eds.), *Social Equality: On What It Means to Be Equals*, pp. 209–225. Oxford: Oxford University Press.

Wright, Erik O. 2019. *How to Be an Anticapitalist in the Twenty-first Century*. London: Verso.

Wright, Erik O. 2010. *Envisioning Real Utopians*. London: Verso.

CONCLUSION

At the end of this journey, I hope that my proposal is quite clear and compelling. If there is anything else to say, I would like to underline some practical implications of the approach of proportional justice. Even under this lens, I think that proportional justice shows considerable advantages over other distributive accounts.

First of all, I would not be surprised if in the end the permissible range for income inequality and wealth inequality in the United States will be different from the 1/29 and 1/400 I proposed. The main purpose is not to provide a final answer, but rather to begin a debate about the acceptable limit ratios of economic inequality within liberal democratic societies and to prove that it is not impossible to identify these limit ratios, as is so often asserted. This also means that a broader intent of the project is to suggest tasks for future research, and ones not only limited to political philosophy. Indeed, the hope is that future multidisciplinary research will go much deeper than I did regarding the constraints that the definition of the permissible range should respect and regarding the limits themselves. In any case, we should not overlap two different tasks: the normative one and the empirical one. We can discuss, and certainly disagree too, about the permissible range for income and wealth inequality which protects us from the *risk of material domination*; and if this is larger or smaller than 1/29 and 1/400, fine. But the normative point of view is that we should not accept, unlike what actually happens in our liberal democracies, that the primary rules are established and shaped in such a way as to allow, *in principle*, an unbounded income and wealth inequality. As I said, this is the difference that exists between a society that ignores the normative significance of the size of economic inequality and another one that, instead, establishes a certain permissible range beyond which inequality is not acceptable, and that consequently arranges political and socioeconomic institutions to ensure that this range is effectively respected. The approach of proportional justice I propose in this book makes explicit this normative prescription.

DOI: 10.4324/9781003189428-6

Someone might remain suspicious about the dimension of 'mathematical quantification' that accompanies the idea of proportionality. However, although it is true that we have to avoid a false sense of precision that proportionality can effectively generate, on the other hand, we cannot embrace indeterminacy with respect to the size of inequality that often characterises other alternative moral and political ideas, such as fairness, reciprocity or relational equality. On the contrary, the dimension of 'quantification', once correctly understood, remains fundamental to our normative evaluations about political and social justice. I do not see in the literature an approach other than that of proportionality which best embodies this normative intuition. My purpose has been to rescue and reformulate the classical idea that proportional justice prescribes that inequality should be contained within a permissible range or a certain *proportion*.

Secondly, I have presented the principle of proportionality as better equipped to condemn the current level of inequality in our liberal democracies than are other competitive distributive principles that are concerned only with people's absolute levels, such as the difference principle, prioritarian and sufficientarian principles, or luck-egalitarian ones. However, I am aware, and I want to emphasise, that the current levels of economic inequality in the USA (and other liberal democracies) are incompatible with almost all of these distributive principles, if correctly applied, because we have strong empirical reasons to believe that it is possible to reduce economic inequality by raising up the absolute level of the less advantaged, while maintaining the efficiency of the economic system and respecting the exercise of individual liberties. This convergence of reasons in favour of a reduction of the current economic inequality seems to be good news. Nonetheless, my effort has been to show that a distributive principle that is normatively insensitive with respect to the gap of economic inequality is unable to orient political and socioeconomic rules and arrangements to protect citizens from material domination. For example, it may easily be proved that the 'Trickle Down' effect is empirically false, but we need a normative argument to exclude *a priori* the pursuit of a political economic strategy that is compatible with an unbounded inequality; that is, if we want to avoid *the risk of material domination*.

There is a great difference between a principle of distributive justice that guides our political actions to raise the absolute level of the worst-off regardless of the width of the gap between them and the best-off, and a principle that explicitly prescribes that this gap should be contained within a certain range. In the first case, we would not be surprised by the incipient empirical studies and data regarding economic elites' influence on politics (particularly for national contexts other than the USA) and about the magnitude of economic inequality between the top and the bottom of distribution. If the size of this gap and the reason why it matters is not seen as a problem of justice, it is very difficult to have an accurate estimate of these phenomena. Not accidentally, the scenario has marginally improved only whereupon the question of the size of inequality between the top 1% and the rest of society emerged in academic and public debate. Much more, although those who advocate distributive principles that are concerned only with people's absolute levels might agree with proportional justice about the reduction of the current economic inequality, this normative prescription risks being, if not a mere coincidence, at best only a short-term convergence. Indeed, there is nothing in those distributive principles that condemns *a priori* shaping the primary rules in a way that raises the material condition of the most disadvantaged at the cost of also increasing the size of inequality in the long term. Thus, the welcome convergence about the prescription for reducing the current economic inequality between those distributive principles that only concern people's absolute levels and the principle of proportionality turns out, in the long term, to be only an optical illusion.

On the other hand, although proportional justice is concerned with the distance in economic resources between the richest and the worst-off, it expresses the moral and political intuition that we do not need to (and should not need to) pursue equality to the furthest extent possible (as with the principle of equality), nor to give up the excess wealth above the line of a supposed fully flourishing life (like with limitarianism). The fact that proportional justice prescribes that inequalities should be contained within some ratio but that it excludes the pursuit of the most egalitarian society possible, and also that it places no absolute limits on wealth, can make a great difference in the public debate and deliberation of our liberal democracies. I think that the approach of proportional justice is able to perfectly exemplify the moral and political intuition in our pluralistic societies that what matters is not being rich, but rather the distance between the richest and the poorest, although not to the point that a modest inequality should be considered problematic. If it is the scale of inequality that we should discuss, we need an approach of justice that explicitly deals with this issue. Again, proportional justice fits within this scope.

Finally, we cannot be so naïve as to believe that all that matters are our reasons for political morality. For sure, a variety of reasons that are not 'moral' also matter to people; i.e., practical or self-interested reasons. I may simply say that the terrain of political philosophy is mainly that of political morality, and in this book I tried to offer my modest contribution regarding this domain. However, I am firmly convinced that we would make a big mistake if we underestimate the normative point of view. For example, given that the 2008 economic crisis was the most powerful and crude proof against the most popular of the neoliberal economic arguments – tax cuts, economic growth, jobs growth, wages rise, and people will be happy – we would be led to believe that neoliberalism is a simple spectre that walks in the world. But unfortunately, if a spectre, it is still a powerful one. For this reason, I think that in the public opinion, the strongest and most pervasive argument against a limitation of economic inequality is based not on economic efficiency and growth, but rather on a moral/political argument which is declined in different ways. For example, imposing constraints on economic inequality violates individual liberties and meritocracy, it impedes the legitimate development of a particular conception of a good life, and, in the most sophisticated argument, economic inequality is not unjust when it is the result of the free market. Although it is true that over the last decade neoliberalism has lost its appeal in many Western countries (particularly in Europe), it is not easy to say if this sentiment is already widespread in the liberal democratic public opinion, and, furthermore, public policies are still oriented toward the same dominant neoliberal doctrine. Even when political authority intervenes heavily in the economy by accomplishing redistributive policies, like during the COVID-19 pandemic, these interventions never put into question the astronomic level of economic inequality of our liberal democracies, nor do they try to attack this inequality. Not surprisingly, the effect of the pandemic was rather to reinforce wealth inequality. Of course, this might be proof of a great distance between the actual political leaders and public opinion, or, more dangerously, that material domination is already with us. In this respect, it is intriguing to speculate that one of the reasons why proportional justice has been neglected so far is precisely the material domination exercised by the wealthy on the public (and scientific) debate: a sort of Gramscian hegemony updated to the times of finance capitalism.

Either way, even if we have reasons to be pessimistic, we should not surrender to pessimism. Maybe because I am Italian and I was influenced by Antonio Gramsci, I truly believe that political philosophers should at least retain the optimism of the will. I think I am not deluding myself into believing we have still room for political actions (and that we should not rule out even civil disobedience) to reshape our liberal democracies towards the most shareable ideals of justice. It is no coincidence that I began this book with the *Occupy Wall Street* movement. Certainly, if we really want to avoid our societies being gripped by *the risk of domination*, we should be ready for radical political, socioeconomic, and cultural changes, and for the same reason we need even more radical, yet reasonable moral and political proposals. I hope that proportional justice can be one of them.

INDEX

For Product Safety Concerns and Information please contact our EU
representative GPSR@taylorandfrancis.com
Taylor & Francis Verlag GmbH, Kaufingerstraße 24, 80331 München, Germany

www.ingramcontent.com/pod-product-compliance
Ingram Content Group UK Ltd.
Pitfield, Milton Keynes, MK11 3LW, UK
UKHW020140200926
475702UK00005B/829
* 9 7 8 0 3 6 7 7 5 6 9 8 7 *